CONNIE MACK

Connie Mack

CONNIE MACK

GRAND OLD MAN OF BASEBALL

FREDERICK G. LIEB

THE KENT STATE UNIVERSITY PRESS

KENT, OHIO

ISBN 978-1-60635-129-1
Manufactured in the United States of America

Cataloging information for this title is available
at the Library of Congress.

16 15 14 13 12 5 4 3 2 1

CONTENTS

ILLUSTRATIONS

FOREWORD

Richard "Pete" Peterson

IN 1945, two years after G.P. Putnam began its celebrated series of baseball team histories, it published a biography of Connie Mack. The Mack biography would have a major impact on the team history series because Putnam went on to publish histories for only fifteen of the sixteen major league teams. Missing from the series was a history of Connie Mack's Philadelphia Athletics, those "White Elephants" of the American League.

Putnam's decision not to publish a team history of the Philadelphia Athletics is understandable because, at that time, a biography of Connie Mack was the equivalent of a history of the Athletics. When Ban Johnson converted his Western League into the American League for the 1901 season and added four eastern teams to challenge the territorial monopoly of the National League, he selected Mack to take over the Philadelphia franchise as manager and part owner. Mack would stay on as manager, while eventually becoming the president of the Athletics in 1937, until he stepped down after the 1959 season at the age of eighty-seven.

Another reason Putnam may have decided against a team history of the Philadelphia Athletics was their extensive working relationship with the prolific and legendary baseball writer Fred Lieb. One of the first members selected for the Baseball Hall of Fame's writers' wing, Lieb broke in as a baseball journalist in 1909 and covered every World Series from 1911 to 1958. He wrote the Connie Mack biography for Putnam and was also the author of six of the fifteen

Putnam team histories. His biography of Mack eventually became, for Putnam's editors, Lieb's seventh team history in the series.

After an opening section on the early life and career of Connie Mack, Lieb's format in the biography is essentially the same as the one he used in each of his team histories. Beginning with the "McGillicuddy Meets Ban Johnson" chapter, the book becomes, until the last section, the history of the Philadelphia Athletics. Once the story of the Athletics franchise begins, the chapters follow the same season-by-season narrative, highlighted by detailed accounts of World Series games, common to all of Lieb's team histories in the Putnam series.

Leib's shift from a portrait of Connie Mack to a narrative of the history of his celebrated teams and colorful players is fortunate for readers of the biography. In his "Preface" Lieb admits that the "tall New Englander was an early hero" and that he "never quite has got over this early hero worship." He also notes that his "personal friendship" with Mack has only increased his respect and admiration.

Not surprisingly, the early chapters of the biography are pure hagiography. Lieb's story of Mack's journey from the shoe factories of Brookfield, Massachusetts, to the baseball diamonds of the major leagues is the stuff of the American Dream. For Lieb, Mack's rise to fame from his humble beginnings is "a saga of American enterprise . . . and opportunity." Praising Mack's "brave heart" and "loftiness of spirit," he describes him as "much more than a great baseball man . . . he is a great American."

However, once Lieb's great baseball man and great American takes over the operation of the Philadelphia Athletics in 1901, he becomes, in the biography, more of a dugout conductor and anecdotal witness to baseball history than one of its major players. Beginning with Mack's acquisition of the alligator-wrestling, fire-engine chasing Rube Waddell and the Athletics' first American League pennant in 1902 (the first of nine for Mack's Athletics), Leib's biography becomes a celebration of two remarkable dynasties in Philadelphia Athletics history and the Hall of Fame ballplayers who shaped those dynasties.

Mack's 1902 American League Champion didn't have the opportunity to play in a World Series (the first was played in 1903), but his 1905 pennant-winner went up against John McGraw's New York Giants in baseball's second World Series (McGraw refused to play a World Series against the American League in 1904). Mack's first World Series, however, ended unhappily when his team lost after Giant pitchers threw four shutouts, including three by Christy Mathewson.

Five years later, the Athletics finally rewarded Connie Mack with his first World Championship when they defeated Frank Chance's Chicago Cubs in the 1910 World Series. Mack's team, led by its "famed $100,000 infield," would go on to win three more pennants in the next four years and gain a measure of revenge against McGraw's New York Giants with World Series victories in 1911 and 1913.

After their surprising and devastating defeat to the miracle Boston Braves in the 1914 World Series, Connie Mack's Athletics plunged into last place and stayed there for the next seven years. It wasn't until Mack slowly rebuilt the Athletics in the 1920s that his team went on to win three more pennants and two World Series championships.

With a powerful lineup, led by sluggers Al Simmons and Jimmy Foxx and the Hall of Fame battery of pitcher Lefty Grove and Mickey Cochrane, the Athletics, in 1928, unseated Babe Ruth's New York Yankees as reigning American League champions and defeated the Chicago Cubs in the World Series. They won the pennant again in 1930 and defeated the St. Louis Cardinals in the World Series. It was Connie Mack's fifth world championship, but it was also his last.

Connie Mack's powerful Philadelphia Athletics won their third straight pennant in 1931, their ninth and last in franchise history, but, this time, lost the World Series to the Cardinals, thanks to the brilliant play of Pepper Martin. The World Series loss was the harbinger of things to come for Connie Mack. With the Great Depression bearing down on the franchise, Mack began to sell off his great players, and, by 1935, his decimated team fell into the American League cellar and stayed there until the 1943 season.

Once Lieb's biography reaches the 1935 season in a chapter called "Riding the Bumps Again," the narrative shifts back from its season-by-season account of the Athletics to a final celebration of Connie Mack's life and career. The last few chapters cover his ascension in 1937, at the age of 75, to the presidency of the franchise and the many honors bestowed on him, including a special Connie Mack Day proclaimed in 1941 by the Pennsylvania state legislature. The last chapter of Lieb's biography, "Still Going Strong at Eighty-two," takes Mack through the 1944 season and the Golden Jubilee celebration of his managerial career.

At the beginning of the 1945 season, Connie Mack said that he was still having fun as manager of the Philadelphia Athletics and wouldn't step down until he "acquire the bad habit" of repeating himself. While Leib's biography ends at that point, Mack continued on as manager of the Athletics until the end of the 1950 season. He died in early 1956 at the age of 93, just a little more than a year after his beloved Philadelphia Athletics franchise moved to Kansas City.

The Methuselah of baseball, Connie Mack managed over 7,000 games in his big league career. His Philadelphia Athletics teams won nine American League pennants and five World Series, though they also finished in last place seventeen times. In 1937, while still managing the Athletics, Mack was elected to the Baseball Hall of Fame. Two years later, in 1939, he was enshrined at Cooperstown with a group of still-living baseball greats that included Cy Young, Honus Wagner, Ty Cobb, and Babe Ruth.

PREFACE

AN ENTERPRISING promoter who had a good sense for publicity thought up the idea of having a reunion of the baseball celebrities training in Florida in March, 1927, and arranged for quite a spread at Venice, Florida. It was after the Florida bubble of the middle twenties had burst, but Venice hadn't heard about it and still was holding open house. Among those who accepted were Connie Mack, whose Athletics trained at Fort Myers; Wilbert Robinson, whose daffy Dodgers dodged line drives at Clearwater; John J. McGraw, whose Giants headquartered at near-by Sarasota; and Miller Huggins of the Yankees, whose Babe Ruth circus had pitched its spring tent in St. Petersburg.

Connie Mack, coming up from Fort Myers, had to make the longest trip to reach the party. Even though national prohibition then was very much on the nation's statute books, the giver of the party felt it incumbent upon himself to extend liquid refreshment in the best of southern traditions. The flowing bowl was given no chance to overflow as the notables of the game awaited the arrival of the safari from Fort Myers. Chubby, cheerful Uncle Robbie, the Brooklyn pilot and former great catcher for the old Orioles, ladled out potent potions for himself and others in his Dodger party.

Tall, spare, six-foot-four-inch Connie Mack, his kindly blue eyes blinking as he came out of the darkness, eventually entered the feast chamber, accompanied by a Philadelphia sports-writing delegation, headed by rotund Jimmy Isaminger.

Catching sight of the tall Philadelphia manager, once one of Robinson's catching rivals in the National League, Uncle Robbie toddled over to Mack and threw his arms around him like a friendly Newfoundland embracing a greyhound. Then, reaching up, he kissed Connie affectionately on both cheeks, saying: "You lovable old son of a sea cook! You lovable old son of a sea cook!"

Now, there wasn't a drop of Latin blood in Uncle Robbie's 275-pound chassis, and he was all he-man—a rough, uncut jewel whose adjectives still were those of the free and easy days of the Baltimore Orioles of the nineties. Professional baseball isn't kissing business, and there wasn't another man in the game upon whose cheeks Wilbert would have planted those vigorous smackers. Can anyone imagine him kissing the ruddy cheeks of John McGraw or the weazened face of little Huggins? Robbie was a man with no inhibitions; he acted on impulse, yet somehow that night he spoke and acted for all baseball—fans, writers, owners, managers, players—past and present, in his impulsive greeting of the great McGillicuddy.

"You loveable old son of a sea cook!" There was love, tenderness, affection, admiration in every syllable. Nearly two decades have passed since that party in Venice; and Uncle Robbie, McGraw, and Huggins have moved on to the Valhalla for America's sport heroes. But Mack remains a majestic figure, who at the age of eighty-two directs his famous club, the Athletics, through its forty-fifth American League season, as he goes into his seventh decade in professional baseball.

They have called him the patron saint of baseball. If the game of the future will have a patron saint, it is sure to be Connie Mack, a man of great kindliness, understanding, tolerance, success—a man who even can make success of a failure.

"My hat is off to Connie Mack," said Sam Breadon, president of the St. Louis Cardinal World's Champions, with unfeigned admiration. "Connie, of course, has won pennants and world's championships, but he can keep the fans coming with a tail-ender. If I finished last twice in succession in my town [St Louis], I would be through. Mack can finish last season after season and still have the fans piling up in front of his turnstiles. That is genius. Why, he drew nearly as much with a tail-ender in 1943 as I did with a championship club."

This writer finds writing the story of Connie Mack an especially pleasant task. To him the tall New Englander was an early hero. He saw his first professional baseball in Connie Mack's bleachers shortly after the turn of the century, and felt a boy's healthy thrill when Connie won his first Philadelphia pennants in 1902 and 1905. Even after years of sports writing, in which he found many popular sports figures to have feet of clay on closer inspection, he admits he never quite has got over this early hero worship.

"In all the years I've known Connie Mack, I've never known him to do a mean thing," said Clark Griffith, president of the Washington club, a lifelong associate. Perhaps Mack couldn't do a mean, or underhanded, thing; it just isn't in his make-up or nature.

A personal friendship increased one's respect and admiration for Connie Mack. For truly the story of Cornelius McGillicuddy, who as a tot worked from 6:30 A.M. to 6:30 P.M. in a New England cotton mill—and became the first figure in the nation's national sport—is a saga of American enterprise, genius in his line, and opportunity. Mack's career has had its deep vales as well as its peaks, but a brave heart never faltered. He has taken his disappointments with his top moments and never has he quit, whined, or lost his loftiness of spirit. Loved, respected, and revered by all in baseball, Connie Mack is much more than a great baseball man—he is a great American.

In writing this book, I had the kindly co-operation of the famous Philadelphia leader, visiting him some half a dozen times in his office in the Shibe Park tower, Philadelphia, and when his club played in St. Louis in 1943 and 1944. Much of the material in this book came graciously from Connie himself, and I am highly appreciative of his warmhearted assistance. I was amazed at his uncanny memory. In checking back some of the games he spoke of in his early major-league days in Washington and Pittsburgh, played over half a century ago, we never scored an error for Mack. He remembered the exact scores—even plays—of games in the eighties and nineties as though they had been played yesterday.

I wish to thank such former Athletic players as Jack Coombs, Eddie Collins, Al Simmons and Jimmy Dykes for their friendly assistance, Jack and Eddie on Mack's earlier champions; the present White Sox manager and Al on the later-day pennant winners. I also am indebted to such Philadelphia sports writers as Bill Dooly and Red Smith of the *Record* for amusing incidents in Connie's colorful career. Bill Brandt, head of the National League Service Bureau and a former Philadelphia baseball writer, was helpful in the period when Mack tried to make his first great comeback in 1925.

The big assist goes to Billy Garvie, veteran of the *Hartford Times* and sports historian of Hartford; another to John Heydler, former

National League president and a young government printer in 1888, on Mack's career in Washington. Frank Stevens, who ran the concessions for his dad, Harry Stevens, in Milwaukee while Connie ran the team, provided material for the Milwaukee chapter, while Charles (Chilly) Doyle of the Pittsburgh *Sun-Telegraph,* also a loyal Connie Mack fan, helped gather the material on Mack's formative years in Pittsburgh. I also express appreciation to J. Taylor Spink, publisher of the *Sporting News,* for permission to browse through the back numbers, files, and valuable clippings of his baseball newspaper.

CONNIE MACK

CHAPTER I

OUR HERO ARRIVES IN EAST BROOKFIELD

1

THE NATION was nearing its second war Christmas, December 22, 1862, in that fratricidal strife known to history as the American Civil War, when a third son was born to Mary McKillop McGillicuddy in the New England mill town of East Brookfield, Mass. Mary's husband, Michael McGillicuddy, a wheelwright by trade, was not home in the modest frame house when this male child arrived on that bleak winter day. Mike McGillicuddy was a "nine-months man," serving with the fifty-first Massachusetts Infantry. When the babe was baptized shortly after the new year, 1863, Mrs. McGillicuddy whispered to the Irish priest: "His name, Father, is Cornelius."

The McGillicuddys came from County Kildare, Ireland, the decade before. "There's a place in Ireland called the McGillicuddy Reeks," said Connie Mack. "A lot of Irish people know about it, and it was named after one of my ancestors. I always had hoped to see the McGillicuddy Reeks some day. I returned from the Orient by way of Suez and the Mediterranean after my baseball trip to Japan in 1934; I wanted to get to Ireland, but I had to get back to look after the affairs of my club and never got there."

Brookfield, Connie Mack's birthplace, was a boom town at the time of Connie's birth. The town's biggest industry was shoes, and the factories were working night and day turning out footwear for the Union armies. There were four Brookfields—Brookfield proper, East Brookfield, North Brookfield, and South Brookfield. Though George M. Cohan was born in Providence, R.I., while his parents were playing there, the Cohans lived in North Brookfield, which was Georgie's early home between theatrical engagements. "Brookfield was the town in George's show, *Fifty Miles from Boston*," said Connie, not unproudly. "It was quite a kick for me when George brought that show to Philadelphia years ago, and I had a chance to show the boys where the McGillicuddys came from."

As to Georgie Cohan, he was one of Connie Mack's first fans to his dying day. When the state of Pennsylvania, by special act of the legislature, set aside May 17, 1941, as "Connie Mack Day," Cohan wrote a song in Mack's honor for the occasion, "Mack Is the Grand Old Name." What's more, while Georgie was quite a Giant fan and for years was a boxholder at the Polo Grounds (once he nearly purchased the Giants), he not only rooted for, but bet on, Mack's Athletics when they met McGraw's New Yorkers in World's Series play. Cohan made sizable cleanups when the Athletics turned back the Giants in the series of 1911 and 1913. Both McGraw and Cohan were members of the Lambs, New York's famous club for theatrical men, and it hurt McGraw that George should bet against him and his team. Most of the Lambs of that time were rabid Giant partisans, and they considered Cohan's conduct next to treason. "But how could I root against a man from Brookfield?" demanded George. The McGillicuddys and Cohans have known each other for years."

Even now, Connie thinks it singular that the small community of Brookfield should have produced three big-leaguers, and all of them catchers—the two Bergens and himself. Marty Bergen was catcher for the great Boston National champions of the late nineties; and his younger brother, Bill, caught for the Brooklyn Dodgers in the first decade of this century. Marty Bergen, second only to Buck Ewing among old-time catchers, died in one of baseball's worst tragedies. He shot his wife and children in his farmhouse near North Brookfield, Massachusetts, in December, 1899, and then killed himself.

A Boston dispatch to the *Sporting News* of that period tells of Marty's cold and sad funeral. Because of the nature of Bergen's death, there was no one there from his church. Most of the players of the Boston champions of 1897-8 lived in the Greater Boston district, but of the entire team only Billy Hamilton attended the catcher's last rites at an undertaker's parlor.

"One other baseball man was in attendance," said the news story, "Connie Mack, the former Pittsburgh catcher and manager, and now manager of the Milwaukee team. Mack, who frequently had been a rival catcher to Marty Bergen, looked at the body of his old friend and one-time opponent, and as he turned away, his sympathetic blue eyes were filled with tears."

How like Connie Mack, never to let a man down, even in death, no matter what his misdeeds!

2

Cornelius was the third of seven McGillicuddy children, five boys and two girls. Of the seven, only Connie and the oldest, Michael, now eighty-eight, still are alive. Michael calls Connie "the Kid." The others were Nellie, two years older than Connie, and Dennis, Thomas, Eugene, and Mary—all younger. Michael, as short as Connie is tall, has an apartment in West Philadelphia and still is a frequent visitor at Shibe Park, where he has a small office.

The McGillicuddy strain has been American for practically a century now. The elder Michael McGillicuddy was brought to America by his parents in 1846 when he was ten years old. Ten years later he married a dark-haired colleen whose parents came to America about the same time as the McGillicuddys. A hard worker in East Brookfield's wagon factory, Michael was thrifty, believed in setting something aside; he was ambitious to do something in the new country and ambitious for his children. He lived until 1892, when Connie was thirty, long enough to realize what a son he had given to the fast-growing national sport of the New World. He gave Mack a heritage of honesty, straight dealing, and hard work; but Connie's character was molded to an even greater degree by his mother. No other person left as deep an impress on the mind and character of the future Athletic leader and America's most beloved baseball figure as Mary McKillop McGillicuddy.

"The children of our family got all of their guidance and

rules for right and wrong from our mother," said Mack. "She was a wonderful woman, and had an uncanny way of knowing what was for our best interests. We never went wrong following her advice."

As for Mrs. McGillicuddy, she found great comfort in her illustrious third son. Connie's first wife died after they had been married only five years, and during his eighteen years as a widower Mrs. McGillicuddy kept house for her tall son. In Connie's early years as manager of the Athletics, Mrs. McGillicuddy was almost as well known to Philadelphia's Columbia Park fans as the young Athletic manager himself. A sweet old lady, she usually carried a sunshade and sat daily in the same place in the grandstand, as she enjoyed victories won by her son's Athletics and the antics of Mack's illustrious early battery, Rube Waddell and Ossie Schreck. With a keen, Irish sense of humor, she would listen with amused seriousness as Connie confided his difficulties with his two problem children, Reuben and Ossie. "But Rube does win the games," Mrs. McGillicuddy would comment.

The courageous soul, who rightly may be called the mother of Mack's kindly philosophy and good sportsmanship, passed from this earth in 1912, at the age of seventy-five.

3

Wages in Brookfield, the Massachusetts shoe town, shortly after the Civil War were small and hours long. It was difficult for Mary McKillop McGillicuddy to feed nine mouths on the meager wages brought home by Michael. When summer vacation time rolled around in 1872, when Connie was nine, there was no loafing around the house, sleeping until nine, diving into a cool swimming hole, or playing ball through the long summer afternoons. At 5:30 Mother Mack got her brood out of bed; Connie was fed his breakfast of mush, and 6:30 he was at work in a near-by cotton mill. He toiled until 6:30 in the evening. Combining with his mother's influence in molding his character, this early experience with child labor gave Mack much of his human sympathy, broad understanding, tolerance, and appreciation of the other fellow's problem, especially when that fellow was the underdog.

"But it didn't seem so bad at the time," said Mack. "Most of the kids in our part of the town had to go to work early. Our parents and grandparents had worked hard in Ireland, also when they came over here, and life wasn't supposed to be easy. And we had fun! We got off an hour in the middle of the day. I hustled through my lunch in a quarter of an hour; that left me forty-five minutes for my ball playing. It wasn't exactly baseball, but a sort of rounders, or town ball.

"The boys of the village made a ring, something on the order of an English cricket field. There were places in the ring for two batsmen. The batter had to hit out of the ring to be safe and keep his time at bat. The boy who didn't hit also was compelled to take the base, or station, of the boy who had just batted. I never was an outstanding hitter in my professional career, but a man who is a ball player at heart enjoys the ring of the bat. I can still recall the thrill of knocking the ball over the heads of the boys, outside of the ring, on that Brookfield field."

Young Cornelius didn't have to work steadily at that early age. After summer vacations in the cotton mill, he returned to the study of the three R's, but he quit school after his grammar grades. For one thing, Connie seemed to grow only one way—up. Neither his father nor his brothers were tall, but the third McGillicuddy boy was nearly six feet when he was fifteen. He was the tallest boy in the school—in the village, for that matter—and he fitted poorly into the desks built for average-sized children. Though no older than the other kids in the class, his head and lean neck extended far above the desk, and his spindly legs constantly were searching for parking space from under his juvenile desk. Pranksters and self-styled wits had a lot of fun at Connie's expense, and he was at an age when these funsters made him self-conscious and awkward. So, the McGillicuddy fortunes being such as to deny the progeny of Michael and Mary the benefits of higher education, Mack left school in his early teens to learn the trade of shaping soles and cutting heels in Brookfield's major industry, the shoe factory. Connie Mack later became one of the greatest managers in America's national game because he is intelligent, quick-witted, and a natural leader. He quickly acquired the knack of making other men work for him. That trait manifested itself early in his career. He mastered his trade well, became a skillful operator, and before he was twenty-one, he was assistant foreman.

Hours at the shoe factory were just as long as at the cotton mill, but the tall lad was packed with energy, and he never lost that kid thrill, felt when a bat came into sharp contact with a baseball. Somehow he found time for ball playing —on Saturdays, Sundays, and after work when the days were long in summer. The game started by Cadet Abner Doubleday, later a Civil War general, in Cooperstown, N.Y., in 1839, found fertile soil in New England. There were no movies, radios, comics, crooners, motorboats, or golf for these hard-working sons of Irish immigrants. They knew only one summer recreation—the comparatively new game of baseball.

Mack kept on growing until he was six feet, four and a half inches tall; later as a National League catcher he weighed little more than 150 pounds. He had a high-pitched, piping voice, but he could play baseball and he could throw that ball around. It was before boys knew the luxury of gloves, and Connie could sting the calloused hands of the other boys as he uncocked those long skinny arms and let go his throws. He didn't care much where he played, so long as it was baseball; but naturally he gravitated in back of the plate. From his human stepladder he could see everything that was going on, and in his piping voice he shouted directions to his teammates.

He became catcher on East Brookfield's leading team; the club played adjoining towns, traveling from town to town in an open wagon. There were lots of quips and wisecracks, as the slender frame of Mack extended far above the sides of the wagon.

"Where ya taking that bean pole?" farmers along the way would call out. Players and fans referred to him as the "slats catcher," but there was nothing funny about Slats when he unlimbered himself and went to work. Only a fair hitter in his best playing years with Washington and Pittsburgh, Connie had no difficulty tanning the shoots fired at him by farm-lad pitchers and boys from other factory towns.

They played Sunday baseball, which shocked the sensibilities of many well-meaning sons and daughters of Massachusetts' Puritan forebears. They decried the fact that the new Irish immigrants were violating the old New England Sabbath. Connie and Mother Mack had much conversation on the subject. Mrs. McGillicuddy had plenty of Irish spunk; she took no one's back talk when she felt she was right, but she wanted to be sure she was right, and she brought up her children to be not only good Christians, but good citizens of the land in which she and Michael had established their home. But after Connie and the other boys had worked hard all week, she could see no harm in their playing the game which gave them so much fun and recreation on their day off, after they had first fulfilled their religious obligations. A parish priest perhaps clinched the matter when he remarked: "There are a lot of worse things idle young scalawags can be putting their minds and time to on a Sunday afternoon than this game of baseball."

Sixty years have seen a tremendous change in the national attitude toward Sunday baseball. Connie has lived to see a later generation of prewar Brookfield boys, whether of Irish or early Pilgrim ancestry, get in their cars on Sunday and drive to Fenway Park, Boston, to root for the Red Sox against his own Athletics. Where those who espoused Sunday baseball and a liberal Sabbath in the early eighties were considered extremists and a minority, those who now frown on it are the minority. In fact, Sunday has become the most important day in the baseball calendar.

4

In 1883 the towns comprising the four Brookfields and others in the surrounding district formed the Central Massachusetts Amateur League. They played a pretty fast game of ball; and Mack, the tall, lanky catcher, got into some keen competition. He still recalls vividly the thrill he felt when his team played exhibition games with the Worcester and Chicago teams of the National League. Worcester, once a baseball hotbed, had a National club in the early eighties, and playing them was a red letter day. Other big-league clubs then jumped out of Boston after the exhibition dollars in the Massachusetts hinterland just as they do today.

Anson's Chicago White Stockings visited Brookfield in 1883, and that was the thrill of thrills for baseball devotees of the shoe town. The Chicagos were the National League champions of 1881 and 1882, and Adrian Anson was the outstanding name among the game's managers and hitters. Probably old Cap, always something of a grouch, looked rather condescendingly at the tall young catcher who caught for East Brookfield as Cap strode to the plate. As for Connie, he couldn't have felt a greater reverence and awe if President Chester Arthur had come to town. Who then would have believed that the names of both Anson and Mack would be entered in a baseball Hall of Fame more than a half century later, and that, as the name of Anson grew faint in the national consciousness, that of Mack would grow brighter and brighter with the passing of the years?

Playing the big-leaguers who called on the town "fifty miles from Boston" was a thrill sure enough, but it was the frosting on the cake; the season's real business was the winning of the Central Massachusetts pennant. And, as such things happen in fact as well as in fiction, the game on which hinged the coveted championship was the final contest of the season between Mack's team, the East Brookfields, and North Brookfield. That was the game to win, and East Brookfield was the victor by a score of 2 to 1.

"I recall that game almost as though it was played yesterday," said Connie, his blue eyes looking out of the windows of his tower at Shibe Park, Philadelphia, as though he was peering over a span of sixty years. Those early shoe-town ball players, most of them no doubt on the other side of the Great Divide, pitched, batted, ran, slid bases again in his memory. "I have enjoyed many victories—games which meant much to me and to my Athletic club," he continued. "But I don't think any other brought me greater joy than when East Brookfield won. At the time, it seemed to be the most important baseball game that ever was played."

The pitcher on the winning East Brookfield club was a strong, stout young Irish lad, with a snapping fast ball, William Hogan. Willie, who would have been Connie's brother-in-law had he lived, was built on exactly opposite lines from the angular Mack; he was constructed on the generous lines of Frank "Shanty" Hogan, of Sommerville, Massachusetts, catcher for the later-day Giants and Boston Braves.

Connie Mack was the only man on his team who wore a

glove. Finger gloves were edging their way into league ball, but most of the East Brookfielders disdained such sissy tactics. The pitching distance then was forty feet, and the catcher stood twelve feet behind the plate; he usually grabbed the ball on the first bounce. Pitchers hurled underhanded, and batters had the privilege of calling for a high or low ball. Mack's teammates each chipped in a dime so he could buy a $2 buckskin glove; he clipped off the fingertips and sewed the ends together. This was all he had to protect his thin "meat hand" from foul tips and Willie Hogan's fast ball.

One of the reasons for Mack's longevity, his eternal youthfulness of spirit, his zest and never-tiring interest in the game, is that his approach today is little different from what it was when the two Brookfields battled in 1883. To the boy from the shoe factory it always has been a ceaseless wonder that some men should pay other men for playing a game—a game which is so much fun.

CHAPTER II

MERIDEN ENGAGES McGILLICUDDY

1

CONNIE'S love for baseball did not interfere with his work in the shoe factory, and Mrs. McGillicuddy's tall son had worked himself up to a pretty good job, as factory jobs went in the eighties. It paid Connie $15 a week. Perhaps Mack did dream of a baseball career when Cap Anson came to town with his white-stockinged, black-mustachioed, hell-raising gladiators; but if it hadn't been for the economic cycles which so often have hit the country—bad times following good times and vice versa—the professional diamond outside of the Brookfields might never have known Connie Mack. But fate took a hand in the election year of 1884. Election years in the eighties and nineties invariably saw the economic pendulum swing low; and, as the nation waited for Grover Cleveland and James Blaine to come to grips, the tariff on leather and shoes became one of the pawns in the struggle. Many of the New England shoe factories shut down. The one in which Connie was employed was among the first to be hit; workers were greeted by closed doors as early as March. There wasn't much use for the cutter of soles to apply to other factories; they, too, were laying off their men.

Though Mack's father still was alive, Connie long since had contributed heavily to the support of his mother and the younger children. There were no other jobs in Brookfield in which he could make decent wages, so he began to think that somebody might care to hire a slim baseball catcher. He read in a Boston newspaper that a group of baseball enthusiasts in Connecticut had met and formed the Connecticut State League. Young McGillicuddy, using some of his little savings, personally called on the managers of the clubs in Willimantic, New Britain, and Hartford, but no one was interested. "Ya ain't got enough flesh on ya bones; they'd be knockin' ya down," one manager said harshly.

"They haven't knocked me down so far," said Connie. "And if they do, I'll lose no time picking myself up."

"Well, it'll be different in this league. There'll be some rough boys playing here," was the rejoinder.

His heart heavy, the disappointed jobless young man returned to East Brookfield to make another effort to see what he might get around town, any job so long as it paid wages.

But a good angel intervened for Mack, and it was his cherubic possible brother-in-law, Willie Hogan. Unlike Mack's catching prowess, word of Willie's smoking fast ball had gotten out of the Brookfields. The new Meriden club had engaged Hogan as its pitcher. Connie, at the time, had a crush on Willie's sister, Margaret; perhaps she wrote to her hefty brother that Cornelius was feeling pretty low. Without Connie's knowledge, Hogan fronted for him with his manager and told him he couldn't promise his best services for Meriden unless he had his old East Brookfield side-kick, Connie Mack, catching for him. Willie was persuasive, and the manager wired Connie to report as soon as he could.

Connie was given his tryout in a preseason exhibition game, which Meriden played with the Yale freshmen. Yale then had powerful baseball teams, and frequently the Blue scheduled games with major- and minor-league teams to get the benefit of stiffer competition. Alternately pitching and catching for the Yale Varsity in those days was the "Grand Old Man of Football," Alonzo Stagg, now coach of the University of the Pacific, but in the eighties as active in Yale baseball as he afterward became in football. Both Mack and Stagg have been awarded the annual medal for outstanding sportsmanship by the Sportsmanship Brotherhood in recognition of the manner in which they played the game and for their part in making this a better world through the medium of clean, red-blooded sport. The venerable pair, both eighty-two, had a pleasant reunion when they were honored guests at the Los Angeles *Times* Sports Award dinner on December 27, 1944. They last had met in 1888 when Yale played an exhibition game with the Washington Nationals in 1888—Alonzo pitched for the Elis and Connie caught for the Senators.

In that earlier Meriden game, Hogan made monkeys out of the Yale frosh, fanning 21 of them. And he had no need to apologize for the catching of his old East Brookfield battery mate. Connie was all over the place, chirping like a cricket. And the Irish fairies must have been working in his behalf that day. After he had experienced no success in interesting anyone in his baseball abilities, offers suddenly tumbled in like manna from heaven. His family forwarded two telegrams which had come to him in East Brookfield. One of them was from Frank Selee of Waltham, offering him $12 a week and board. Selee later was the famous Boston and Chicago National League manager. And another from New Britain offered him $60 a month. Connie carefully read over the telegrams on the bus going out to the ball park, so that the Meriden manager, Tom Reilly, could glance over his shoulder.

"Do you want to sign now?" Reilly asked before the game.

"No," said Connie, feeling he had the job in his pocket; "Let's wait until after the game."

When he did sign, it was for $90 a month, without board, which wasn't bad at all. Willie Hogan was top man on the club with $100 a month; most of the other players received only $40 to $50. To Mack, in the spring of 1884, that $90 seemed more like $900.

2

Though twenty-one the previous December, young Cornelius didn't enter professional baseball for keeps without going into a long huddle with Mother Mack. She had a lot of wisdom and a pretty good picture of the life her son was entering. Professional baseball of the eighties wasn't exactly the kind of a profession a God-fearing Christian mother cared to see her son launch his life's ship upon. The game was full of booze-fighters and crude, boisterous, blasphemous roughnecks. A bunch of crooks were thrown out of the National League in 1877, but gamblers still had their slimy fingers on the game. Ball players were the sporting boys of the town by day; they had little or no social standing, so naturally they cavorted with the sporting girls of their respective towns at night. Even the big-league clubs were welcome at nothing better than the fourth-class hotels of that day, and in 1884 they really were fourth class.

"You'll find drinkers there—hard drinkers. They'll be wanting you to join them," Mrs. McGillicuddy said. "There'll be men saying things to you who will want to make you fight. I'll not ask you to make any promises, but you'll never get anywhere drinking and fighting."

Mack never forgot her words. And Connie was a good boy, with a sort of inherent goodness and decency. It never took the form of self-righteousness or a holier-than-thou attitude toward his fellow men. Vulgarity, filth, and shabbiness just repulsed him. At twenty-one he was an unusual young man, especially for one raised in a factory town of the eighties—he didn't drink, smoke, or swear.

In the years that followed, he hasn't always been an absolute teetotaler, as has been reported. As a player he took an occasional glass of beer, and in later years he has been seen taking a sip of wine to celebrate the winning of a World's Championship. "But I never liked the taste of the stuff, so for years I haven't touched anything," he said.

The same was true of his swearing. "I don't like profanity or obscenity around a ball club, or anywhere else," he said. "Once, when we didn't have much of a crowd, and the park for some reason or other was surprisingly still, Stuffy McInnis, my old first baseman, called out: 'Jesus Christ.' I called him to the bench and spoke to him about it. 'Did I say that, Mr. Mack?' he said in surprise. 'Only so loud that everyone in the grandstand and bleachers heard you,' I replied. 'Don't do it again.'" But occasionally, in a time of great stress, Connie himself has blown up with some vigorous language.

3

Both Mack and the Meriden club enjoyed a fine season in 1884. Connie was smart; he hit fairly well, and the fans enjoyed a good laugh when he unwound his long legs and tore around the bases. He wasn't overly fast, but he had a tremendous stride. And he won an early reputation for his repartee behind the plate. Connie wasn't mean or vindictive, but he wasn't tongue-tied either; and in his piping voice he fired many good-natured jibes at his opponents. With the catcher playing back, he stood almost with his back braced against the little grandstand, and the fans got a great kick out of his chatter. "You tell 'em, Connie; you tell 'em," they would encourage him.

Meriden finished second to Waterbury in a good race, and the club's high position was attributed to the early work of the Irish battery from East Brookfield, Hogan and McGillicuddy. Yet the season had tragedy for young Mack and the Meriden fans. In the late summer Willie Hogan, the strong boy, contracted what used to be called galloping consumption, and in a few days breathed his last. His sister, Margaret, found solace in the comforting presence of Connie Mack. The husky Hogan, whose fast ball had blinded those twenty-one Yale freshmen only a few brief months before, went to an early grave; while his skinny battery mate, Mack, who helped in this victory, is a healthy octogenarian today.

Reilly, the Meriden manager, dug up another pitcher, Jumping Jack Jones of Yale, and the team continued to win a good percentage of its games. The fans were so appreciative of Connie's efforts in his freshman year as a full-fledged professional that they presented him with a gold watch on the last day of the season. It was the first of a whole houseful of gifts presented to the tall New Englander at the home plate. Years later the watch was stolen in the Pittsburgh clubhouse, and its loss could not have touched Connie more deeply if it had been studded with rubies and diamonds.

That following winter, 1884-5, was the first in which Mack had loafed since leaving school, and one of the few in which he had no cares during his long professional career. He skated on Lake Lashaway, played cards with Brookfield cronies, went to Boston to do some shopping, and returned to East Brookfield wearing his first Derby hat.

4

The inscription in that watch was: "To Connie Mack from the fans of Meriden." It is interesting to note that since that early engagement Cornelius McGillicuddy always has played under the name of Mack. "Except when we voted, our people always called themselves Mack," explained Connie. "There is an idea that I shortened the name when I started to play professionally, but even in school the boys called me Mack.

"In fact, I never saw the name McGillicuddy in print until 1895, when I was manager of the Pittsburgh Pirates and we were playing a series at the Polo Grounds in New York. A well-known sports writer of that time, O. P. Caylor of the *New York Herald,* had a streamer across his sports page: 'McGillicuddy and his Pirates in Town Today.'

"Naturally I was curious to know how Caylor came to know my legal name, so I looked him up and asked him where he had heard it. The *Herald* man quickly explained the mystery. He told me he used to own a newspaper in Carthage, Missouri, and sold it to Eugene Roach, who was my first cousin.

"Roach and Caylor started to fan about baseball, and Gene told him he was a cousin of a well-known National League player. When Caylor asked who the player was, Roach replied: 'Why, McGillicuddy of the Pirates.'

" 'I don't know anyone on the Pirates by that name,' said Caylor.

" 'Oh, he's on the Pittsburgh team, all right; in fact, he manages it,' my cousin Eugene said. Caylor then understood that I was McGillicuddy.

"The Giants seemed to think it was funny, and they yelled: 'McGillicuddy' at me all through the game. It also was printed in the Pittsburgh papers, and when I got back home the fans in the stands yelled: 'McGillicuddy! Hey, McGillicuddy!' Somehow it seemed to strike them funny, or they thought that I had been hiding something. After the game a crowd of small boys followed me down the street from the ball park to my home, calling: 'Look, look; there goes Mr. McGillicuddy.' "

Connie's Missouri cousins, the Roaches, are real people in the Show-Me state. Eugene Roach made his paper a far greater power than its size. His brother, Cornelius Roach, the father of fifteen children, became secretary of state of Missouri. He was named after the same Irish forebear as was Connie. When the Cardinals of St. Louis played the Athletics in the World's Series of 1930 and 1931, the Roaches were torn between two loyalties—whether to root for the team of Cousin Cornelius McGillicuddy or for the Redbirds of Missouri, then led by Gabby Street of Joplin. There always are Roaches to call on Mack whenever he brings his Athletics to St. Louis.

CHAPTER III

NEXT STOP: HARTFORD

1

The newly formed Connecticut State League had no reserve clause; and in 1885 Connie was free to accept a job with Hartford in the South New England League. This proved quite a boost for the McGillicuddy finances, as the salary paid the young catcher was $125 a month. When word of it got around East Brookfield, they really thought Cornelius was a big shot. Why, that was well above the stipend paid the best shoe foreman in the Brookfields!

Before the season was over, Connie found himself one of the most talked-of young catchers in New England. The name of Connie Mack was getting around. He stuffed more wadding in his buckskin glove and had the open fingers sewed together. People were beginning to say: "Keep your eyes on that Mack; he's a smart one, and headed for the big league."

Later, in Hartford, Connie was the first to wear a rubber catching pad, invented by Bill Gray of Hartford. Gray had Mack and White, the Boston catcher, try it out in an exhibition game. Boston's White said: "It never will do," but Connie's verdict was: "It's all right; I think it will help the catchers." Gray sold his patent to Spalding's for $5,000; it eventually evolved into the catcher's mitt of today.

If Mack had been reared in a family of British cricketers, in which sportsmanship is a tradition, Connie couldn't have been a better sportsman. But if you can outwit the other side—and the umpire—in baseball, it always has been permissible, even though you cut corners on a rule here and there. Under the rules of the eighties, a caught foul tip was an out, regardless of the number of outs. As the batsman swung, Connie learned to make a noise with his bare hand slapped in his buckskin glove that sounded just like a foul tip. Frequently the umpire called the batter out, much to the latter's indignation and Connie's amusement. Later he was so successful with this trick in the National League that the rule was changed so that a batter is retired only if a catcher holds a foul tip on the third strike.

At Hartford, Mack was hooked up with a tall, skinny, right-handed pitcher, Frank Gilmore. Gilmore, another lean New Englander, had as little meat on his gaunt frame as Connie had, and Connecticut fans dubbed them the "Bones Battery."

In an early preseason exhibition game with the Mets (Metropolitans) of New York, Gilmore shut out the big-leaguers with three hits and struck out thirteen. "Gilmore will be a good pitcher when he combs some of the hayseed out of his hair," commented a New York scorer to Mack.

"Well, I didn't see any hayseed in his delivery," responded Connie dryly.

2

Mack never missed a chance to make an honest dollar; and, following the 1885 season in Hartford, the Bones Battery was invited to do its stuff for Poughkeepsie, New York, which had a strong independent team, playing other Hudson River towns and teams from the Catskills.

Connie's nearness to Manhattan proved another good break. The Mets were finished with their American Association championship season and were picking up exhibition dollars in the surrounding country. Football then was still wholly a college sport; there were no present-day restrictions against barnstorming by major-league clubs; and teams remained intact until the snow fell. In fact, the big-league club owners held players under contract until the end of the fall exhibition season. The Mets were in need of a catcher—their regular was out with an injury—and the manager, remembering Connie from the spring exhibition game, wired him, asking if he cared to come down to New York and give his team a hand.

It was with the Mets that Connie had his first taste of how they do things in the big leagues. Many of the exhibition games were played in what then were the New York suburbs, and the players traveled on the old Sixth and Third Avenue "L" lines, pulled by steam locomotives, to reach their destinations. The Mets were an aggregation of sturdy young baseball roughnecks of that period; they swore, sang, played pranks, and guzzled beer to their hearts' content. Seemingly they had plenty of money and liked to spend it. Instead of each hefty paying his nickel at the "L" window, some opulent Met plunked down a half-dollar and smaller change and paid for the crowd. Young Mack was impressed but never joined in the competition to be first at the window. He still was a green kid, but this sort of thing was upsetting him.

One day he sat on the bench with another player, a big catcher named Ripschlager. Connie confided: "I hope the fellows don't think I'm cheap; it seems somebody always is paying my fare."

"Don't let that worry you, Slats," said the big-hearted "Rip." "Sometime when you come into a saloon with the boys, buy a round of drinks, and that'll make you all right."

So, after the day's game, when the Mets hustled for a saloon, Connie edged his long skinny elbows up to the bar and piped: "This round is on me."

There were a few sly winks and amused grunts as Connie laid a dollar bill on the bar. No one then thought of eleven-cent beers; they came to only a nickel a throw. And a throw was a "schooner," with a real handle. But the little gesture went well with the ball team. "You're all right, Connie," they said. Connie had established himself as a man and a regular fellow; he had set 'em up for the team.

3

Connie was back with Hartford in 1886; and that season the Connecticut capital was taken into the Eastern League. It was a pretty snug compact loop, and included Newark, Jersey City, Bridgeport, Waterbury, and Meriden. Connie's pay was advanced to $200 a month, and in East Brookfield they were looking on the McGillicuddys as plutocrats. That was impressive money! Mack continued to catch Frank Gilmore in all of his games. He also helped out at first base when Billy Kreig caught. However, his 1886 batting average of .248 for 69 Eastern League games was scarcely enough to have big-league owners camping on his doorstep.

Washington then was in the National League and having difficulty in holding its own with the more opulent clubs with greater populations to draw from. The Senators were roosting at the bottom when Walter F. Hewitt, the Washington owner, went to Hartford on a September scouting trip. Club owners and their managers then did their own scouting. Reports had reached the big leagues of some pretty lively talent in Hartford, especially the long slim pitcher, Frank Gilmore. He had struck out more than 300 batsmen that season. However, Gilmore and Mack had made an agreement that they would stick together; if one got a chance at the majors, he wouldn't go unless his partner also was purchased.

After sitting in the Hartford stands for several days, Hewitt made Jack Remsen, the Hartford manager, a proposition for several players, headed by Gilmore. The Hartford players knew the Washington owner was looking them over, and Gilmore got wind of the players he wanted. Mack's name wasn't on the list. The string-bean right-hander called on Hewitt at his hotel.

"I hear you're ready to buy me, but don't want my catcher, Mack," Gilmore said. "I just came to say that wherever I go, he goes."

"Mack don't hit enough," protested Hewitt. "He couldn't hit National League pitching."

"He'll hit enough," insisted the pitcher loyally. "We go together, or I don't go to Washington."

Hewitt was impressed with this spirit of loyalty and decided it would be a mistake to separate the Bones Battery. He included Mack in his offer and purchased Pitchers Gilmore and John Henry, Catchers Mack and Billy Kreig, and George Shoch, who played either infield or outfield, for $3,500. Today Connie couldn't buy an obscure second-string Hartford catcher for that amount.

The Hartford fans gave Connie, and Gilmore, his battery mate, a great send-off. In their final game as a battery for the Connecticut Senators, the Hartford rooters presented Mack with a gold-headed cane and a diamond stickpin and Gilmore with a gold watch. Thanks to the Meriden fans, Connie already had a watch.

"They surely like us here," said Mack to his lean associate. "Too bad we have to leave such fine people."

But Connie Mack found fine people to appreciate him wherever he went in the next fifty-nine years!

CHAPTER IV

BONES BATTERY GOES TO WASHINGTON

1

THE FIVE Hartford players purchased by Hewitt were ordered to report immediately to Manager Mike Scanlon of the Washington team, and Gilmore and Mack were put to work as soon as they reported to the club. The man who was to see more big-league baseball than any other made his major debut with the Senators at old Capital Park, Washington, on September 11, 1886, nearly six decades ago.

Shoch and Kreig, two of the other players purchased from Hartford, also were in the game; and, thanks to a three-run rally in the eighth inning—started by Mack's single—Washington won the ball game from Philadelphia, Connie's home town for the last forty-five years, by a score of 4 to 3. While Gilmore struck out ten Phillies, the tall pitcher was fidgety and nervous and guilty of four errors. Throughout the game Connie had to steady him with words of encouragement. "Steady now, Frank; they're no tougher here than they were in Hartford," he called back to his pitcher.

When Manager Scanlon looked at the two bean poles in poorly fitting uniforms walking to their respective places at the start of the game, he grinned and remarked: "The Shadow Battery, eh!" It was a new one to go with the "Bones Battery" and promptly found favor in Washington.

Writing of the game in a Washington newspaper of 1886, an old-time baseball writer had this to say of Mack's first big-league game: "Mack's single started Washington's winning rally in the eighth inning, as the score was 3 to 1 in favor of Philadelphia when the Senators found use for their bats." Relating the rally in greater detail, he wrote: "Mack made a hit, and Gilmore took first on Shortstop Irwin's error; both were advanced on a passed ball, and scored on Hines' rattling three-bagger. Carroll's single then sent Hines across the plate with the winning run."

Of Connie, the catcher, he said: "Mack received Gilmore's delivery in masterly manner and threw in fine style."

Among the Philadelphia players who played against Mack on the day of his major debut were Jack Clements, one of baseball's few left-handed catchers; First Baseman Sid Farrar, father of Geraldine Farrar, the opera singer; and Arthur Irwin, later manager of the Phillies and Giants and a well-known baseball coach at the University of Pennsylvania.

Only a fortnight remained of the 1886 season, but Mike Scanlon's new Shadow Battery quickly did itself proud. Shortly after his inaugural game, lanky Gilmore pitched a one-hit game against Kansas City, in which he fanned twelve men, and he followed that by striking out sixteen St. Louis batsmen, September 28, even though Washington was on the losing side, 5 to 2.

Gilmore had a preliminary motion, which was part of his stock in trade, and most amusing to the fans of the eighties. It was an amazing procedure. With his long arms and spindly legs, this half of the Bones-Shadow Battery twisted himself into a pretzel, and then, untangling himself, would shoot the ball with terrific force to the waiting Mack. Frank also knew how to pitch a pretty good early version of the curve ball. The Washington fans guffawed as batsmen swung futilely at the fast pitch, which came to rest in the skinny paws of the grinning Mack, standing a dozen feet behind the plate.

In Hartford, Walter Hewitt had expressed a doubt that Mack would hit in the National League; Frank Gilmore had insisted he would. Frank won that argument hands down. Connie was hotter than a firecracker in his ten games before the Senators rang down their 1886 curtain; he cracked out 13 hits for an average of .361, which was to be far above his pace in later years. Hewitt paid Mack $800 for finishing that

Box-Score of Connie Mack's First Game in the Majors at Capital Park, Washington, September 11, 1886

PHILADELPHIA (N. L.)

	A.B.	R.	H.	O.	A.	E.
Wood, L. F.	5	0	2	4	0	0
Andrews, C. F.	5	0	0	0	0	0
Mulvey, 3B.	5	1	1	0	1	0
Fogarty, 2B.	4	1	0	3	2	1
Ferguson, R. F.	2	1	1	1	0	0
Irwin, S.S.	3	0	0	1	7	1
Dailey, P.	4	0	2	1	6	1
Clements, C.	4	0	0	4	2	0
Farrar, 1B.	3	0	1	10	1	0
	35	3	7	24	19	3

WASHINGTON (N. L.)

	A.B.	R.	H.	O.	A.	E.
Hines, C. F.	3	1	2	3	0	0
Carroll, L. F.	4	0	1	2	0	0
Farrell, 2B.	4	0	0	4	3	0
Kreig, 1B.	4	0	1	6	0	0
Shoch, R. F.	3	0	0	0	0	0
Houck, S.S.	3	1	1	1	2	1
Knowles, 3B.	3	0	0	0	1	1
MACK, C.	3	1	1	11	1	0
Gilmore, P.	3	1	0	0	11	4
	30	4	6	27	18	6

Philadelphia	0	0	0	2	0	1	0	0	0—3
Washington	0	0	0	0	1	0	0	3	x—4

Two-base hits—Hines, Houck, Wood. Three-base hit—Hines. Stolen base—Fogarty. Double play—Fogarty, Irwin, and Farrar. Earned runs—Philadelphia, 1; Washington, 2. First base on errors—Philadelphia, 2; Washington, 1. Bases on balls—off Gilmore, 4; off Dailey, 1. Struck out—by Gilmore, 10; by Dailey, 2. Wild pitch—Dailey. Passed ball—Clements. Umpire—Pearce.

EDITOR'S NOTE: Under 1886 scoring rules, pitchers were given assists for strike-outs, accounting for Gilmore's large total of assists.

season with Washington, and Connie impressed the club owner so favorably that he signed the young New England catcher to a $2,750 contract for 1887. By this time East Brookfield bracketed the former assistant shoe-factory foreman with the Astors and Vanderbilts.

2

The season of 1887 was a busy and happy one for Connie Mack. Washington again had a mediocre club, but things were going Connie's way. He was proving himself to be a shrewd, crafty workman behind the plate. He had a chance to compare himself with other National League catchers. Some were better hitters, but Connie learned he could catch and throw with the best of them. He had keen wit and chattered continuously to his pitcher and opponents. The little Washington grandstand egged him on. "Give 'em some of your mind, Connie," the fans would shout as his high-pitched voice could be heard above the din and bustle of the ball game.

On May 17, when Cap Anson's Chicago White Stockings played in Washington, Marty Sullivan, the Chicago outfielder, slapped out three triples. The next day Connie kidded Marty so much about his display of power that the Chicagoan made five errors. "Well, you surely did hit that ball yesterday. You're quite a hitter," complimented Mack. "Good thing for us you don't bat against us every day." "Is that tall guy kidding me?" Sullivan asked himself as he went to his outfield post and dropped a fly. "Well, you don't often muff flys," consoled Mack as Sullivan again came to the plate. "But, then, a feller can't do everything—hit three-baggers and catch all those difficult line drives." Connie had Marty so that he didn't know whether he was coming or going, and before the game was over he couldn't catch a ball with a butterfly net.

Gilmore and Mack, the Bones Battery of Hartford and Scanlon's Shadow Battery, acquired a new name; fans from all over the country now were speaking of them as the "Hartford Battery." They became an attraction not only in the National League, but on the exhibition belt. The Washington club was besieged with requests for exhibition dates, the big stipulation being that it bring along the angular Hartford Battery.

Playing with Washington in Connie's first full season as a big-leaguer was Paul Hines, the outfielder credited with being the first picket man to make an unassisted triple play with the Providence National League Grays in 1878. Another teammate was Pitcher Hank O'Day, a young Chicago Irishman who had come to Washington in 1887 from the Savannah club. Hank came up with a good fast ball and a bag of pitching tricks. Connie also caught the Chicagoan and started a friendship which lasted until the day of O'Day's death in 1935. Baseball fans, of course, know that Hank became a great National League umpire—one of the best in a century of baseball. What soothsayer could have predicted in 1887 that eighteen years later Mack would be directing a team against the pennant-winning club of the National League for the World's Championship, and that O'Day would be one of the umpires!

Mack, with that lifelong knack of making people like him, made himself so popular with the Washington fans by his heady catching and all-around worthiness that late in the season they presented him with a silver tea set. Nick Young, the president of the National League, who lived in Washington, made the presentation.

Connie had immediate use for the tea set, for following the season he contracted his first marriage—to Margaret Hogan of Spencer, Massachusetts, sister to Connie's early battery partner, Willie Hogan, the fat boy, who put in the plug for Mack with Meriden. Mrs. McGillicuddy lived only five years after her marriage, and three children blessed the union—two sons, Roy and Earle, and a daughter, Margaret. Earle is assistant manager of the Athletics and Roy is vice-president and secretary. Margaret died at the age of forty, leaving two sons.

3

The season of 1888 started as a glorious adventure for Connie Mack. Ted Sullivan, one of the picture-book characters of baseball, had succeeded Mike Scanlon to the management of the Senators. Like Mack, when he became a manager, Ted had the spirit of the pioneer. He always was introducing special innovations and seeking new baseball worlds to conquer. Ball players still speak of day coaches as "Sullivan Sleepers."

Wherever a railroad would lay its tracks, Ted would day-coach his players.

There has been some dispute as to which club was the first to train in the South. Cap Anson, the old Chicago White Stockings leader, is credited by some with being the first to take a major-league club into the deep Southland for preseason conditioning. But in 1888 Ted put his Washington club in a Jacksonville-bound Sullivan Sleeper. It wasn't exactly Florida training de luxe, as experienced by many big-leaguers prior to Pearl Harbor. The hotel where the Washington club was housed consisted of two shacks in the outskirts of Jacksonville—near the ball park. There the housekeeper—a lady who wasn't too particular about her guests—put up Sullivan's players for $1 a day for three meals and a bed.

Yet for the young New Englander it was fun, diversion, and adventure. It wasn't so long before that he had had to report at 6:30 A.M. at the shoe plant. As he basked in the semitropical sun, listened to the raucous cries of angry mockingbirds, the croaks of frogs—even of distant alligators—he knew he was living, seeing his country and the world. And again he chuckled that he was being paid good money for all this. Married to a sweet girl, he thought he was the luckiest lad in all the land. The Senators played exhibition games in Jacksonville for the swells down in St. Augustine, and in places where Yankee troops from the Brookfields had been only two decades before—Savannah, Charleston, and Raleigh.

The actual season of 1888, however, was a dismal failure for Washington and gave Mack his first real baseball heartache. Sullivan always was a better promoter than he was a manager. His club promptly sank into the cellar and stayed there, and comedians of the vaudeville and burlesque stage first started drinking their toasts to Washington, "first in war, first in peace, and always last in the National League." Yet Sullivan had one good alibi—the skinny right arm of Frank Gilmore, pitching member of the Hartford Bones Battery, suddenly lost its snap.

With a Florida training season behind him, Gilmore should have had an edge on other pitchers and enjoyed his best season. Perhaps in untangling himself from his acrobatic windup he put too much of a strain on his long, lean whip of an arm, and a tendon—or something—gave way. He couldn't get the ball up to the plate, let alone break a pane of glass with it.

Clubs didn't go in for the luxury of a trainer in those days, and players rubbed their arms with anything from liniment to snake oil acquired from traveling Indian—or paleface—medicine men who wore feathers and rubbed clay-colored chalk on their cheeks. Players then slept two in a bed; and, though the smell usually operated against a restful night, Connie faithfully rubbed in whatever remedies his battery mate could lay hands on. But all to no avail. The great Gilmore arm failed to come back. With three- and four-man pitching staffs, no club could afford to carry a sore-armed pitcher. Much to the distress of Connie, one half of the Bones Battery was released, and he was left to catch the deliveries of Hank O'Day, George Haddock, and Aleck Ferson. As for Connie, it was a bad season at bat. Try as he might, he couldn't get that ball safe and finished with the anemic average of .186. Perhaps concern for his wife, who was expecting, had much to do with the slump. Connie's eldest son, Roy, was born in Washington, August 27.

At the close of the 1888 season the spirit of adventure still was with him. Instead of returning to Massachusetts for the cold New England winter, he took the young mother, who was none too robust, to the sunny climes of southern California. There he took part in exhibition games with resident big-leaguers and lesser players wintering there and managed to make expenses.

Washington had another poor team in 1889 and again finished in the eighth slot. However, if the Senators again were down, Mack was up—up over 100 points in his batting. His average sprouted like Jack's bean pole; it soared from .186 to .292. And Connie was quite busy, playing ninety-seven games—helping out in the infield positions when he wasn't catching.

"It's odd about players, how they hit in cycles," reminisced Connie, discussing his "high, low, and the jack" hitting of 1888 and 1889. "They will go through a stretch when everything they do is wrong. They meet the ball well but line it directly into the hands of the fielders. At other times the fielders just can't get them out. I seemed to hit just the same in 1889 as in my lean season the year before, but this time the ball just fell safe."

4

Speaking of the Washington club of Mack's day, John Heydler, for many years president of the National League, who went to Washington in 1888 as a young government printer, recalled: "Washington was in the big league then, but you would hardly believe it from present-day standards. The Hewitt brothers, grain merchants on Seventh Street, owned the club, and they had a small and primitive grandstand at G and North Capitol Street, which they called Capital Park. We could see the games from the upper floors of the Government Printing Office, as it was only a block from the ball park.

"Everybody around the printing office knew and loved Connie Mack. He was one of our favorite players. There was a small butcher shop opposite the park on G Street, where Mack used to have a daily small steak cut to put in his left finger glove. Then we younger fellows also would buy steaks to put into our gloves. The butcher didn't know his baseball too well and expressed wonder that we should eat up all his steaks. Also he never could understand why Connie's daily steak didn't put more flesh on his bones.

"In those days, which were prior to the big-glove period, it was no fun for the catcher to come up behind the bat, and the small steak that Connie stuck into his glove felt very good. Catchers, especially in one-sided games, then kept as far back as the stand would permit. And in Mack's Washington days he stood with his back against the grandstand. But there was a sound method in playing so far back. A foul tip caught was out. The Washington pitchers kept the pitch on the inside and high, which helped the tip. Connie's size and long reach did the rest. I recall three men going out in one inning on foul tips to the long, angular Mack."

CHAPTER V

CONNIE GOES RADICAL

1

THE YEAR 1889 was a year of agitation, secret meetings, and dissatisfaction among the players of the National League and the old major American Association. The Baseball Brotherhood, a union of ball players with strong Leftist tendencies, was formed. Players were getting tired of having the club owners make all the money—or so they believed. It was time for the players to get a better reward for their toil and sweat. And Mack, the former East Brookfield shoe hand, was right in there with them.

Procuring backers for clubs in New York, Brooklyn, Philadelphia, Boston, Buffalo, Chicago, Cleveland, and Pittsburgh, the seceding players launched the Players League. The idea of the league was 'that the promoters would divide their profits evenly with the players. Maybe it was just a share-the-profits organization, but the National League club owners of that time, and also those who followed, regarded it as next door to baseball communism.

Most of the leading National League players of 1889 threw in their lot with the new league. The Players League war ruined the famous Chicago White Stockings; it was years before they regained their old-time skill and prestige. It broke the New York owner, John B. Day, whose Giants had won the National League pennants and World's Championships of 1888 and 1889.

Men who later became conservative club owners and league officials were ringleaders in the new league—which was to line the players' pockets. Charles Comiskey, later the opulent owner of the Chicago White Sox, left Von Der Ahe's St. Louis Browns of the American Association to manage the Players League club in Chicago. John K. Tener, later anything but a pink as a Republican Congressman, governor of Pennsylvania and president of the National League, jumped from Chicago to the Pittsburgh club and became treasurer of the Brotherhood. John Montgomery Ward, later a New York attorney and president of the Boston Braves, jumped the Giants and was one of the shining lights of the Brotherhood in New York.

The Washington National League players of 1889, almost to a man, went to Buffalo to form the Players League team in that city. So naturally Mack went with the Washington rebels. Even today Connie has no regrets for having jumped to the Players League, even though the experience wiped out his first bank account.

"I was younger then, and things looked different to me," he said. "I was an enthusiastic Brotherhood and Players League man. It seemed to me then that we had a good cause, and the Brotherhood intended to correct some of the inequalities and abuses which then existed in baseball. No doubt today, having some idea of the difficulties of operating a major-league club, I would take a different view of such a movement."

Mack signed with the Buffalo Players League club for the same sum he received in Washington in 1889. What is more, he took all the money he had saved from six years of catching and "invested" it in the Buffalo club. Connie was going to play it both ways. As a player, he was to share in the profits; as an investor, he was to take down a piece of the club's profit.

2

Connie Mack worked hard for his investment in 1890. Maybe if other players had worked as hard, the Players League would not have been such a fiasco. Mack was not a great player, nor is his name included among the catching knights of the game—the immortal Buck Ewing, greatest of the old-timers; Roger Bresnahan, Johnny Kling, Bill Dickey, and Mack's later-day

Mickey Cochrane. But in that single Players League season he established a major-league record for catching 119 games, a mark which stood up all through the nineteenth century. The record held until 1902, when Johnny Kling of the Cubs caught 128 games. Ray Schalk of the White Sox, nearly a foot shorter than Mack, advanced the record to 151 games in 1920. And Connie's present-day sturdy Athletic catcher, Frank Hayes, tied Ray Mueller of the Reds for a new record by catching all of his team's 155 games in the war year of 1944.

That Buffalo Brotherhood club started off in a scoring frenzy. No club in baseball ever broke from the barrier with such a rush of runs to the head, as the Bisons swept a series with Cleveland by scores of 23 to 22, 15 to 8, 19 to 7, and 18 to 15. "They just couldn't get us out," chuckled Connie. The Bisons scored 75 runs on 73 hits and 44 Cleveland bases on balls, but Connie had to be satisfied with 5 of the hits. However, the Brotherhood Buffalos, recruited as they were largely from Senators, soon brought their Washington tail-end habits to the big New York town, and the club slipped rapidly to the bottom.

Despite Connie's zeal and hard work, that season of 1890 was a sad one for the little family of McGillicuddy. Buffalo had made several attempts to support a major-league club, but the lake city soon became cool toward the new venture. With the National League, Players League, and American Association all claiming to possess major-league status—and bidding for patronage—the fans became surfeited with the whole business. They remained away from the many ball parks in droves, and in late-season games the players outnumbered the spectators.

Players League promoters soon ran out of money, and the Buffalo tap was one of the first to run dry. The little which trickled in at the gate was insufficient to meet the pay roll. Mack and his mates played the last month of the season for fun—and expensive fun. Instead of drawing a fat dividend on his cash investment, Connie saw his nest egg go up in smoke when the ill-fated league blew up after one season. So, at the age of twenty-eight, Mack, now a young family man, had no more than when he left East Brookfield in 1884 to catch Willie Hogan on the Meriden team.

CHAPTER VI

MACK BECOMES A PIRATE

1

FOLLOWING THE crackup of the Brotherhood and Players League, Connie Mack was assigned to the Pittsburgh National League club, a team which had been hit hard by the baseball war; it finished a miserable last under the management of Guy Hecker in 1890. Ned Hanlon, a former great outfielder who managed the Pittsburghs in 1889 and jumped to the Brotherhood, was back in command in 1891. Before the season was over, Ned was succeeded by Bill McGunnigle, who had led pennant winners in Brooklyn in both the American Association and the National League. Hanlon then went on to manage the great Baltimore Orioles, National League champions of 1894, 1895, and 1896. Connie always had a wholesome respect for his 1891 leader.

"Hanlon was one of the really great managers of baseball," said Mack," and I am proud that I once played under him. He later was fortunate in getting such great—and brainy—players as John McGraw, Hugh Jennings, Joe Kelley, and Willie Keeler; but Hanlon was smart, one of the great generals of baseball. He thought up many of the plays which McGraw, Jennings, and Keeler executed. All three had been around the league for several seasons before Hanlon brought out their full ability."

The 1891 Pittsburghs (they then were the Stogies) trained at St. Augustine, where Mack had another chance to see Florida in the spring. The Stogies traveled in a little better style than Tim Sullivan's Washington caravan to Jacksonville three years before. J. Palmer O'Neil, who ran the club, felt that a ball club should show some signs of opulence. He never smoked anything less than 25-cent cigars, and even when receipts were low he retained an affable disposition.

Among the pitchers Connie handled in Pittsburgh that year were Jim Galvin, Harry Staley, Al Maul, Mark Baldwin, C. Scott Stratton, and "Silver" King. "Silver" was the great pitcher of the old St. Louis Browns, who had jumped to the Chicago Brotherhood team and was assigned to Pittsburgh. Mack's companion catcher was George Miller; and the infielders to whom Connie snapped his throws were Jake Beckley, Louis Bierbauer, Charley Reilly, Sam LaRoque, Ed Spurney, and Frank (Piggy) Ward. The outfield was manned by Hanlon, Roger (Pete) Browning, the old Louisville slugger, Fred Carroll, John Corkill, and Dan Lally.

2

The signing of Bierbauer by the Pittsburgh club started a new baseball war and gave the team with which Mack then was associated the nickname which it has carried down through the years—the Pirates. After the Players League tossed in the sponge, players who had jumped from National League or American Association teams were ordered back to the clubs with which they had played in 1889, unless otherwise assigned. Through an oversight, the Philadelphia Athletics, an earlier edition of the club which in this century was to be synonymous with the very words, Connie Mack, failed to reserve two players —Bierbauer, a second baseman, and Harry Stovey, an outfielder and famous speed-boy. The Pittsburgh Nationals then signed Bierbauer, and the Bostons engaged Stovey.

The American Association shouted its indignation to the high heavens and charged the Pittsburgh club with piracy—hence the Pirates. A board of arbitration awarded the two disputed players to Pittsburgh and Boston, respectively. The Association refused to accept the verdict and started a new baseball war, which ended the following winter with the National League and American Association merging into a twelve-club league. In the merger the old Philadelphia Athletics passed out of the baseball picture. Had someone then told Mack, the young Pittsburgh catcher, that he would bring back the famous Gothic "A" of the Athletics to major-league baseball and lead the team to its greatest laurels, Connie would have replied in the vernacular of that day: "Tell that to my Aunt Fanny."

3

In 1892, Pittsburgh's first season in the newly formed twelve-club league, Mack's new bosses were Tommy Burns, the old Chicago third baseman, who was named Pirate manager; and William C. Temple, who succeeded Palmer O'Neil to the club presidency. Temple was a well-known figure in American sports during the nineties and later offered the Temple Cup to the winners of a postseason series between the first- and second-place National League clubs, which developed into a sort of an early World's Series.

A smart catcher in Washington, Connie, profiting by experience, became an even more cagey workman behind the plate. It was about this time that the catcher moved in close behind the batter; and Mack, who had won an earlier reputation for simulating foul tips, now won a new one for tipping bats. Always he would apologize most humbly and profusely. He was known as "the talking catcher," but his talk didn't go into personalities, such as maligning a man's antecedents and casting aspersions on his character, a practice freely indulged in, especially by the Orioles and Pat Tebeau's Cleveland Spiders.

"But don't let anyone kid you that Connie was a little tin god behind the plate," Wilbert Robinson, Mack's Baltimore catching rival and the man who kissed Connie in Venice, once said. "He could do and say things that got more under your skin than the cuss words used by other catchers," said Robby.

As in the case of Marty Sullivan in Washington, Mack's favorite method was to engage a rival batsman in conversation and praise him as he came to bat. "Say, Cap, you surely made a fine hit the last time you were up," he would say to Cap Anson, then slowing up but still a constant threat at the plate.

"How did you hit that ball so far? Why, when I called for that pitch, I thought it would strike you out."

Mack coached his pitchers to give him a quick delivery. His strategy was to take the batter's mind off the next pitch by making him think over Connie's compliment and a proper rejoinder. Often, when the hitter's attention was thus distracted, the pitcher shot in a quick third strike, and the umpire bellowed: "Yer out!"

"When I played ball, I often remembered an old expression of my boyhood days in East Brookfield, that you can catch more flys with honey than with vinegar," recalled Connie.

In later years Mack had his jockeys, especially Jimmy Dykes, Eddie Rommel, and Mule Haas of his last great champions. He had a chattering bench. But his players knew how far they could go, even though in the 1929 World's Series Judge Landis had to call in Mack and request him to put a gag on his team.

Bill Wambsganss, the fellow who made the unassisted World's Series triple play and played with the Athletics late in his career, once related a conversation Connie had with his players in the Athletic clubhouse.

"There is room for gentlemen in any profession, and baseball is my profession," Mack told his players. "I don't know of many games that have been won by rowdy tactics, and I've seen a lot of them. I will not permit my players to indulge in rough jockeying, as they call it. There always is an exchange of joshing before and during a game. The average player is a good-natured chap and a practical joker. But I have told our boys that there never can be anything personal or malicious shouted at our opponents.

"We face the possibility of a charge that we are timid, but I always will insist as long as I am manager of the club that my boys be gentlemen. They may kid back and forth, but I will not tolerate profanity, obscene language, or personal insults from my bench."

4

Feeling that he was delivering for the Pirates and bringing in his share of the fans, Mack figured a raise might be in order, but his hopes for greater financial security were dashed rudely late in the 1892 season. Twelve of the leading Pittsburgh players were called to the front office, where they were addressed by Colonel W. W. Kerr, who soon was to relieve Temple and take over the Pirate presidency. Kerr didn't mince his words.

"You know what we've been up against, men," he said. "It has been a tough year for us here in Pittsburgh, as well as for the other club owners in the league. We can pay you fellows just a certain amount of money, and no more. We have contracts made out for each one of you here for $2,400 for the 1893 season. And those who don't sign now will get contracts calling for $2,100 in the spring."

Rather bitter at the action of the club, the grumbling players, still subdued by the quick collapse of the Players League, signed the $2,400 contracts. But Mack did so with a heavy heart. He felt the game which he had made his life's work was going back instead of moving forward. The baseball wars, first between the Players League and the National and later between the National and the American Association, had left the fans indifferent and gave some justification for the $2,400 limit. Yet that limit, which was adopted by all twelve National League clubs, was to remain in Mack's mind and figure heavily in the start of the American League less than a decade later.

That winter a discouraged fellow player wrote to Mack and talked of quitting the game. "My only fear is that the game may quit," wrote back Connie Mack.

5

The season of 1893, the first of the $2,400 top salary limit, was one which made Pittsburgh a hotbed of excitement, and it is one of which Mack still speaks today with a certain pang of regret. For the 1893 Pirates it was a season of might-have-beens. Under the new leadership of Al Buckenberger, the Pittsburghers—long a baseball underdog, as were the Browns of 1944—became a real fighting contender; they ran first a good part of the season, had the entire nation pulling for them, and eventually finished a good second to a strong Boston club in the twelve-club grind.

However, the season saw Mack meet with a serious accident, which he feels shortened his playing career by five years.

"We were playing the Bostons, our leading rival, and I threw down to second to break up a double steal," Connie recalled. "Bierbauer's return throw to the plate was hurried and a bit on the inside. Herman Long, the crack Boston shortstop, was the man coming in, and he hit me hard. My left leg was ripped open between the knee and the ankle, and I was carried off the field with a torn leg and a fractured ankle. It was about ten years before Roger Bresnahan, as a member of the Giants, introduced shin guards; and I often think what a blessing they are for present-day catchers. They could have saved me from the severity of this accident. Long also was out for three weeks, but I was out much longer. I played only thirty-six games that season, and it promised to be one of my best batting years, as I hit .325. I never was the same player after that. I was slower on the bases and couldn't stoop as well behind the plate. It would catch me in the calf, where I had been spiked. Buckenberger and some of the players were kind enough to say that my injury cost the team the pennant."

6

Following their strong season of 1893, Pittsburgh expected big things from the club in 1894. But the upstart club in Baltimore, the Orioles, handled by the Pirate castoff, Hanlon, were turning the league race upside down. The Giants, with Rusie enjoying a great year, were up there, as were the scrappy Cleveland Spiders; but the Pirates were back in the muck. William W. Kerr, the president, sent for Mack in midseason.

"I don't like the way this club is being run," said Kerr. "We should be winning more games. Mack, I've been watching you, and I like your work. I think you're smart. How would you like to manage the club?"

Loyal, fair-dealing Connie Mack, instead of thinking of himself, thought of the great fight of 1893 and immediately began making excuses for Buckenberger.

"I don't think you can blame Al for our poor showing," he said. "Buckenberger is a good manager and knows his baseball.

But we've had a lot of bad breaks. I, for one, am not catching the ball I did last year before I was spiked."

"All right," said Colonel Kerr. "I will give the matter some more consideration."

However, another six weeks went by, and there was no improvement in the club; in fact, the Pirates, 1893 runners-up, sank deeper into the second division. Kerr again sent for Mack.

"Connie, I am offering you the management of the Pittsburgh club," he said. "There isn't any use in your turning it down, as I definitely have decided on a change. Buckenberger is out, and if you do not take it, it will have to go to someone else."

Mack had given much thought to Kerr's first offer. It was hurting him more and more to crouch behind the plate, and he knew he was being thrown out on plays which he once beat with ease. He realized his days as a hundred-game-a-season catcher were over, and he had to think of his future and the three children he was bringing up.

"Colonel Kerr, I accept," he said. "I am sorry to see Al go, but I will do the best I can for you."

CHAPTER VII

A 22-1 INAUGURAL

1

MACK TOOK charge of the Pittsburgh club on September 3, 1894; and approximately fifty years later all Pennsylvania, from Lieutenant Governor Bell down, filed into Shibe Park, Philadelphia, to celebrate Mack's golden jubilee as a big-league manager. Furthermore, that 1894 inaugural was a gala day, one worthy to be fittingly celebrated a half-century afterward. The Pirates ushered in their new skipper most impressively, defeating Washington, Connie's old alma mater, 22 to 1. "My, we made runs that day," laughed Mack. "The scoreboard almost ran out of numbers."

The 1894 club perked up in the month in which Mack was in charge and finished seventh. But the tall New Englander's 1895 team had a splendid chance to put the young manager over the top in his first complete season in charge.

"We had a pretty fair club," reminisced Connie, "and were in first place on the Fourth of July. That meant 11 other clubs were trailing us. I believe we would have won, too, if Frank Killen, the great left-hander, hadn't been badly spiked in Baltimore on June 11. He had his leg ripped open while covering the home plate, and we had to leave him in a Baltimore hospital for 49 days. You can guess what that meant to my club when I say Killen won 36 games in 1893, and in 1896, my last year in Pittsburgh, he won 31 and lost 19. I also had difficulty in keeping some of the men in condition, but we stayed up in the race until late in the summer, and Killen's injury really beat me. Had I won that pennant, it would have made me a real big shot in Pittsburgh; for, with the exception of 1893, Pirate fans had known nothing but second-division baseball."

2

Mack's 1895 Pirates, who trained at Hot Springs, were made up of Pitchers Frank Killen, Emerson (Pink) Hawley, Billy Hart, Tom Colcolough, Jock Menefee, Gussie Gannon, James Gardner, Guy Wehing, John Foreman, Dave Wright, Jake Hewitt and Sam Moran; Catchers Mack, Joe Sugden, Tom Kinslow, Bill Merritt; First Baseman Jake Beckley; Second Baseman Louis Bierbauer; Shortstop Montford (Monte) Cross; Third Basemen William Clingman and Billy Niles; Outfielders Elmer Smith, Jake Stenzel, and Patsy Donovan; utility, Frank Genins and Bill "Chauncey" Stuart.

After Killen's injury, Connie certainly worked the knuckles off "Pink" Hawley, and he became the headliner of the staff. He finished with 29 victories and 21 defeats, and for a spell he worked every other day. How do present-day pitchers like that for a busy season! Monte Cross later became Mack's early shortstop on the Athletics in Philadelphia, while Genins was so versatile that he appeared in five different positions during the season. All through the "literature" penned by Pittsburgh sports scribes in 1895 runs the suggestion that Connie had his full share of trials and tribulations in keeping his merry Pirates on the straight and narrow. If they are not criticized for not being in condition, they are praised for tending to business. It also is interesting to note that they frequently wrote of Mack as Con Mack and spelled his familiar nickname "Conny."

The *Sporting News*'s Pittsburgh correspondent that year signed himself by the not-too-savory cognomen of "Foul Tip." His weekly letters recite the tale of the rise and fall of the club, Con's difficulties with his boys, and his penalty for raising the hopes of his fans too high.

On June 8, with Pittsburgh in first place, we read: "The Pittsburgh players never behaved better, and if they continue to take as good care of themselves, they are bound to win many games and stay in front."

A week later in the issue of June 15, Foul Tip had this to say: "Another week has passed and we are in second place. The boys are not knocking many boards off the fence for Conny Mack, and if they can only brace a little at bat, the world is ours.

"In spite of all that has been said about Frank Killen, that young man has been conducting himself in a very praiseworthy manner of late. Conny has no fault to find with him. His pitching in Boston was of the triple-X brand and his many friends in Pittsburgh hailed the change with exclamations of delight. With three such pitchers as Hawley, Hart, and Killen in form, Mack and the Pirates have little to fear." (Before the ink on that issue was dry, Killen had met his serious injury in Baltimore.)

By June 22 we find this head over Foul Tip's column: "KNOCKING THE PIRATES. Disappointed Fans Are Using the Deadly Hammer on Mack's Team." The column follows: "The Mighty have fallen and are now in third place, and if the Smoky City boys don't take a brace in their batting, they'll not be able to hold even that position very long. The miserable exhibition at Philadelphia last Saturday was fruit for that class of fickle fans known as 'knockers' and they now are making life miserable for Mack and loyal supporters of the club.

"The club has but one active catcher, Merritt. Tom Kinslow has been laid off for a time, and is paying a fine of $25 a day. He is playing truant in a most disgusting manner. He was given permission to go to his home in Washington from Baltimore, promising to report in time for the next day's game. He did not join the club until Mack had sent word that it would cost him three times his daily salary until he returned."

On July 19 the club again bobbed up in first place, and the next two weeks the Corsairs ran second. Yet about that time we read: "There was a general shaking up among Pittsburgh's second-rate pitching staff, and Mack doesn't know which way to turn. Gannon, the left-hander from Erie, has been adjudged too light for big-league company, and he was farmed to Syracuse. [Sounds familiar.] Jordan was released unconditionally, and Pitcher Gardner of Pittsburgh was signed conditionally. He is a wealthy law student and refuses to pitch professional ball regularly; he will pitch only at home. [The law student's 1895 record was 8 victories and 2 defeats.] Tom Colcolough has gone to Syracuse. Frank Killen may not pitch again this season; he still is in his hospital bed in Baltimore."

Yet, despite all this, August 9 found Connie and his Pirates again leading the league. But it was the last rose of summer! Connie was working Hawley almost every other day to stay in front; "Pink" felt the strain; he no longer could win, and from then on the descent was rapid. By August 30 the club had toppled down the ladder to sixth, and eventually Pittsburgh wound up in the seventh slot with 71 victories, 61 defeats, and a percentage of .536.

3

Old George Moreland, the Pittsburgh baseball statistician, once told the author of the wiles and inside baseball tricks practiced by Connie during his managerial days in Pittsburgh.

"There used to be an icebox in the Pittsburgh club's office," said George, "and Connie got the idea of freezing baseballs in the box. The scheme was to take the life out of the baseballs by this freezing process, and it really deadened the balls. So, during the game, Connie contrived to work the frozen balls into the game while the visiting team was at bat, and then substituted the unfrozen variety when the Pittsburgh club had its innings at the plate."

When asked whether George's tale was true, an amused twinkle came into Mack's blue eyes. "We had to use a lot of tricks to win games," he said, "and maybe that was one of them."

And though Kerr, the Pirate owner, was exacting, though the players were difficult to handle and the fans unreasonable and often belligerent, there was fun in managing that Pittsburgh club. The old warrior broke into a hearty laugh as he recalled an amusing incident in one of those nineties games between his Pirates and the Cincinnati Reds.

"I was catching for our side that day," said Connie, "and Tim Hurst, one of the famous early umpires who later came into the American League, was the only umpire in charge. Tim was calling 'em from behind the plate. A close play came up at third base, and Hurst called the Red player out.

"Arlie Latham dashed off the Cincinnati bench to the plate,

yelled something at Tim, and threw his cap to the ground. Tim kicked the cap. Arlie picked it up, slammed it down again, and Tim gave it another kick. This went on for some time, Latham slapping it down and Tim kicking it, until he had kicked it all the way down the line to third base. The crowd and players howled with glee, and I know my sides ached from laughing. I think it was the funniest thing I ever saw on the ball field. Hurst was serious at first, and then he broke out laughing, but all the time Arlie was fit to be tied."

And then as an afterthought Connie remarked with a grin: "I really thought that Red player was safe."

4

In connection with Mack's 1895 season in Pittsburgh, a little incident which took place the winter before last bears repetition. Connie Mack, the former Pirate manager-catcher, and John K. Tener, former Pennsylvania governor and an old Chicago pitcher, were honor guests of the Pittsburgh Chapter of the Baseball Writers' Association at their annual dinner. The committee which welcomed Mack at the Pittsburgh station included Doc Billy Thompson, an old-time Brooklyn pitcher; Elmer Smith, one of Mack's 1895 Pirate outfielders; and Chilly Doyle, the Pittsburgh baseball writer, to whom I am indebted for this little sidelight.

Connie recognized Thompson and Smith immediately and shook hands all around. Thompson had in his hand a letter which Mack had written to him on the old Pittsburgh club's stationery nearly fifty years before, and asked: "Do you remember sending me this?"

"You bet," replied Connie, "and that Gannon was a pretty good pitcher, too."

The letter, written in Connie's well-known East Brookfield script, follows:

Pittsburgh Athletic Club
Exposition Park,
Allegheny, Pa., May 27, 1895

Mr. William Thompson,
Sharon, Pa.

Dear Doc: As you, Doc, no doubt are a little interested in the Pittsburghs, would like to ask a favor of you. Have heard such good reports of Gussie Gannon, the Sharon pitcher, that I would like to give him a trial. And if you will kindly speak to him in our favor, will be very thankful to you. Would like to hear from you on what you think of him.

Address me at Willard Hotel, Washington. See you are having some pretty good games. Remember me to Harry, and I hope you will meet with good success.

Sincerely,
CONNIE MACK

The pitcher, Gussie Gannon, a left-hander, joined the Pirates that season and was the chap Foul Tip had farmed to Syracuse. Gussie became the father of a sports-loving priest of the Pittsburgh district, Father James Gannon, and uncle of Bishop Mark Gannon of the Diocese of Erie, Pennsylvania. Perhaps that's one reason they say that every Catholic priest is an unofficial scout for Connie Mack.

Prior to that Pittsburgh dinner, Connie took a taxicab over to Allegheny, where the Pirates played at Exposition Park before Forbes Field was built in 1909. With his long legs he walked over the old neighborhood where he had caught and first directed ball players. At the dinner he said: "Pittsburgh is off the American League trail; I haven't been here much since I played and managed over in Allegheny a half-century ago. But I have a love for Pittsburgh and its industrial throb that I never have gotten over. And I still am in the same state with Pittsburgh."

5

Connie Mack's last season in Pittsburgh was not a happy one. After the team's fine promise in 1895, much was expected from the 1896 Pirates, and there was optimism by the carload at the club's Charleston training camp. However, the club made little headway and soon fell back into its old second-division rut. Some trades panned out poorly, and Mack had more difficulty with his players, especially one of his pitchers, Jack Foreman. When Connie called at the office, he noticed a decided chill. President Kerr was not nearly as amiable as he had been the preceding season, and a coolness developed between Mack and other stockholders.

Before Connie took charge of the club in 1894, he had noted that Kerr repeatedly second-guessed his predecessor, Al Buckenberger, when things went badly. When the job first was offered to Mack, he said he knew he would be second-guessed, and before he signed his first managerial contract in 1894 he exacted a pledge from Kerr that the club owner never would second-guess him. Even so Mack was skeptical.

When, after a heartbreaking defeat on the road, which had Mack feeling badly enough, he received a wire from Kerr asking why this and that hadn't been done, the young manager made no attempt to explain his moves but brazenly shot back a wire: "I told you so."

Late in the season Kerr and Connie came to a definite parting of the ways. The president advised the young manager that he had decided upon another managerial change for the 1897 season, but that Mack could remain with the club as catcher and coach. Connie thanked him, but told him he was not interested. Mack's managerial successor was the team's right fielder, Patsy Donovan; but Pittsburgh remained a second-division club until Barney Dreyfuss and Fred Clarke moved into Exposition Park in 1900.

Years later, Kerr admitted to Mack that he was hasty and used poor judgment in releasing him. "It was the mistake of my life—letting you go," the Colonel said.

In September, 1896, Kerr, after notifying Mack that his contract would not be renewed, made several changes on the club without consulting Connie. He traded Jake Beckley, the club's veteran first baseman, to the Giants for a young Philadelphian from Girard College, Harry Davis.

"I didn't make the deal for Davis," recalled Mack, "but I still recall people hollering at me from Pittsburgh windows: "Why did you trade Jake Beckley?"

Who then could have known that the same Harry Davis would become Mack's first-base-playing captain on a team which many persons regard as the greatest ever assembled in baseball?

CHAPTER VIII

McGILLICUDDY MEETS BAN JOHNSON

1

EVEN THOUGH William Kerr said his action in releasing Mack was a mistake, the error was entirely Kerr's, and it proved a great break for the tall catcher from East Brookfield, then at the very twilight of his career as an active player. It brought McGillicuddy into close contact with that dynamic organizer and fighter for clean baseball, Byron Bancroft Johnson, then the ambitious young president of the Western League, with headquarters in Chicago. Connie had known Ban as a Cincinnati baseball writer, but the acquaintance was casual. Before Mack left Pittsburgh he received a letter from Johnson, saying he had read that Connie's managerial contract would not be renewed. Ban asked Mack to come to Chicago for a chat, intimating that he had something in mind which might interest the released Pirate skipper.

Connie was ushered into Ban's Chicago office and met the steady gaze of a sturdy, broad-shouldered man who even at that time filled his office chair. The conversation which followed was fraught with importance for Mack; his subsequent great career was the aftermath.

"I've followed your National League career pretty well, Connie, and I long have admired your way of doing things," said Johnson. "I've a managerial vacancy in Milwaukee that I would like to have you fill. If you are interested, we would give you an interest in the club. We're not a big league, but

I've a strong, well-balanced circuit, and I think you would find real competition. What's more, I have plans for the future of the Western League."

Mack was impressed. He wanted to know more about the Milwaukee proposition, and Johnson laid his cards on the table. "You'll be your own boss up there; you'll run everything," he said.

After some of his experiences in Pittsburgh, Mack found the prospect of being in full charge much to his liking. He felt that he could shop around the National League, but he was impressed with Johnson, his sincerity of purpose and his candid words. And perhaps McGillicuddy's Irish intuition made him sense that Ban was a good man to tie up with. He accepted the managerial post in Milwaukee.

2

Mack since has said that his four seasons in Milwaukee were among the most interesting and educational in his career. He learned much about baseball in those four years—of managing men and running the business end of the game.

"Ban was right about me running the Milwaukee club," laughed Mack. "I did most everything up there but sell tickets. We didn't have the luxury of a road secretary or business manager. Managing the ball club on the field was only part of my job; I signed the players, made the trades, arranged our railroad transportation, found hotels for the players, and paid all the bills. It surely was an education!"

While Mack was in Pittsburgh, he became quite friendly with Harry Stevens, the peanut and score-card king of Exposition Park. It was before the elder Stevens took his talents to the Polo Grounds, New York, where he later became the nation's first sports caterer, with a concessions empire which, according to the letterhead of Harry Stevens, Inc., reaches "from the Hudson to the Rio Grande." Harry's second son, Frank Stevens, now a power in the dynasty, was only sixteen when his Dad sent him to Milwaukee with Connie to look after the Milwaukee club's concessions.

"Baseball wasn't big business then," said Frank, "but at the time the Milwaukee club looked like the biggest business in the world to me. Nearly a half-century has rolled by since those Milwaukee days, but I can recall Mack as a real leader of that team. Connie still got into uniform and occasionally caught. However, even more, I recall his kindly feeling toward me, and how I went to him with some of my problems. Dad told me, 'If you need advice, go to Connie Mack.' I did, and never went wrong following the sound counsel Connie gave me."

3

Ban Johnson was no teetotaler. In fact, during his later years as the most powerful figure in baseball, he was a pretty good two-fisted drinker. But during Mack's Milwaukee days Ban gave him a more powerful temperance lecture—as far as baseball is concerned—than any he ever has heard. Not that the well-behaved Mack needed it personally, but it sank in deeply.

"A ball player, or a manager, is a public figure," Johnson told Connie. "Everybody knows him, especially if he is a success. And a player, or manager, who isn't known intimately by his public isn't worth his salt. Once a ball player gets drunk in public, it isn't long before the entire town knows about it. An average person can get drunk, and his friends quietly put him to bed. But, once a player gets drunk and boisterous, he immediately is put down as a drunkard. He will make an error on the field, and everyone will say: 'Oh, yes, he was drunk again last night.' The ball player doesn't have to be as decent in his private life as the average man; he must be more so."

Connie thinks this observation of Johnson's fits ball players and baseball as well today as when Ban uttered these remarks in the gay and lighthearted late nineties. Mack never was a bluenose, and during national prohibition he was strongly opposed to the statute. His observation was that it did young people far more harm than good. In his early years as a manager he was more tolerant of the drinkers, the chronic offenders. As he grows older the job of nursing along a drinking ball player or "bad actor" would take too much out of him. He talks to the boy once or twice like a Dutch uncle; and then, when the lad disobeys again, Connie has the player marked off his team. Then fans often are surprised to hear that a pretty good Athletic player has been released to another club on waivers.

4

During his career as manager of the Milwaukee club, Mack decided on another step which is unique among baseball managers. For many years he hasn't dressed with his players and doesn't go into the clubhouse unless it is to hold a meeting or give his players some last-minute instructions.

"In my early years in Milwaukee I still was in uniform; in fact, in 1897, my first season with the Brewers, I did a little catching and helped out at first base," said Mack. "I then dressed with the players, and there were the usual arguments after we lost a tough game. And in trying to fix the blame, hot words often were spoken on both sides.

"Then one day something came up that made me real sore; I was so mad I knew I couldn't talk calmly. So I waited around until all the players had dressed and gone home. Then I changed my clothes in the solitude of the clubhouse and was alone with my thoughts. I still was hot as I went home, but when I awoke the next morning it was just another ball game we had lost. It was a bonehead play, yes; but ball players are human, and it was all part of baseball.

"From that time on, I never again dressed with my players, either in Milwaukee or afterward in Philadelphia. My coaches are in the clubhouse, but I do not go near the players unless I have something I especially want to take up with them. I save my own feelings as well as theirs. If we are on the road, I see the player who may have made a mistake in the hotel lobby or call him to my room. If we are home, I let it go until the next day. By then we both are calm and can discuss the matter with no bitterness. Often I am able to point out to the player his mistakes, show him how the play should have been made; and, if the player has the natural ability, he may learn from his mistake."

5

Mack was in a minor league in Milwaukee, but he was with men of major-league stature, most of whom had been in the National League or the old major American Association. Next to Ban Johnson, the leading spirit of the Western League was Charley Comiskey, the owner-manager of the St. Paul club. Commy, leader of the old picturesque St. Louis Browns, won four straight pennants for Chris Von Der Ahe in the eccentric German's Sportsman's Park *Bierstube*. Later the Old Roman managed the Reds in Cincinnati, where began his intimacy with Johnson, the former Cincinnati baseball writer. W. K. Watkins, who managed the famous Detroits, National League and World's Champions of 1887, ran the Indianapolis club; Jimmy Manning held title to the Kansas City franchise; and Tom Loftus, old-time outfielder, was owner-manager of the club in Grand Rapids, which Ban had shifted from Columbus. Detroit, vacated by the National League, also was later added to the circuit.

"The Western League was a pretty good league in the late nineties," said Mack. "About the strength of the present American Association before the war. I had some good men in Milwaukee, men who later played for me on the Athletics or with other American and National League teams—Dave Fultz, Rube Waddell, Wid Conroy, Frank Sparks, and Ginger Beaumont. Comiskey had Frank Isbell and Roy Patterson in St. Paul. Other Western League players who later made big-league reputations were Topsy Hartsel, Socks Seybold, and Ollie Pickering, all of whom played in my Athletic outfield; Jimmy Slagle, Harry Steinfeldt, Deacon Phillippe, George Davis, Sandow Mertes, Bill Coughlin, and some other good men."

In 1887 Connie had a third baseman in Milwaukee, Charlie Myers, who believed one good nip deserved another nip. His drinking became one of Connie's infield problems. "Charlie just liked to drink, and I couldn't do a thing with him," said Mack. "But he was a good player, and I tried all the stunts I could think of. When we came to a series that didn't amount to much, I would stick a fine on him and suspend him. Then I would reinstate him for an important series. Myers would be penitent and play his head off, until I would have to suspend him again."

Mack's best hitter in Milwaukee was an outfielder named Buck Weaver. He wasn't the White Sox player involved in the 1919 scandal. He was the original Buck Weaver, and all subsequent Buck Weavers were nicknamed after him. In the National League, Weaver had played for Cleveland and Louisville, and he had a feud with Mack, then of the Pirates. It has been said that Connie was an expert at bat tipping, pushing the bat just as the batsman took his swing, throwing him off his stride. He did it several times to Weaver. So one day, instead of swinging at the ball, Buck swung at Mack's meat hand and knocked the Pittsburgh catcher out. But Connie knew about Weaver's ability to whale a baseball; he held no grudge, and in his Western League years he was happy to have Buck working for him in his Milwaukee outfield garden.

Mack's Milwaukee Brewers finished third in 1897 and 1898, fourth in 1899, and second in 1900, when Ban Johnson changed the name of the Western to the American League.

Connie recalls vividly the Spanish-American War year of 1898. "We really thought that was quite a war," he recalled. "In riding out on the bus to the ball parks, we would instruct the driver to go by a route which took him past the newspaper offices. There we read the latest bulletins, all about the fighting in Cuba and the Philippines, and the sinking of the Spanish fleet in Santiago harbor. Compared to the present war they were skirmishes, but it was very important news in 1898."

Then, with his delightful sense of humor, Connie enjoyed a chuckle as he added: "You know, there were bigger crowds in front of those bulletin boards than we had at our ball parks."

CHAPTER IX

SNARES RUBE IN PUNXSUTAWNEY

1

THOSE AMBITIOUS schemers, Ban Johnson and Charley Comiskey, had ideas and plans for their newly termed American League in 1900. And they pulled a fast one on Jim Hart, then the owner of the Chicago Cubs. Despite its new high-sounding name, the American League still had minor-league rating; since the merger of the National League and American Association into the twelve-club National League, that was the one and only big league. And it was cocky and cocksure. Following a mediocre season in the Spanish-American War year and also in 1899, the National League reduced to eight clubs, clipping off Washington and Baltimore in the East and Cleveland and Louisville in the West. It left vacant some good baseball territory, and threw seventy-five big-league players on the market, most of them to be absorbed by the higher minor leagues.

Comiskey and Johnson asked Hart's permission to put an American League club into Chicago's South Side. Big-hearted Hart, well located in a residential district on the West Side—and never smelling a mouse—agreed when he learned that Comiskey planned to build his wooden park in the midst of the odoriferous stockyards district. "If Commy can play in that smell, he's good," said Jim. Hart also was to have the privilege of drafting one of the Chicago American players.

To further strengthen his league, Johnson took up the

recently vacated Cleveland territory and also moved into Buffalo, which once had had National League ball and where Mack played during the Brotherhood war.

It was while Rube Waddell was with the Detroit Western League team in 1898 that Mack first saw the great left-hander, who later was to become his pitching ace and No. 1 problem child. In 1897 Waddell had been with Louisville in the National League for a stretch, long enough sorely to vex his manager, Fred Clarke. Connie became a Waddell fan in 1899, when Rube, pitching for Tom Loftus' club in Columbus and Grand Rapids, won 26 games and lost only 8 and struck out an even 200 batsmen.

In 1900 Mack's Milwaukee club was involved in a great pennant battle with the team which Comiskey had shifted from St. Paul to Chicago. "Now, if I could only get one more winning pitcher, I think I could beat out Commy," Mack mused.

In Cleveland, Connie ran into Tom Loftus, who had left the league during Johnson's shifts of the preceding winter and was running a saloon in Dubuque, Iowa. "I think Rube Waddell could help you, Connie," Tom said. "He's a very peculiar character, but he surely can pitch. I understand he's in a Pennsylvania coal town by the name of Punxsutawney. Why don't you try to get him?"

Waddell, by this time, had become the property of Barney Dreyfuss' Pittsburgh club as a result of the merger of the Louisville and Pittsburgh teams; but Clarke, manager of the merged club, still had no patience with the Rube and didn't want him around. Mack checked up on Waddell and learned that he was pitching great ball for Punxsutawney's independent team. Mack's next procedure was to go to Pittsburgh and ask Dreyfuss' permission to dicker with Waddell. "Go ahead," said Barney. "We can't do anything with him. If you can handle Rube, you're welcome to him."

Mack called up Waddell in the Punxsutawney hotel where he was told the pitcher was stopping, and after some delay Rube was fetched to the telephone.

"Is that you, Rube?" asked Connie.

"Who the hell are you?" Waddell demanded.

Connie realized then that he had made a mistake in his

approach. The left-hander didn't like strangers calling him Rube. So he changed his tactics, and in his best sugary voice said: "Eddie, this is Connie Mack of the Milwaukee club; I'd like to have you do a little pitching for me."

"I like it here," Rube replied, almost belligerently.

"But I would pay you good money. You could pitch my club to a pennant, and I know you would like Milwaukee, and the people there would like you."

"I told you I like it here," Waddell said sharply as he hung up.

2

Mack went back to Milwaukee empty-handed and a little put out. But Connie always was a persevering cuss, and his recent years in the cellar show that he isn't easily discouraged. For a fortnight he shot the Rube nightly wires saying how badly he was needed, and bombarded the pitcher with letters. Eventually his forbearance bore fruit, as a wire came from Waddell: "Come and get me."

"I had to get a train out of Pittsburgh at three o'clock in the morning, and I arrived at Punxsutawney around eight," related Mack. "The hotel proprietor directed me to Rube's door; I rapped a couple of times and said: 'It's me, Connie Mack, coming to get you.'

"Waddell finally agreed to get up, and then I took him to breakfast, and he had one of those Elmer the Great appetites. Then he suggested we take a stroll down Main Street, saying he had a few things he wanted to do. The little things were for me to pay bills for shirts and ties, for settling his account at a saloon and at a pants-pressing place. Next he took me to the express office, where he owed $7.50 for a dog, which a friend has sent C.O.D.

"I began to get alarmed, as my cash was running low. They weren't too opulent days in baseball, and I said: 'Rube, I can't pay for much more, or there won't be enough left to get us back to Milwaukee.'

" 'Well, I just want to make one more stop,' he said rather meekly. He led me to one of those places where they have three balls outside, and I paid another $25 to get his watch out of hock.

"Finally we had everything paid up and I got him on the station platform. There was a train leaving at three in the afternoon. As we stood on the platform, I noticed about half a dozen fellows gathering and looking over at Rube and myself. They were big fellows, too, and looked sort of surly. Eventually they started moving over toward us, I thought: 'Here it comes; they're going to get nasty, because I am taking Rube Waddell away from their club.'

"The leader asked: 'You're Connie Mack that used to manage Pittsburgh and now are in Milwaukee, ain't you?'

"I replied: 'Yes, I am,' wondering what was to be the next move.

" 'Well, the boys and I want to offer our congratulations and shake hands with you. And we want to thank you for taking Rube out of town. He's a great pitcher, but Punxsutawney just couldn't stand having him here any longer.' "

3

"Waddell was everything I expected him to be in Milwaukee," added Mack. "He was colorful, soon became a big favorite with the crowd, and we had good turnouts every time he pitched. I still used to put on a glove in those days and warmed up with Rube in front of the grandstand. Every now and then I'd step aside and let one of his fast balls go through and rattle off the grandstand. 'That's right, Rube, kill 'im,' the crowd would yell, thinking his fast one had torn right through me. Of course, it was all meant in fun. Then the Rube would go out to the bleachers, cut a piece off his sleeve, and then really cut loose.

"Eventually Waddell became too good, and I guess I also outsmarted myself. He had a record of 8 games won and 3 lost, when I started him against Comiskey's White Sox in the first game of an important double-header. Well, the first game went 17 innings, and Rube helped win it with a triple. After he struck out the last White Sox hitters, he turned handsprings all the way from the pitcher's box to the bench.

"That gave me an idea. I thought if he was that frisky after pitching 17 innings, maybe he would like to work a little bit more. It was well along in the afternoon, and Comiskey sent his captain, Dick Padden, over to me, asking if I would agree to limit the second game to five innings. I, of course, gave my consent.

"We were to leave that night for Kansas City, so I said to Rube: 'How would you like to go to Pewaukee Lake for a few days instead of going to Kansas City?' Pewaukee was one of his favorite fishing spots, and he loved to fish. 'If you go in and pitch the second game, you can go to Pewaukee for a few days and join up with us in Indianapolis.'

" 'Gimme that ball,' he said. He also won the second game by a 1-to-0 shutout.

"But that is where I outsmarted myself. The press associations didn't carry our box scores, and there wasn't much about our games in the eastern papers. But Waddell pitching and winning a 17-inning game and then following it up with a 1-to-0 victory, all in one day, made a big story. The Associated Press ran quite a piece on it, and Barney Dreyfuss read it in a Pittsburgh newspaper. His club then was in a stiff battle with Brooklyn for the National League pennant. Mind you, Waddell still was his property, and he sent me a wire: 'Have Waddell join the Pittsburgh club in Boston.'

"Sorrowfully I wired Rube at Pewaukee that he was to report to the Pirates. He telegraphed back: 'I'll quit baseball before joining Clarke and the Pittsburgh club again.' Fred never would take from him what I did. And, sure enough, when we arrived in Indianapolis, Rube was waiting for us there.

"I wasn't pleased at losing Waddell, but Barney Dreyfuss had treated me all right. There then was no friction between the leagues, and under baseball law Rube was his property. So I didn't encourage Waddell in his revolt, but this time it was I who wired to the Pittsburgh club: 'Come and get him.'

"Dreyfuss sent his veteran catcher, Chief Zimmer, to Indianapolis to bring Rube back. He made little progress and appealed to me for help, asking: 'What can I do?' I replied: 'Try buying him a suit of clothes, some ties and socks, and maybe some fishing tackle, and perhaps you'll win your way into his good graces.' Zimmer followed instructions; Rube yielded, and I lost a pitcher who had won me 10 out of 13 games and struck out 75 men in 15 contests."

Without him the Milwaukee team couldn't offset Comiskey's superior pitching in Chicago, and Mack's Brewers had to be content with second place, trailing the White Sox by 4 games.

CHAPTER X

BAN'S DREAM COMES TO REALITY

1

WHEN Connie Mack first went to Milwaukee in 1897, he had no idea that in back of Ban Johnson's mind there lurked the daring thought of expanding his Western League into a major circuit. "I had no idea such a thing would happen," he said. "At the time I was released by Pittsburgh, I was thirty-five, a widower with three children, and I looked upon going to Milwaukee in much the same way as a present-day young manager would consider an offer to manage the Milwaukee American Association team of today. I still had to make a living, and it looked like a good field and opportunity."

But Ban Johnson had opportunities beyond Mack's expectations, though perhaps Connie began suspecting something when Ban changed the name of the Western League to the American in 1900 and moved into Chicago. Certainly John McGraw, the old Oriole, had a strong inkling that Ban would have an American League club in Baltimore when he signed with Frank DeHaas Robison, owner of the St. Louis Cardinals, for only one season in 1900 and insisted that the reserve clause be stricken out of his contract.

A five-year agreement among clubs of the Western League, by this time the American League, expired October 14, 1900, and Ban Johnson held a meeting in Chicago on that date to clean up the business of that league. Those in attendance, in addition to Ban, were Connie Mack, Charley Comiskey, Charles Somers, and Tom Manning.

When a new league was formed, it was voted to expand the league to eastern territory. The most important changes recommended by Johnson were to go into Philadelphia, which had had two clubs when the Athletics represented the Quaker City in the American Association, and to take up the territory vacated by the National League a year before in Washington and Baltimore. A fourth eastern city was to be selected later. Ban advised his club owners he would ask the consent of the National League to his changes; but, whether or not it acceded, he would move east.

"I think you are the man to take over in Philadelphia, Connie," Johnson said to Mack. "They know you in Pennsylvania, and I think the fans will be receptive. Of course, we'll revive the name of the old Philadelphia American Association team—the Athletics."

Johnson handed the Washington club to Tom Manning and said the Baltimore franchise would go to John McGraw and Wilbert Robinson, former great players of the Baltimore National League Orioles, who in 1900 played with the St. Louis Cardinals. McGraw and Robbie ran a café, bowling alley, and sports rendezvous in Baltimore called the Diamond Café.

While the Philadelphia franchise was awarded to Mack, he received only one-quarter of the stock. The other three-quarters went to Charles Somers, Johnson's angel, who also was financially interested in several of the other clubs. Somers wasn't a wealthy man as baseball millionaires now are considered, but his bank roll went a long way in helping Johnson, Comiskey, and Mack put over the American League. He was the first president of the Boston Red Sox and later headed the Cleveland club. Later much of Charley Somers' fortune was swept away, and he was forced to relinquish his Cleveland holdings in 1915.

2

Johnson claimed that his expansion was to frustrate plans of some baseball interests to revive the old American Association, the major rival of the National League before the 1892 merger. In fact, McGraw supposedly was fronting for an American Association crowd in Baltimore before he was taken into the new American League. In Chicago, Ban made no bones about it—his league would take on full major status. Deliberately the American League refrained from asking protection under the old National Agreement for the season of 1901.

Nick Young, who was president of the National League and also secretary of the National Board, wired Johnson on October 31, 1900, that he had not forwarded his protection fees for 1901, and please to do so. It brought the issue to a head.

Johnson wrote back, also on October 31: "Your telegram received. I wired in reply that I should write you concerning the matter. The plan of the American League to occupy the Eastern territory has been well defined, and I think the men of the National League thoroughly understand our position in the matter.

"For two years we have been menaced by the possible formation of a league hostile to our interest and detrimental in many ways to organized baseball. This annual agitation is hurtful and we propose to so shape our organization as to check it in the future.

"In extending our circuit to the far East, it is unreasonable to assume we could continue along the old lines prescribed by the National Agreement. New conditions must alter, in part, our relations with the National League. This is a matter I have discussed informally with some of your members."

Nick Young never answered the letter; and, when it was presented at the National League's annual meeting in New York in November, it was decided, practically to a man, to ignore the communication and to oppose any circuit changes proposed by the American League upstarts. The National Leaguers felt that if there was to be a baseball war, the American League would stand before the baseball public as the guilty party as the result of their secession from the National Agreement.

Two weeks after the National League meeting, delegates for a new American Association met in Chicago, formed a temporary organization, and appointed a committee to form an alliance with the National League under the National Agreement. It also had its eye on Philadelphia and Baltimore as possible eastern cities.

From then on, Ban Johnson moved quickly. He had stayed out of Boston so as not to antagonize the old league too much, but now he shifted the Buffalo franchise to Boston and rushed Somers to the Hub to take a five-year lease on a piece of ground on Huntington Avenue, which still is the site of present-day Fenway Park.

3

At one of the early American League meetings in Chicago, Johnson said to Mack: "I want you to go to Philadelphia and contact Ben Shibe, who manufactures baseballs and is one of the owners of A. J. Reach and Co. I think he will be helpful to you in Philadelphia and may become interested."

Connie looked up Ben Shibe at his ball factory in Philadelphia's Kensington district. One of the inducements to get Ben into the new league was the promise that the American League would make his baseballs the official ball of the new circuit. Shibe was one of the nation's pioneer baseball manufacturers. As a young man he was a Philadelphia horse-car driver. In his spare time he made baseballs, letting them out to neighborhood women who sewed on the covers by hand. Eventually Ben got a little plant; it grew into a great factory; and for many years the Shibe concern, now run by the heirs of Uncle Ben's two sons, John and Tom, has been manufacturing the baseballs used by both major leagues.

In his youth Ben was an ardent follower of the early Athletics of the seventies, when Al Reach was a member of the team. The two men then formed a partnership in their sporting-goods house, known later as A. J. Reach & Co. Ben Shibe also became a small stockholder in the Athletics when they were in the American Association but lost his investment during the Brotherhood war. Later he had an interest in the Athletics when they were represented in the Eastern League for one year and backed a semipro club in Philadelphia. He always was a strong believer in the two-league principle, and thought that big cities such as New York, Philadelphia, Chicago and Boston should have continuous ball.

Ben Shibe showed considerable interest during Mack's first

visit and wanted to know more about the new league and where it would obtain its players. "We'll get them wherever we find them," said Connie; "the Phillies have a few good men that we can use."

"You mean you're going after Reach's and Rogers' players," said Ben, a little aghast. Reach was president of the Philadelphia Nationals, but the more loquacious Colonel Rogers owned most of the stock and was active head of the club.

"If they make us fight, we'll raid them," said Connie.

4

Shortly before the new year, Ban Johnson sent word around that all hopes for a peaceful settlement with the National League were over, and his raiding parties could begin. Mack, Comiskey, John McGraw, Clark Griffith, and Jimmy McAleer were Johnson's biggest raiders, though Ban occasionally tried a one-man raid himself—for example, when he took a freight elevator in a Pittsburgh hotel and tried to snatch Hans Wagner from under Barney Dreyfuss' nose.

Mack concentrated on Napoleon (King Larry) Lajoie, the great Philadelphia National second baseman and Wagner's foremost rival as top National League hitter and drawing card. Connie also went after two of the star Philly pitchers, Chick Fraser and Bill Bernard, and snared Lave Cross, his first Athletic captain, from the St. Louis Cardinals.

Lajoie listened to siren Connie's voice. Mack won the great King Larry with a munificent contract of $4,000, chicken feed for such later-day stars as Ruth and DiMaggio or Mack's Simmons and Foxx.

"Larry was getting only $2,400," explained Mack. "Under the National Agreement, adopted when I was in Pittsburgh in 1893, that still was the top salary for ball players. Of course, there were a few ways of getting around it, but that was Lajoie's pay with the Phillies.

"That is one reason why I never felt badly about going after the National League stars. As a player I resented that $2,400 rule, and I felt the start of a new major league, even though it meant a ruinous baseball war, would help the case of the players.

"Lajoie, however, was cagey, and was going to make sure he would get that much money. We had to deposit the entire sum in the Northwestern National Bank of Philadelphia in the name of Frank Hough, sports editor of the *Philadelphia Inquirer,* and a man named Johnson, with whom Larry boarded. On pay day they would draw checks against the amount and then pay Larry."

Mack brought along Dave Fultz from his 1900 Milwaukee club and also signed a batch of other 1900 American League players, including Ralph (Socks) Seybold and Maurice (Mike) Powers, soon to become strong Philadelphia favorites. And Mack signed a tall handsome pitcher who had played brilliant football and baseball for Bucknell College, and who had pitched for the 1900 tail-end Giants—Christy Mathewson—for a sum of $1,500. Always with his ear close to the ground, Connie felt that young Mathewson's showing with the then mediocre Giants was no criterion of his true ability and sensed that the Bucknell boy would go far in baseball.

5

After several conferences, Ben Shibe decided to come in, and took over 50 per cent of the stock, from the 75 per cent originally assigned to Charley Somers. The remainder of the Somers holdings was transferred to Hough, Lajoie's sports editor–paymaster, and Sam Jones, then in the Philadelphia office of the Associated Press. Shibe was elected president of the new club.

It was during those early struggling days, when Mack was trying to complete his organization, to find additional backers, sign players, and get a suitable site for a ball park, that the impetuous John McGraw, the leading light in the new American League Orioles, remarked: "The Athletics are going to be the white elephants of the league."

Ever since, the white elephant has been the symbol of the Athletic Baseball Club. There is a white elephant on the windbreaker of every Athletic player; a white elephant flutters from the center-field flagpole, and Sir Cornelius has one in ivory on his desk as a paperweight, while other elephants (none of them pink) adorn his walls.

It wasn't so easy to find a new park. In Washington and

Baltimore Johnson had an easy task—all he had to do was to take over the parks vacated by National League clubs in 1900. There were satisfactory parks in Chicago, Cleveland, Detroit, and Milwaukee. The only new construction needed was in Philadelphia and Boston. Ben Shibe, Mack, Johnson, Hough, and Jones looked at a number of locations and eventually decided on the rental of a piece of ground at Twenty-ninth Street and Columbia Avenue, in a part of Philadelphia then known as Brewerytown. Frequently the smell of hops, yeast, and newly brewed beer permeated the atmosphere over the new ball yard, named Columbia Park—an odor which never offended the nostrils of a famous Athletic battery, Rube Waddell and Ossie Schreckengost.

It is interesting to recall that, when the various promoters of the new team made their recommendations for a ball park site, Mack voted for a lot at the corner of Twenty-first Street and Lehigh Avenue, which now is the location of Shibe Park.

Building a ball park in 1901 wasn't the enterprise that it is today. One put a grading crew to work to level off the field, sodded the field, and, needing to buck no priorities, purchased sufficient lumber to erect a wooden grandstand and bleachers. By paying the carpenters a little overtime, one had his stands up in a jiffy. The new Columbia Park seated about 9,500, running largely to bleachers. The American League, in its bid for patronage, stressed 25-cent ball, and for years the Athletics had a greater percentage of bleacher seats than any other club in major-league baseball.

CHAPTER XI

THERE ALWAYS WERE ATHLETICS

1

TAKING UP the early name of Athletics was one of the smartest things done by Johnson and Mack. The very name endeared the new team to Philadelphia fandom. The nickname, Athletics, is one of the oldest in baseball; it goes back almost to Abner Doubleday himself. Except for a brief span in the nineties, there has been a Philadelphia team wearing the Gothic "A" of the Athletics for eighty-six years. The first Athletic team took the field in 1859, two years before the Civil War and three before the birth of Mack, taking its name from Philadelphia's famous Athletic Club.

Many of the players fought in the Civil War, but in 1865 the returning soldiers put aside their blue uniforms and got into the strange diamond regalia of that period. The 1865 Athletics played and won more games than any other club in the country. In 1866 the only team to beat them were the Unions and Atlantics of Brooklyn. Their particular stars were McBride, the pitcher; Al Reach (the same man who headed the sporting-goods house and was 1901 president of the Phillies), second base; and "Lip" Pike, third base. In 1867 the Athletics won 43 games and lost only 3. In 1869 Brooklyn's Atlantics defeated them in a memorable struggle, 51-48, but the Athletics made history by defeating the unbeatable Reds of Cincinnati in a game in Philadelphia. The following year the

A's again defeated the great Reds and won 4 out of 5 in a hotly contested series with the Atlantics.

In 1871 the Athletics won the pennant in the first professional league, the National Association—the parent of the present-day National League. They nosed out the famous White Stockings of Chicago, a late-season Athletic victory over Chicago, by the more moderate score of 4 to 1, clinching the championship for the Philadelphians.

This club was made up of McBride, pitcher; Malone, catcher; Fisler, Reach, and Meyrle on the bases; Radcliffe, shortstop; and Cuthbert, Sensenderfer, and Heubel in the outfield.

The A of Philadelphia also was one of the first baseball uniforms exhibited in foreign lands. In 1874 the Athletics and George Wright's Boston Red Stockings, champions of the National Association, made a trip to England, Ireland, and Scotland. The Britishers couldn't get the drift of the new game of baseball, so the Athletics and Red Stockings took them on and beat them at their own game—cricket.

By this time Adrian Anson, later the famous Cap Anson of Chicago, joined the Athletics from Rockford, Illinois, as did Tim Murnane, later a great baseball figure and sports writer in New England. The Athletics of Philadelphia were charter members of the National League in 1876 but soon dropped out, and when the Quaker City again was taken into the league the club became known as the Phillies.

A club calling itself the Athletics entered the old American Association in 1881 and played at Twenty-seventh and Jefferson streets. It won the championship of 1883, defeating the Eclipse team of Brooklyn in a hot September finish. Other clubs in the Association were the Metropolitans of New York, Von Der Ahe's St. Louis Browns, the Cincinnati Reds, Louisville Colonels, and the Allegheny club of Pittsburgh. The 1883 Athletics were made up of Matthews and Corey, pitchers; Rowen and O'Brien, catchers; Stricker, Bradley, and Monahan on the bases; Corey, shortstop; and Birchall, Blakiston, and Knight, outfielders. Jumping Jack Jones of Yale joined the club during the season, and his victory over the Eclipse team, September 28, gave the A's the pennant.

Later famous Association Athletics were Wilbert Robinson, the doughty Oriole catcher and Brooklyn manager; Harry

Stovey, who stole 156 bases for the 1888 A's for the major-league record; and Louie Bierbauer, Mack's Pittsburgh second baseman. During Robbie's stay with the team, the Athletics had a Ladies' Auxiliary. Some of the girls had reputations slightly tainted; they called themselves the "Big Bosom 'A' gals."

It was this name, "the Athletics," which Connie Mack gave back to Philadelphia and the fans of America. He injected new life into it and gave the name glory and renown beyond the fondest dreams of Athletic fans of the last century.

2

After Connie's Herculean efforts, his fight to get his field ready and to put together a winning team, the business of opening the first American League season in Philadelphia in 1901 was not an overly happy one. The Athletics were scheduled to pry the lid off the season with Jim Manning's Washington club on April 24, and Connie had to sit in his water-soaked clubhouse office as the rain dripped through the grandstand. It was a beautiful rain for spring crops, but a difficult one for a young manager opening in a new town, in a new league, and with a new team. What made it worse was that the rain wasn't a one-day affair; it carried right through to the twenty-fifth. It seemed an unhappy omen! After a baseball inaugural is twice postponed, it usually loses much of its enthusiasm; but when the sky finally cleared on the twenty-sixth, a Friday crowd of 10,547, which overflowed into the soggy right field, was on hand. And Mayor Ashbridge welcomed the new league into Philadelphia by throwing out the first ball.

Connie Mack, who has since seen his Athletics play some 6,600 games, did not enjoy that first Philadelphia American League game at all. Chick Fraser, the Philly jumper, was on the mound for Mack, and was opposed by Doughnut Bill Carrick of the Washingtons. There were some good names in that new Athletic line-up, but the team slithered around on that soft field and piled up seven errors, six of them by the infield. No wonder the A's lost, 5 to 1. However, the club's big magnet, Larry Lajoie, started to lay the foundation for his robust .405 batting average by getting three of the eight Philadelphia hits.

Mack's opening Philadelphia line-up was John Hayden, left field; Phil Geier, center field; Dave Fultz, shortstop; Nap Lajoie, second base; Ralph (Socks) Seybold, right field; Lave Cross, third base; Charley Carr, first base; Maurice (Mike) Powers, catcher; and Chick Fraser, pitcher.

The last four players on Manning's Washington line-up were Bills—Bill Clingman, shortstop; Bill Coughlin, third base; Bill Clarke, catcher; Bill Carrick, pitcher; and in the second slot Manning had Bill Everett at second base. "There were just too damn' many Bills on that Washington club," said Captain Lave Cross.

3

Connie Mack's first season in Philadelphia wasn't a bad one. Even without Lajoie, Bernhard, and Fraser, the Phillies still had a good ball club in the National League and finished second, but Mack gave them good competition with his new-old Athletics. He was in the race most of the way; and, though he had to be content with fourth, his 1901 Athletics trailed the first-place White Sox, led by Clark Griffith, by only nine games. The Detroit club, managed by George Stallings, nosed Mack out for third place by a half-game on the last day of the season. An early disappointment for Connie was the failure of Christy Mathewson, the Bucknell collegian, to report. Before the season started, Matty jumped back to the Giants, a common practice during that unsettled wartime period. With Mathewson on his staff, Connie might readily have started his long Philadelphia sojourn with a pennant victory.

Mack engaged no less than fifty-five players in that first American League campaign, though he stuck pretty well to his starting line-up. His only important change was the replacement of Charley Carr at first base by Harry Davis, the Girard College boy, and the same player acquired by Pittsburgh from the Giants in 1896, when Connie was abused for the trade engineered by Colonel Kerr.

"Somehow the Philadelphia fans didn't seem to like Charley Carr," said Mack. "Fans then expressed themselves more noisily than they do today, so I decided I had better get myself a new first baseman. My thoughts ran to Harry Davis, who was a

Philadelphian. Harry had decided to give up baseball and was then employed as a clerk by the Pennsylvania Railroad. Davis always was good at figures and is an accountant. I finally succeeded in convincing him that I needed him and had a good opening for him. It was one of my best moves and made possible my first three pennants. And I feel that Harry never regretted that he signed with me. It started a pleasant association which has endured through the years."

4

Another fine prospect came to Mack a few weeks after the 1901 season started; in fact, though he came from only a minor college, Gettysburg, he was a front-line hurler from the time he joined the Athletics and made up to some degree the loss of Mathewson. The twirler was the great southpaw, Eddie Plank, one of the two left-handers in baseball history to win 300 or more games. The other was to be another Mack-developed pitcher, Bob (Lefty) Grove, who was to write Athletic history over two decades later.

"The Gettysburg coach, Frank Foreman, lived in Baltimore and was a good friend of mine," recalled Connie. "He was a brother of John Foreman, the pitcher with the thirst that I had in Pittsburgh. Frank told me he had two pitchers, each of whom he thought could win in the new American League—Plank, a left-hander, and George Winters, a right-hander. Foreman was correct on both of them. I picked Plank, and he became a star on my club; Boston signed Winters, and he was a winning pitcher on the Red Sox."

And then Connie sighed as he remarked: "I wonder why we can't come up with college pitchers like Plank and Winters these days."

Plank, a Pennsylvania farm boy, was a little old for a collegian—twenty-five—when he joined the Athletics. He never played ball until he went to college,.but as a boy had amused himself by knocking birds off rails with stones. That helped him develop his great arm and control.

Mack first called on Plank to relieve a pitcher named Baker in a game with Washington, May 13, which the Athletics lost,

14 to 5. Five days later Connie started Gettysburg Eddie against the Orioles. He held them to six hits; and, as he had some hefty batting behind him, he won by a score of 11 to 6. It was the first of a great collection of Athletic victories. Plank wound up that season with 17 victories and 11 defeats.

The two jumpers from the Phillies, Bill Bernhard and Chick Fraser, however, were the bellwethers of Connie's first Athletic staff. Bill had a record almost similar to that of Plank—17 wins and 10 reverses—and Fraser, work horse of the corps, won 20 and lost 15. Lew Wiltse, a brother of southpaw George Wiltse, later to win fame with McGraw's Giants, brought in 13 games for Connie and lost 5. Three other pitchers, Loose, Baker, and Milligan, helped out.

The power of the club was built largely around Lajoie, Socks Seybold, and the aggressive captain, Lave Cross. In addition to leading the league with his .405 average, Larry lashed out 48 doubles, 13 triples, and 13 home runs. Socks hit .332, and Captain Lave 1 point less. Socks was a roly-poly fellow who played right field with a first-baseman's mitt, by Ban Johnson's special permission. He won as much fame with his omnivorous appetite as with his home-run bat. Ball players with reputations as trenchermen still look back at Ralph Seybold's feats with envy.

Lave Cross was captain in more ways than on the ball field. He was always the first one in the old horse-drawn bus, which used to haul the Athletics from their third-rate hotels to the ball parks. The ritual went both for leaving the hotel and after the ball game, and anyone trying to scramble in ahead of Lave had a fight on his hands. Lave was so bowlegged it was a wonder those hot ones down the third-base line didn't roll right through the hoop which he made with his legs as he stooped for grounders.

During the 1901 playing season, Colonel Rogers of the Phillies made several efforts to get out an injunction restraining Lajoie, Bernhard, and Fraser from playing with the Athletics on the ground that they violated options in their Philadelphia National contracts, but Mack won the first round in the lower courts.

And Connie finally said good-by to the Brookfields and

New England and became a full-fledged Philadelphian. He took up his residence at 2932 Oxford Street, directly across the street from the north side of Columbia Park. The first Mrs. Mack had died in 1892, and in the Oxford Street dwelling his mother kept house and helped him to bring up Roy, Earle, and Margaret.

CHAPTER XII

A JUDICIAL THUNDERBOLT

1

IN THE winter following the 1901 season, the war between the young American League and the old National increased in intensity. Players were convinced that the new major league, started by Johnson and supported by such vigorous and able lieutenants as Mack, Griffith, Jimmy Collins, Comiskey, and McAleer, was in the field to stay. The Milwaukee club was shifted to St. Louis, and the American promoters showed bank rolls such as the players of that time never before had seen. The most severe raids were directed at the remaining stars of the second-place Phillies and the fourth-place Cardinals.

Mack signed up Elmer Flick, the Phillies' hard-hitting right fielder; Bill Duggleby, the Quakers' big right-hander; and Monte Cross, their shortstop. Monte is the same player that Connie had for a while in Pittsburgh, and was no relation to Lave Cross. The Washington club put a big bunch of lettuce before the great Philadelphia slugger, Ed Delehanty, and signed him to a Senator contract; and the new Browns snatched Donohue, the Phillies' 1901 pitching leader.

During the off season, Mack also had braced his club in other departments. He obtained the little tow-headed outfielder, Fred Tully (Topsy) Hartsel, for left field. Hartsel, who died a few months ago, was almost an Albino; hence the nickname Topsy. He had played with Seybold on the 1900 Indianapolis American League club, but Connie had induced him to jump the Chicago Cubs. Ossie Schreckengost, which was usually condensed to Schreck in box scores, came from Boston to help Powers in the catching department.

The Athletics trained in Chapel Hill, North Carolina, for the 1902 season, and Connie felt pretty good as he brought his club to Baltimore to open his second American League season. He felt surer of a pennant than at any time since his 1895 Pirates blew up on the stretch. Then the big blow fell! On April 21 a Baltimore sports writer showed Mack an Associated Press flash announcing that the Pennsylvania Supreme Court had handed down a decision affirming the validity of the option clause in the Philadelphia National contracts and reversed a decision of the lower Philadelphia court which had refused to grant the injunction restraining Lajoie, Bernhard, and Fraser from playing with the Athletics. While the decision did not name Flick and Duggleby, Phillies who jumped to Mack after the 1901 season, they naturally fell into the same category. For some reason, Colonel Rogers did not try to regain the services of Monte Cross, a mediocre hitter.

It was a trying period for the ambitious young manager. All of his carefully laid plans for building a winner in Philadelphia came tumbling around his ears. "I felt as though they had swept my ball club right from under me," Mack said.

Ban Johnson promptly called a special meeting of the league in Cleveland, April 30. The young league had received a stiff judicial wallop, but it was full of fight; it voted to ask for a new trial and to carry the case to the highest court in the land if that was necessary. The big fear was that the Pennsylvania ruling might set a precedent for other states, but clubs were advised to stand firm and hold their contract- and reserve-jumpers. And Johnson recommended that Mack be given help in his difficulty.

"The league was swell to me," said Connie. "My big need was pitchers, as I was losing the best men I had. The Boston club let me have Fred Mitchell and Howard Wilson. Mitchell later turned catcher, and then managed the Cubs and the Braves in the National League. Wilson was a former Philadelphia high-school boy. And the league awarded me Bert Hustings, who had been with the Milwaukee club in 1901. They all helped me that season."

Mack, Ben Shibe, and Johnson also saw a ray of hope when their attorney felt the Athletics could play the Philadelphia National jumpers, pending the club's appeal; but a judge knocked this slender prop from under them by refusing such permission.

Though Fraser and Duggleby pitched a few out-of-town games for Mack in the early spring, they eventually returned to the Phillies. After some dickering with Colonel Rogers, in which there was an atmosphere of ill-feeling on both sides, Elmer Flick joined the Cleveland Americans and soon was followed by Lajoie and Bernhard. The Athletics' loss was Cleveland's gain, as the famous Phillie trio set the lake city afire with renewed baseball interest. However, during the entire 1902 season, Lajoie, Flick, and Bernhard played no games at Columbia Park, as it was necessary for them to remain outside Pennsylvania jurisdiction.

Special officers frequently set traps for Lajoie, thinking he was concealed at the hotel where the Cleveland club was housed in Philadelphia. They were so busy looking for King Larry under the beds that they neglected to watch the Camden ferry. Several times Larry, traveling by himself, went through the state, unobserved and unmolested, on his way to Atlantic City, where he basked in the sun while his teammates were playing the Athletics at Columbia Park.

2

If a soothsayer had told Mack on April 21 that he still would win his first flag in 1902, Connie would have considered him crazy, a fool, or both. Yet the acquisition of two players, Rube Waddell and Danny Murphy, made that first modern Athletic championship possible.

Mack made a fair start, and with Plank the new anchor man of the pitching staff, and Lave Cross, Seybold, and Davis driving in the runs, the A's won their share of early-season games; but no one considered them a pennant threat. If Tom Loftus gave Connie Mack the idea that Rube Waddell might help his Milwaukee club in 1900, it was Jack Sheridan, the ace American League umpire, who started the bee buzzing in Mack's brain that the big Rube wouldn't look so bad wearing the big A of the Athletics on his ample chest.

"Rube Waddell is going great out in Los Angeles," Sheridan confided to Mack before a game in Detroit. "I've got a tip from some friends out there that he is faster than ever. You got some great pitching out of Rube and learned how to handle him in Milwaukee. Why don't you go after him? He might be the solution to your pitching problem."

Dreyfuss of the Pirates had released the eccentric Waddell to the Chicago Cubs; but Rube got into an argument with Jim Hart, the Chicago boss, left the club in a huff, and hooked on with Los Angeles. But the baseball war was on, and no one was paying any attention to contracts, major or minor. If you wanted someone, you just tried offering him more money.

Connie, acting on Sheridan's suggestion, sent Waddell a wire: "How would you like to pitch for me again?"

Rube wired back from L. A.: "Send me $100 and transportation."

Mack sent the money and ordered the left-hander to report in Chicago, but when the Athletics arrived in the Illinois metropolis there was no Rube. An acquaintance told Mack that he had seen Rube board a Chicago-bound train at Los Angeles, when several men got on the train and started to talk about the good old times. Finally the Rube broke down in tears and said: "I never did want to leave you fellows anyway." He got off the train and boarded another for San Francisco, where the L.A. club was playing.

Connie walked over to Ban Johnson's office and related his Waddell troubles. "I think I know just how to handle it," said Ban and led Mack to the Pinkerton detective agency. With Connie giving instructions on how to bait Waddell, two detectives left for San Francisco that night to conduct Rube to St. Louis, the Athletics' next stop.

From Dodge City the dicks sent Mack a wire: "We've got him this far, but you better come along to Kansas City and bring him the rest of the way."

"Young Corbett had just beaten Terry McGovern in Dodge City," related Mack, "and Rube wanted to stick with Corbett. He had worked up a great admiration for the little fighter and struck up quite a friendship with Corbett's trainer, Frank Newhouse.

"To make matters worse, there were two clubs in Kansas City at the time, one managed by Pat Tebeau and the other by Jim Manning. Rube promised both he would pitch for them; and, as he had seen young Corbett fight, he was most anxious that the boxer see him pitch.

"Following the distress sign from the detectives, I took a train for Kansas City. I still don't know how I did it, but I told Rube he belonged in the big league, that thousands wanted to see him pitch, and persuaded him to pack his $1 cardboard bag and his fishing pole and come down to the station with me. By this time the Athletics had finished their western trip, so I personally conducted Rube to our next stop, which was Baltimore.

"I put him in a game against the Baltimore Orioles, then still managed by John McGraw. I had Doc Powers catch Waddell, and the pair didn't get along too well. Waddell was beaten by a score of 7 to 3. However, in his next game, we played McGraw's club in Columbia Park, and quite a crowd came out to welcome Rube to Philadelphia. The papers already were full of Rube Waddell stories. This time I had Ossie Schreck catch Rube, and he won by a score of 2 to 0. With two out in the ninth, he beamed at me and yelled: 'Send the crowd home; it's all over.' And sure enough, he struck out the last man. From that time on Schreck was Waddell's regular catcher, and they were a great battery."

Though Waddell didn't join the club until June 26, he was a hard, willing worker and won 23 games while losing only 7. And in 33 games he struck out 210 men. Though he had the brain of a juvenile, Waddell had an inherent pitching smartness and probably threw the fastest ball ever hurled by a left-hander, with the possible exception of Bob Grove. And Rube loved to buzz that fast one past the hitter's letters. He gave Connie both headaches and heartaches—Mack says present-day baseball wouldn't tolerate Waddell a week; but there still is a great warmth in his heart for this colorful and baseball-talented child of nature. Mack's eyes light up with a merry twinkle when he spins Waddell yarns, and invariably he speaks of him as "the Rube."

Schreckengost was made to order as Waddell's catcher. Before the baseball war, Ossie had caught for the Cleveland Spiders and St. Louis Cardinals. He was as much of a character in his way as was Rube, and they made the ideal battery. Schreck was amusing to look at, with his big round face and curly dark hair. He was not a great catcher, but a good one, and the fans enjoyed seeing him work. He invariably caught one-handed and was a master in teaching control to Waddell and Plank, and later to Chief Bender. He would hold up his glove hand and have the pitchers pitch not at the mitt, but to a spot in the mitt. After Bender joined the staff, he had an amusing trick which made even Connie laugh. Schreck would have Waddell, Plank, and Bender pitch to him from different parts of the infield, one firing almost as soon as the other. Schreck would snatch the ball out of the glove with his bare hand and then await the next pitch until he had all three balls. Then he threw them all back at once, and he never missed returning a baseball to all three pitchers.

3

Almost as important to Mack's success as the snatch of Rube Waddell was the midseason acquisition of Danny Murphy as the club's second baseman. Four decades before Clark Griffith of Washington engaged his colony of Central and South American Latins, Connie Mack played his early 1902 games with a Venezuelan, Jud Castro, at second base. Castro had studied at Holy Cross and Manhattan; and, in the language of a later-day baseball Latin, Miguel Gonzales of the Cardinals, Jud was "Good field, no hit." So in July Connie landed Danny Murphy from the Norwich, Connecticut, club. Though born in Philadelphia, Danny had grown up in Connecticut and had played a little major-league ball in 1901 with the New York Giants.

Murphy's debut with the Athletics was the most brilliant of any player in the long history of the club. It took place in Boston, July 8, 1902; and the new infielder, reaching the park late, did not get into the game until the second inning. Even so, the Norwich recruit lashed out 6 hits in as many times at bat, including a "Grand Slam" homer, one with a mate on every base. His victims were George Prentiss, Cy Young, and

Merle Adkins. The new second baseman also had a busy time of it in the field, handling 12 out of 14 chances, as the Athletics won with runs to spare—22 to 9.

"Goodness gracious, but we had a batting day that afternoon," laughed Connie. "I guess Jimmy Collins, the Boston manager, wondered how he ever was going to get Murphy, my new man, out."

4

The Athletics were in first place for a few days in May, and they were just under the top as Chicago led from June 9 to August 12. Then the new St. Louis Browns set the pace for a few days, only to have the A's, feeling the added strength of Waddell and Murphy, take the lead on August 15, and hold it for the balance of the season. Eventually Connie beat out the second-place Browns, .610 to .574, to win his first of nine American League championships.

It was a happy season for the new manager, as he had everything that year—pitching, hitting, and base-running. Waddell and Plank were high up among the new league's pitchers; Connie had six .300 hitters, led appropriately enough by Captain Lave Cross .339. Rotund Socks Seybold was the early Babe Ruth of the league, smacking 16 round-trippers; they stood as the league's high for 17 years until the mighty Bambino raised it to 29 in 1919.

And Connie liked to see his speed-boys race around the bases. He always enjoyed directing a base-running attack. Mack's club stole 239 bases that season, and he had the two top men, Topsy Hartsel, the league leader, and Dave Fultz, with 54 and 48 steals, respectively. They also were the league's No. 1 and 2 scorers; Fultz tallied 110 runs, and Hartsel was on his heels with 108.

Yes, when they feted the Athletics after that season, Connie really was genuinely happy. Despite the adverse Supreme Court ruling and the loss of Lajoie, Flick, Bernhard, Fraser, and Duggleby, he had given Philadelphia a real team of champions.

5

Always a pioneer and willing to venture into new fields, Mack sensed the possibilities of football as a professional sport and thought of ways to capitalize on Rube Waddell's popularity and drawing powers after the baseball season had been put in camphor. He and Tom Shibe, older son of Ben and business manager of the Athletics, thought up the idea of assembling an Athletic professional football team for postseason games at Columbia Park. Big husky 200-pound Rube Waddell was the most publicized of the Athletic players. Others on the team were Ed Bader, later mayor of Atlantic City; Blondy Wallace, Phil Draper, Bryan Hayes, and former sturdy ex-collegians of the turn of the century. Connie and Tom even put in a primitive lighting system for night games. Their opponents were the Phillies and Pirates—those ball clubs also put in football teams—and a few other early professional teams from the coal and iron country.

It wasn't a profitable venture, and as a football player the Rube was a great southpaw pitcher. He didn't care much about the way those rough college boys mauled him when they got him at the bottom of a scrimmage. It was much easier smoking in that fast one. The Athletic football club went about $4,000 in the red. Uncle Ben called Connie and Tom to his office. "I've paid all of those football bills," he said, "but from now on I think you boys had better stick to a business you know something about—baseball."

CHAPTER XIII

A TRAINING TRIP IN JAX

1

THE BASEBALL war ended in the winter of 1902-3, with the National League recognizing the American as a full major with all the rights of the National, and baseball put under a three-man government headed by Garry Herrmann, Cincinnati's club president, Ban Johnson, and Harry Pulliam, the youthful president of the National League. Connie and his boss, Ben Shibe, were most happy. "We had won everything we were fighting for, and we knew the American League was in the field to stay," said Mack. "How well it has progressed since then, everyone knows."

Mack confidentially expected to repeat with his pennant winner of 1902, though he anticipated stiff competition from the new club in New York. As one of his last war moves, Johnson put an American League club in New York, shifting the Baltimore club to the nation's metropolis. Ban tried to put an all-star team in New York, and Mack contributed his fast-running center fielder, Dave Fultz, to Griff's new Highlanders. To fill Dave's place, Connie purchased Ollie Pickering from Cleveland and acquired a great young outfield prospect, Danny Hoffman, from Springfield, Massachusetts. Danny, one of Mack's early favorites, joined the A's with a good pitching record, but the tall tactician quickly told him to forget about his pitching and concentrate on outfield play. Danny was as fast as Fultz and a hard left-handed hitter. He would have been one of the league's all-time greats but for an injury which nearly wrecked his career and almost took his life the following season.

If 1901 produced Eddie Plank, and 1902 saw the development of the eccentric Waddell into a full-fledged major-league star, the 1903 season saw the great Indian, Chief Charles Albert Bender, blossom into early stardom. Though he joined Mack's colors several months before his twentieth birthday, the Chief was a star almost from the day he put on his first Athletic uniform. The luck of Connie with untried youngsters, especially collegians, in his first decade at the helm of the Athletics was uncanny.

Though Bender's features are those of an Indian, and in his heyday as a pitcher he had all the coolness under fire of the traditional bronzed aborigine, the Chief has only one-quarter Indian blood. His father was of Dutch descent and his mother a half-Chippewa. Born at Brainerd, Minnesota, Bender was educated at the old Carlisle Indian School, where Pop Warner then coached baseball as well as football. Later the pitcher enrolled at Dickinson College. Mack heard of him when he pitched for the Harrisburg A.C. under the name of Albert. Connie's scout, Jess Fresinger, signed Bender at $300 a month, and the Chief thought he was on his way to becoming a millionaire. "I also paid the manager of the Harrisburg club $100," said Connie. "I've forgotten the man's name, but should remember it, because that was one of the greatest bargains in baseball."

Bender really is quite a remarkable fellow and combined an amazing eye with the steadiest of nerves. He was one of baseball's greatest trap-shots—both of live and clay birds—and the game has had some good ones. He plays a good game of golf or billiards and can tell the genuineness of a precious stone at a glance. In his early Athletic years he learned the jewelry business during the off season.

2

Mack went farther south for his training in 1903—back to Jacksonville, where Connie had trained with the Washington Nationals fifteen years before. Tom Shibe put up the A's a

© Sporting News

RUBE WADDELL

Letting go that left-handed thunder ball.

© Sporting News

OSSIE SCHRECK

He caught one-handed and nailed steak to dining room wall.

© Sporting News

HARRY DAVIS

As he looked in 1905

© Charles M. Conlon

DANNY MURPHY

Broke in with six hits on Connie's 1902 champions.

little better than did Tim Sullivan when he quartered his Senators in two shacks at $1 a day, but it still wasn't training de luxe. The Athletics stopped at the Casino, which a year before had been a gambling hall. There were no beds, but cots were installed in the big barnlike structure. The players would have considered themselves dudes had the hotel provided individual bathrooms.

The A's ate at a near-by beanery, called Wolfe's Café. It was there that Ossie Schreck first pulled his famous steak trick. Whenever an Athletic player ordered a steak, Wolfe would go back to the kitchen and yell: "One baseball steak." Then the players heard the sound of a wooden mallet as Wolfe's cook mashed the steak. The players got the idea that "baseball steaks" were delivered to the less desirable trade. A steak was placed on Ossie's plate, which he soon decided was just as tough as before it took its beating, so Schreck nailed it on the wall.

"It created quite a commotion," recalled Chief Bender. "Wolfe was awfully sore, and for a while it looked as though we would lose our eating place, but Connie finally talked the proprietor into letting us stay."

3

Waddell quite naturally had his share of adventures in Jax, including wrestling with a live alligator and suffering from a case of unrequited love. Rube fell hard for a sprightly North Florida brunette, paid her much attention, and in the early part of the training stay he was as faithful as a big St. Bernard. Then one day, after practice, he went to meet his date at a café which both frequented, only to find her sitting at a table with a stranger. And when the angry Rube barged over, she not only refused to leave, but gave him a ladylike neigh which was intended for a horse laugh.

Rube was heartbroken. He said: "I don't wanna live no more. I'm goin' to kill myself. I'm goin' down to the dock and jump off."

Sure enough, he went straight to the old Clyde Line dock, with Schreck, fearing the worst, at his heels. And without pausing the big 200-pounder dove in head first. But his "suicide" attempt came at absolutely low tide. Instead of the usual five to ten feet of water at the dock, there was only about a foot. So Waddell plunged into the river's muck almost to his shoulders and nearly choked before faithful Schreck and several dock hands, grabbing him by the feet, could pull him out.

On another occasion Rube disappeared on Connie Mack for two days. What's more, Connie was much annoyed; in those days a manager carried a small staff, and the absence of one pitcher upset his entire schedule.

Connie was standing outside of his hotel, with two of his players, Danny Murphy and Socks Seybold, when they heard a band coming down the street. "It's the minstrel show that's in town," said Danny. "Let's watch the parade."

As the band approached, there was Rube leading it, tossing his baton thirty feet into the air and catching it as it came down.

"Don't let him see you," said Murphy to Mack. "It will spoil the fun."

Connie ducked and tried to hide his lean frame behind a sign, but Rube spied him and was undisturbed and unabashed.

"Hello, Connie," he called, and kept right on marching. Mack, Murphy, and Socks then followed the band and troupe to the hall where the show was to be held; there Rube held the big bass drum for the drummer. Connie told Waddell it was nice of him to show such interest in music, but added: "After all, Rube, you're down here to get that left arm in shape to strike out American League hitters." Next day Waddell was back at the ball park, ready for work.

4

The Athletics opened the 1903 season with morning and afternoon Patriot's Day games in Boston. The Red Sox bunted Waddell all over Fenway Park in the morning and won by a score of 9 to 4. Finally, in the fourth inning, the still-sleepy Rube fell on his left shoulder chasing a bunt. He got up, rubbed it, groaned, and wanted to leave the game. "Get in there and pitch, you big so-and-so," yelled Harry Davis. The Rube looked appealingly at Mack; but Connie, suspecting that he had trained for the game with Boston cronies the night before, made Waddell stay in and take it. Connie didn't even put his hands to his ears to avoid hearing Davis' explosion.

Philadelphia's cause didn't look so good in the second game either, as Boston drubbed Eddie Plank, Mack's other ace, early. Connie sent Bender, the young Indian, who had won a city-series game from the Phillies, out to the bull pen, saying: "I think I'll soon be needing you." After Bender was called in, the copper-skinned youngster held the Red Sox to one additional run, a homer by Buck Freeman, while the Athletics batted out a 10-to-7 victory. In his first American League start, April 27, the Chief drew the wily Clark Griffith, pitcher-manager of the New York stars, as his opponent. Bender held the Highlanders to 4 hits and won by a score of 6 to 0.

When Bender finished his day's chores, Connie's comment was: "Nice work, Albert." Though Mack occasionally refers to his great Indian hurler as "the Chief," whenever he speaks to him personally he still calls him "Albert."

The Athletics led from the opening week of the season until July, and for a spell in midsummer it was a close, interesting tussle, when Jimmy Collins' Boston team began to pull away and eventually beat out the second-place A's by 14 games. It was one of the few runaways in the early years of the league. Griffith's stellar New York team never clicked and had to be satisfied with a poor fourth.

Waddell won 21 games that season and lost 16, and in his first full season with the A's boosted his strike-outs to 301. Plank did a little better—23 victories against 16 defeats; while Bender won 17 and lost 15 in his freshman year. Even with this fine pitching, Mack couldn't follow the steady pace of Collins' strong Boston team.

The A's did get one fall out of the champion Red Sox, however. When the players arrived at the park one day, Waddell and big George (Candy) LaChance, the Boston first baseman, got into quite an argument. So they decided to wrestle it out; and neither Connie nor Jimmy Collins, the Boston manager, tried to interfere. For a half-hour the two big men tussled all over the field, until Rube finally pinned "Candy's" shoulders to the turf and sat on him, saying: "How do you like it?" LaChance didn't play first for Boston that day, but Rube pitched a whale of a game for the Athletics.

5

While the Athletics of 1904 finished with a percentage only 20 points less than that of the second-place club of 1903, the club dropped to fifth, Mack's first second-division club in Philadelphia. Even so, Connie stayed up in the race for the greater part of the season and didn't fall out of the running until September. It was the year Boston defeated the New York Highlanders for the pennant on the last day of the season, when Jack Chesbro uncorked a fatal wild pitch. They still remember the wild pitch but have almost forgotten that Happy Jack won 41 games for New York that year. It was a year of great pitching feats. On May 5 Cy Young, opposing Waddell, pitched a perfect game for the Red Sox, no Athletic player reaching base. Cy fanned 8 that day, against Rube's 6, but at the end of the season Waddell had 343 strike-outs, the major league record for this century.

Always ready to praise the other fellow, Mack still can enthuse over Young's perfect game against his team. "Cy was just great that day; we couldn't touch him. We might as well have been East Brookfield that afternoon. In my long career, it is the only perfect game I ever have seen."

The Holy Cross battery of Andy Coakley and Pete Noonan joined Mack that year, though Andy had tossed a few vacation games for Mack under the name of McAllister while he still was at college. Andy and Pete long since have settled in New York, the pitcher as an insurance man and baseball coach at Columbia and the catcher as one of the managers of the Hotel New Yorker, where Mack stays with Pete whenever he is in the big town. Other acquisitions were an unlucky hurler, Weldon Henley, and an Indian outfielder named Bruce. For a while Connie held high hopes for Bruce, but he never developed as did Bender.

Injuries had much to do with throwing the 1904 A's into the second division. Harry Davis was out twice with injuries to his legs, and Socks Seybold was subbing for him when a near fatal accident almost ended the career of the brilliant youngster, Danny Hoffman. Jesse Tannehill, Boston left-hander, pitched a fast inshoot, and the ball struck Hoffman directly under the right eye, almost forcing it out of the socket. The player went down like a felled steer. All night long Mack waited at the hospital until he was told that everything possible was being done for Danny, and that there was a good chance of saving the eye. He was as much affected as though the accident had happened to Earle or Roy.

"Danny looked terrible with that eye out," said Mack, "but he seemed in a trance at the plate, and just couldn't get out of the way of that pitch. Hoffman was out for most of the remaining games of that season, and when he returned to my line-up I had to do what looked like a heartless thing. I had to let him bat against Tannehill, when Jesse next pitched against us. I hated like anything to do it, and Hoffman was pathetic at the plate; Jesse struck him out four times. But I had to do it to restore Danny's confidence and keep him in the league."

Even though the Athletics slipped into the second division, Waddell's strike-outs made the club a great attraction. In many respects Rube's whiffs of enemy hitters were like Babe Ruth's later-day home runs. Only, where the customers paid to see Babe knock one out of the lot, they paid earlier to see Rube buzz his left-handed curve across the chests of opposing sluggers. And, like Ruth, Waddell was a great draw on the exhibition belt, both before and after the championship season. It was there that Waddell used to call in his fielders, sometimes keeping Davis on first base, in the ninth inning, and then strike out the side.

There still are legends that Rube performed this feat in American League play, but Connie says no. "Ban Johnson was quite strict, and his umpires never would have permitted it in a league game," he added. "But Waddell did it quite often in exhibition games, and usually it worked."

"There was a game in Memphis in which, for some reason I've forgotten, Mike Powers caught Rube instead of Schreck. Harry Davis was managing the club for me that day. We led, 6 to 0, in the ninth inning, so Rube called in all of his fielders, including Davis. Rube struck out the first two batters and also fanned the third, but Powers dropped the ball, and the Memphis player reached first. Then the next two batters popped little flies over Rube's head, and his tongue hung out chasing the ball. He appealed to Davis to return the men to their positions, but Harry said: "No, you wanted it that way." So poor Rube had to work it out the best he could, and eventually struck out the side with the bases full. But he was all in when the game was over."

CHAPTER XIV

WHITE ELEPHANTS WIN AGAIN

1

CONNIE MACK rallied his forces quickly after his second-division season, and a second White Elephant pennant fluttered from Columbia Park's center-field flagpole after the 1905 race was over. The lanky New Englander nailed it down with much the same club which won for him in 1902, and he still admits he was lucky to win it.

"Cleveland had the ball club that year," said Connie, "and, but for a lot of bad breaks, they would have been the champions. By the end of June they led us by 100 points, and it looked as though nothing could stop them."

Then Larry Lajoie, Mack's 1901 second baseman and by this time Cleveland's playing manager, broke a leg, and he played in only 65 games. Second base was Cleveland's jinx position, as Elmer Flick, the outfielder, brought in to play the bag, promptly broke a finger; then Catcher Bemis tried it and also got hurt. George Stovall, the club's first baseman, took a crack at second; and Charley Carr, Mack's original Athletic first baseman, covered first base. Speed-boy Bay also was injured, as were other key players, and in one series in Philadelphia the Cleveland club, then called the Naps, was forced to play Pitcher Otto Hess in left field and Catcher Bemis in right.

That kind of a patchwork Cleveland line-up made things much easier for Mack; as Cleveland's percentage melted away, the A's forged into the lead on August 2, displacing Lajoie's distressed team. From that point on, the Mackmen never were dislodged from the front seat, though on the September home stretch the White Sox, now managed by Fielder Jones, gave Connie Mack an awful scare.

2

In a prank on the platform of the station at Providence, Rhode Island, on September 1, Rube Waddell injured his valuable left shoulder. It later put him out of the 1905 World's Series; but, more important to Mack at the time, it almost cost him his chance to get into the series. Connie still speaks of the incident with a trace of regret in his voice; it prevented him from opposing the great Mathewson, the big fish which got away from him in 1901, with his crack southpaw in Connie's first World's Series.

The Athletics had been playing in Boston, but Mack had given his young college pitcher, Andy Coakley, permission to visit his folks in Providence. Coakley picked up the club as the Federal Express rolled into the station. It was New England's closed season for straw hats; and Gene Mack, Connie's brother, whispered to Andy: "The Rube has declared war on straw hats. Better watch yours."

In those days players carried their own suit rolls, and there was a special compartment in the suitcases for the spiked shoes. Andy placed his straw skimmer under his coat, but the Rube saw him try to reach his Pullman and started in hot pursuit. Andy raised up his bag for protection, and the spiked shoe grazed Waddell's chin. That made Rube mad and more determined than ever to smash Coakley's hat. In the scuffle Rube tripped over a bag and fell heavily on the shoulder.

After they got on the train, the Pullman conductor, an Athletic partisan, who had seen the incident, suggested they kiss and make up. At the time Rube's dignity was hurt more than his painful shoulder; he frowned for a while, but his pout did not last. His face broadened into a grimace as he said: "I'll shake hands with Andy, but I'll be damned if I kiss him."

During the night he slept by an open window, and the next morning he couldn't raise his arm above his collar. It stayed that way for the balance of the season. With the World's Series a month away, ugly rumors started to circulate that gamblers had gotten to Rube. Connie still gets annoyed at such rumors. "Anyone who knew Waddell knew how silly and ridiculous such rumors were. Money meant little to the Rube. He loved to play ball and to win, and he always was loyal to me. As a matter of fact, at the time of Rube's injury I wasn't thinking of the World's Series, but of the pennant we were trying to win. We still were far from being out of the woods."

3

Mack was right that he wasn't out of the woods; a comfortable lead which his team had piled up by Labor Day almost vanished as the White Sox ripped through the Atlantic seaboard on their last eastern trip. By capturing nine games out of eleven in Boston and New York, Comiskey's white-hosed Chicagoans whittled Connie's lead down to three points by the time they reached Philadelphia, September 28.

The three-game series with the White Sox was the biggest baseball excitement Philadelphia had known up to that time, and one which Mack still remembers with keen relish. "We just had to win that series, and winning it was more important to me than anything else in the world," he laughed.

Little Columbia Park was jammed to the gunwales for all three games, and ropes were stretched all around the outfield. With a livelier ball there would have been a shower of extra-base hits. The roofs of all the houses on Twenty-ninth Street did a land-office business, as house owners took care of those who couldn't get in the ball yard at two bits a head.

Faithful Eddie Plank won the first game, September 28, from Roy Patterson, 3 to 2. Then, on September 29, Connie really had a chance to sit back, relax, and enjoy a ball game. While Chief Bender held the White Sox helpless, the Athletics unloosed an extra-base shower at the expense of Nick Altrock, Ed Walsh, and Piano Legs Smith, and won 11 to 1. "That was the vital game for us," observed Connie. But he didn't fool around and asked Plank whether he could take care of the third game after only one day's rest.

"Do you think you can beat them again, Eddie?" he asked. "If your arm doesn't feel rested, tell me and I'll pitch Coakley."

"I'll be all right," said Plank, but he wasn't quite as effective, September 30, and he lost to George Owen, 4 to 3. Chicago, therefore, left Philadelphia a game and a half behind, with only a week to go. That was the approximate winning margin of the Athletics at the finish. Both clubs won 92 games, but Chicago lost 60 against only 56 defeats for the 1905 A's.

4

Mack didn't have a .300 hitter on his 1905 champions, as Harry Davis was high man with .284, and his eight homers were enough to lead the league. Harry wore the American League's home-run crown from 1904 to 1907, inclusive. Batting averages that year were the lowest in A.L. history, with Flick, the almost-Athletic of 1902, and "Hit 'em where they ain't" Willie Keeler, the only .300 hitters among hundred-game players.

Connie made a sensational midseason move, and only a man with Mack's spirit of daring would have attempted it during a hot pennant fight. He benched Monte Cross and played Jack Knight, a lanky lad plucked right from Philadelphia's own Central High School, at shortstop. Jack had a reputation in Philadelphia scholastic athletics similar to that of Lou Gehrig in New York two decades later. Knight was tall and rangy and hit only .234 in 88 games against Monte Cross's .270 for 78 games. Late in the season, in the close hand-to-hand fighting with the White Sox and in the World's Series, Connie returned Cross to his infield because of Monte's greater experience.

Danny Hoffman never was quite the same player after that near-fatal Tannehill pitch, and during the season Mack replaced him in center field with Briscoe Lord, a chunky boy from Upland, Pennsylvania, just outside of Chester.

Coakley came fast that season: won 17 games and lost 10. Henley remained Mack's unluckiest pitcher, though one of the tall right-hander's 4 victories was the first no-hitter pitched by one of Mack's pitchers. In August the Athletic director purchased Jimmy Dygert, a pony spitball pitcher, from the New Orleans club. And Connie got a great thrill on July 4, when Waddell defeated Cy Young, 4 to 2, in 20 innings. "That sort of made Rube feel that he had squared matters with Cy for the perfect game Young pitched against him the year before," said Mack.

Waddell's September 1 injury cost him a chance for his greatest record, for with the season still 6 weeks to go, he already had won 27 games against only 10 defeats, while he had struck out 286 men. And it was another season of Waddell peccadilloes! A favorite stunt was to go into a saloon, take off the bartender's apron, put it on himself, and start dispensing beer. Fire engines still had their allure; and once, as the horsedrawn apparatus passed Columbia Park, Rube disappeared between innings to ride to the fire on the engine. Between games, Mack often gave him a day off so that he could fish; fishing was his great delight and kept him out of mischief. The Camden, New Jersey, saloons always had an especial attraction for him; and one evening, as he was crossing the Delaware on a ferry, Rube thought he heard someone say, "A woman's overboard." Seeing something afloat on the water, Waddell, a good swimmer, dove overboard without removing his clothes and came up with a greasy black log.

Ossie Schreck had a complaint to file with Mack on Rube's bed behavior. At that time players slept two in a bed on the road. "The Rube eats crackers in bed," Ossie complained to his manager. "I don't like to sleep dunked in cracker dust."

"I'll speak to Rube about it," said Connie.

"I want you to put it in his contract that he can't eat crackers in bed," persisted Schreck.

Charley Dryden, that genius of the press box, then was at his height as baseball writer for the old *Philadelphia North American,* and the Athletics gave him rich color to display his talents. If Ossie objected to Rube's crackers, Charley wrote that Waddell had his own grievance in Schreck's midnight snack, which the catcher termed a Pizzazza sandwich. Quoting Dryden, "A Pizzazza is made of two slices of rye bread; in between is a thick smear of Limburger cheese, freely sprinkled with raw onions. The smellier the cheese, and the stronger the onions, the better is the Pizzazza."

At his peak, Waddell's salary was said to have been $2,200. Tom Shibe, Ben's son, used to pay Rube in one-dollar bills—not to make it seem more, as has been reported, but to make it last longer. A ten-spot would go as quickly with Rube as a one.

5

Despite the loss of Waddell, neither Mack, the Athletics, nor their followers were discouraged as the White Elephants prepared to play the Giants, McGraw's scrappy New York team, in the 1905 World's Series. After all, Connie still had Plank and Bender. It was the first series played under the so-called John T. Brush rules, in which the original split of the players' pool called for 70 per cent for the winners and only 30 for the losers. That the Giants felt their chances no better than 50-50 was evident from the fact that the New York players were willing to make side agreements with individual Athletics to pool a winning and losing share and then divide it two ways. McGraw, Mathewson, and Bresnahan of the Giants alone refused to come in on it; and, of course, Mack did not enter such an agreement. He had no objection to his players making the side agreements; he knew what the absence of Waddell meant to his staff, and felt the 70-30 split was all out of proportion. After the 1906 all-Chicago World's Series, it was changed to the present division of 60 and 40.

Yet the result of Connie's first World's Series was one of his early disappointments. It wasn't that he lost, but how he lost; for in four defeats, three inflicted by Christy Mathewson, his team was shut out. That he once had Matty under contract didn't sweeten matters, and he extracted little comfort from the fact that his lone victory, pitched by Bender, also was a shutout. His A's came out of the series with the rather ignoble team average of .162. There still was little love between the American League and McGraw at the time, the Giants' aggressive chief having left the Baltimore Americans in midseason of 1902 to accept a job under Andy Freedman as manager of the Giants, taking a parcel of American League players with him. Connie never was one to hold grudges, and he saw that McGraw had his side in the matter; but, after only two and a half years of baseball peace, losing to McGraw was like swallowing gall and wormwood for any loyal American Leaguer.

An amusing sidelight on the 1905 series was that the Philadelphia *North American* put up a big gong west of City Hall at Fifteenth and Market streets. During the series they were to ring it once for Athletic doubles, twice for triples, three times for home runs. The bell ringer was about as busy as Santa Claus on Fourth of July Eve. In five games he had only five chances to sound his gong, and then for paltry two-baggers.

6

In those days the opening World's Series city was decided by the flip of a coin. Garry Herrmann, the National Commission chairman, tossed up a half-dollar, and Ben Shibe called "Heads." Heads it was. Mack, who attended the meeting with Shibe, was pleased and thought it was a good omen. He preferred opening at home. "Well, we won the first round," he chuckled to Uncle Ben.

The schedule for the series called for alternate games between Philadelphia and New York. In a clubhouse talk to his players, Connie said to Plank: "You'll take the first one, Eddie," and then to Bender, "and you'll go in New York, Albert." In Bender's three seasons with the team, the observing manager had noted the Indian's amazing coolness under all circumstances, and preferred to have him face the hostile—and then very partisan—crowd at the Polo Grounds.

McGraw started with Mathewson, as was expected. Plank had met him before in Pennsylvania college ball, when he pitched for Gettysburg and Matty starred for Bucknell. "My, what a crowd!" said Connie, as his little stands quickly overflowed and spilled behind outfield ropes in both left and right fields. The official attendance for that first authorized modern World's Series game was 17,955. The Athletics only doubled their regular admissions, a dollar for the grandstand and four bits for the bleachers or for parking space for one's dogs behind the ropes. In honor of the occasion, John T. Brush, the Giants owner, dressed his players in a specially made black uniform with white box-shaped caps and stockings and a big white N.Y. on the blouses. Connie said: "Brush's uniforms are all right, but my players will wear their regular home and road suits."

The Giants won, 3 to 0, on October 9, getting ten hits off Plank against only four Athletic bingles off McGraw's Big Six, three of them being ground-rule doubles. Trying to get more batting strength into his line-up, Mack had Schreck catch Plank, which he rarely did in the season; but Ossie was not in good form, and McGraw's speeders stole four bases on him. Plank held off Matty for four innings, but the black-uniformed New Yorks bunched hits and steals on the left-hander for two runs in the fifth inning and added another in the ninth on Gilbert's single, Matty's sacrifice, and Bresnahan's one-base hit.

The next day, before 24,992 New Yorkers at the Polo Grounds, the Athletics exactly reversed the result of the previous day. The score was the same, 3 to 0; and Mack's winning pitcher, Bender, held the losers to four hits. The A's made only six hits themselves off Iron Man McGinnity and Red Ames, who pitched the ninth, but Mack's players profited by two New York errors in their two scoring innings. Alas, it was the last Philadelphia scoring Mack was to see during the series!

Not knowing what was ahead, Connie was fairly content as his players sped back to Philadelphia the night of the second game. "We're as well off now as McGraw," he told his men, "and we should win in our park tomorrow." But it rained that next day; it complicated the schedule and was a break for McGraw. The National Commission then decided to play the third game in Philadelphia and the fourth and fifth games in New York, so as to get in a Saturday contest at the Polo Grounds. The rainy day gave Mathewson two days of rest, and he was available for the third game. Mack then sorely felt the loss of Waddell and had to call on Andy Coakley to oppose McGraw's ace.

The play of the Athletics that day brought Bronx cheers from the stands. Of Mack's 43 World's Series games, it was the most unpleasant he ever sat through. His team again was blanked by Mathewson; for the second time Christy pitched a four-hit game, while the Giants won by the overwhelming score of 9 to 0. Coakley wasn't nearly as bad as the score indicated, as the Athletics made five errors, three by Murphy, and only one of New York's runs was earned. The Giants stole five bases; and, though Schreck was not charged with any errors, Connie became so displeased with his poor throwing and erratic work behind the plate that he yanked him in the middle of an inning and sent Powers to catch. From then on Mike, though a lesser hitter, caught the remainder of the series.

The fourth game, played in New York on October 13, also left a bitter taste in Connie's mouth. Plank, making his second start, opposed Iron Man McGinnity and lost another shutout, this time by 1 to 0. "You can't win if they don't get you any runs," Mack consoled Eddie. Plank gave up only four hits, and McGinnity five, with New York's lone run being a gift by the two Athletic Crosses. "Sandow" Mertes led off with a grounder to Monte, which the shortstop fumbled. Seybold caught Dahlen's fly, and Plank tossed out Devlin, the strong man going to second. Eddie got two strikes on Gilbert when Billy hit a ball right at Lave Cross. "My goodness," ejaculated Connie as the ball rolled between Lave's bow legs, Mertes scoring the only run of the game. Then and there Connie decided that old Father Time had crept up on Lave, and that his captain would not be on his 1906 club.

When Connie saw that ball trickle through Lave's legs, he had a sinking feeling that the play spelled disaster. He wasn't wrong, as the series ended the next day with Mathewson defeating Bender, Mack's only winner, 2 to 0, before another great Polo Grounds crowd of that period—24,187 fans. The Chief went down valiantly, yielding only five hits against six off Mathewson—and, though the partisan New York crowd exulted over its World's Championship, there were times when Bender was cheered almost as much as the Bucknell star. The first run off the Chippewa came without a hit, as Bender walked Mertes and Dahlen in the fifth. Devlin pushed them along a base with a sacrifice, and Gilbert's fly drove in Mertes.

7

In the three games which Mathewson pitched within a period of 6 days, he held the Athletics runless in 27 innings, gave up only 14 hits, walked only one man, and struck out 18—Bris Lord, the Upland boy, falling a victim five times to Matty's fade-away. It was the greatest pitching of World's Series history and made Connie wonder over the vagaries of baseball fate and what would have happened had the Bucknell boy joined his club in 1901.

The figures of that series make Mack smile today. The five games drew 91,723, for a total gate of $68,436.81. In 1943 the first game of the Yankee-Cardinal World's Series in New York drew a gate of $265,980. Both 1905 clubs had many 50-cent admissions. The share of the winning Giant players was $1,142, while that of the Athletics was only a little over $300. Mack went to see Ben Shibe and suggested that they throw the Athletic club owner's share of the gate into the players' pot. "We've had a pretty good season," Connie said. "The boys put us into the series, and they'll appreciate it." Ben readily consented, and it brought the "A" shares up to $823. Later, when they settled up their side agreements with the rather annoyed Giants, the Philadelphia players fared better than the winning New Yorkers.

Philadelphia did not take the World's Series defeat to its heart. It comforted itself with the thought that if Rube Waddell had been available, the result would have been different, but Connie always says: "I got great pitching in 1905, and even Rube couldn't have won without any runs."

Even though the A's blew the series, six Philadelphia newspapers combined to stage a great baseball parade for Mack and his 1905 Athletic American League champions—perhaps the most unusual parade ever held for a ball club. Ball teams, semipro and amateur, paraded from Pennsylvania, New Jersey, and Delaware. There were many bands, and fireworks flared along the full length of the parade on Broad Street. There were figures made up as an old-fashioned farmer, depicting Rube Waddell; a robed ghost for Ossie Schreckengost; a black-faced, curly-haired minx for Topsy Hartsel; a roly-poly fat boy for Socks Seybold; a monocled Britisher for Bris Lord; an armored knight for Jack Knight; two chaps carrying big crosses labeled "Lave" and "Monte"; a whooping redskin for Chief Bender; and a great plank for Southpaw Eddie. They even borrowed an elephant from the Philadelphia zoo. It was proposed to whitewash him, but the zoo objected, so a great white sheet was hung over him, and the paraders had a white elephant after all.

Highlighting the parade were open barouches drawing not only the Athletic American League champs, but their World's Series victors, the Giants. And the one who took the biggest cheers from the sidewalks was the tall, lean manager of the Athletics—Connie Mack. After the parade both clubs were wined and dined at a great baseball banquet.

CHAPTER XV

A'S GET TOSSED OUT ON EAR

1

FOLLOWING his quick decision during the fifth game of the 1905 World's Series that Lave Cross had slowed up too much to cover third base satisfactorily, Mack released his veteran captain to Washington. Connie elevated Harry Davis to the captaincy; and "Old Jasper," as he was called, became one of the most popular of those to wear the Athletic "shoulder straps." Danny Hoffman also was released, to New York. Mack acquired Arthur Brouthers from Montgomery to replace Lave Cross and picked up another lively young infielder, Rube Oldring, a former Bronx semipro, who had played a few games with Griffith's New York Highlanders in 1905.

Mack felt pretty good about his 1906 chances and thought he had a good chance to repeat. Shortly before leaving Philadelphia for his Montgomery, Alabama, training camp, Connie gave the following optimistic forecast to the Philadelphia correspondent of the *Sporting News:* "If the reports which come to me concerning Rube Waddell's arm are true, I don't fear any team in the league; and, while I don't wish to make a prediction or boast of our chances, yet I can say we will be either at the top or thereabouts at the finish.

"I've had personal conversations with Rube, and he assures me he can throw as well as ever. I feel Brouthers, the new infielder, can hold down third base. If he can't, I have several other good prospects. Everyone knows what Plank, Bender, and Coakley can do; and, if I can get another winning pitcher from among Henley, Dygert, or Myers, I am set."

2

Connie Mack's training expedition again was enlivened by the antics of that colorful battery, Waddell and Schreck. The manager was younger then; the situations weren't so funny when they actually occurred, but Connie could enjoy many a laugh later in recounting them.

The club played an exhibition game in Birmingham, and the following dispatch appeared in the *Sporting News* in a March, 1906, issue:

"BIRMINGHAM, ALA.—Rube Waddell, the Athletic pitcher, was held up and robbed on Allen Street. He was found and revived by two fellow players, Art Brouthers and Monte Cross. Waddell claimed that he had been hit on the head with a sandbag and robbed of $40. He has a gash six inches long in his head. The case is being handled by Birmingham detectives. Rube declares that he will be able to identify his assailants."

Connie wasn't overly sympathetic with the plight of his big pitcher. "Can I help it if somebody socks me on the bean?" asked Rube.

"If you'd stay away from back streets and alleys, it wouldn't have happened," said the angry Mack.

"But, Connie, that wasn't a back street, and I can't stay around the hotel all the time. I'd get nervous."

And, while playing some exhibitions at New Orleans, Schreck repeated his steak-nailing-to-the-wall trick, but this time it wasn't at Wolfe's in Jacksonville, and the entire club was thrown out on its collective ear. Ball clubs still weren't welcome at the best hotels, but the A's were American League champions and Connie had obtained quarters at a fairly swank New Orleans hostelry.

Schreck didn't like the steak they brought him. After trying to hack away at it, he called the Negro waiter and said: "This steak is too tough; I can't eat it."

"Dat's too bad, suh; I'll bring you another one," replied the waiter.

Ten minutes later he reappeared with another platter, and

Ossie again attacked the steak. He beckoned to the waiter. "That's the same steak you brought me before—only it's cooked more. Can you bring me a hammer and some nails?"

The waiter scratched his head and asked: "Did you say hammer and nails, suh?"

"Yes, that's what I said, and be mighty quick about it."

Anxious to please, and having decided that he could expect anything of Schreck and Waddell, the waiter brought the hammer and nails.

Then, with some one hundred ball players and other guests looking on, Ossie nailed the steak to the wall of the dining room.

Word of the exploit reached the hotel manager and, summoning Mack, he said: "You'll have to get your ball club out of here."

"Oh, Schreck is just a little playful; he didn't mean any harm," said Connie. "I'll gladly pay for any damage."

"No, Mr. Mack, we want your rooms—and at once," insisted the manager. Connie's persuasive eloquence failed, and at that time of the night he and Tom Shibe had to find new quarters for the ball club.

"And next time you keep your steaks on your plate," said Connie sternly to his frolicsome catcher.

Under training-camp notes in the *Sporting News* issue following the incident we read: "Connie Mack's American League Champions have stacked up against a little roughhouse at New Orleans. It always has been that way. Those countrymen never did have any respect for a champion."

3

Mack said he'd be on top or thereabouts in 1906, but he wasn't. Brouthers didn't make the grade at third base, and Mack eventually finished the season with the young New Yorker, Oldring, at the hot corner. The latter part of the season was given over to experimentation, as the club came home fourth, behind the "Hitless Wonder" White Sox, Yankees, and Indians.

However, the season was noteworthy in that two of Connie's greatest ball players, Jack Coombs and Eddie Collins, joined the A's that season and broke for the first time into Connie's line-up.

"My brother, Tom, who used to run the Franklin Hotel in Worcester, was the one who first told me about Coombs," said Connie. "He kept his eye on New England players for me. The college teams which played Holy Cross stopped at Tom's hotel. Coombs went to Colby College in Maine; he was big and strong, and Tom wrote me about him. So I had him sign Jack to one of our contracts."

As Chief Bender pitched a shutout against New York for Mack in his first starting engagement, so Coombs, the tall hurler from Kennebunk, Maine, broke in with a shutout against Washington.

However, before Colby Jack entered that early shutout into Ban Johnson's records, he had many interesting adventures. A Maine country boy, Coombs left for Philadelphia the afternoon of the day he received his sheepskin at Colby; and, arriving in the Quaker City, he soon was lost in its maze of trolleys. He took three wrong ones before a kindly policeman helped him find his way to Columbia Park.

Nervous but excited, the young collegian was given an "A" uniform in the clubhouse and introduced to another player by the name of Mike Powers, who was changing his clothes. Mack then got the Maine country boy acquainted with the other players. Another big husky citizen came into the dressing room; but, as no one bothered to introduce the newcomer to Coombs, Jack concluded he must be a rookie like himself. Connie then said to Jack: "Go out and throw a few."

So Coombs started to toss a few preliminary pitches to Powers, limbering up his shoulders and body muscles, which were stiff from his long trip. The big fellow who had come late into the clubhouse joined them and also started to take a few kinks out of his arm. Pretty soon Jack started to let out and put some zip behind his throws; the big man followed suit. But the harder Coombs threw, so did the big man. Finally Jack gave it all he had, but his delivery looked like a slow freight compared with the fast express the other sent roaring into Powers's glove. Perspiration stood on Coombs's brow, and dreary thoughts ran through his mind. "So that's how they throw them in the big league," he concluded, thinking of returning to the farm and getting back to college in the fall and concentrating on chemistry, which he had thought of making his life's work.

Then Connie walked over and said rather sharply to the big fellow: "Reuben, what are you trying to do, show that boy what a fool you are? He will see that speed often enough when he watches you pitch ball games. Needn't show off to him now." It was Coombs's first inkling that the big guy was Rube Waddell.

Jack was in the league only a little more than two months when he pitched the longest American League game on record, September 1, a 24-inning game, in which he defeated another young pitcher, Joe Harris, of the Boston Red Sox, by a score of 4 to 1. The Athletics scored a run in the third inning; Boston tied in the sixth; and the Mackmen finally broke through with three runs in the twenty-fourth.

"I had a lot of stuff that day," reminisced Coombs; "but was young and inexperienced and never could have won the decision without Connie Mack's perfect strategy. That was especially true of the nineteenth inning when Freddy Parent opened with a two-base hit and Chick Stahl sacrificed him to third. Here Mr. Mack ordered me to walk the next two batters, Ferris and Hoey, filling the bases. Mr. Mack then brought his infield in, to try for a force play at the plate, or for a possible double play. But you can imagine my thrill when I walked off the rubber after striking out Grimshaw and Morgan, both of them swinging hard at a third strike. Experience by the older man, Mr. Mack, had saved the situation."

"My, you had a mighty long day, Jack," said Connie with a smile when it was over. But he slapped Jack on the back as he remarked: "That was a great job."

4

Late in the season of 1906 Connie exhibited the greatest jewel among his many baseball finds, Edward Trowbridge Collins, the Columbia University shortstop. Eddie glistened only faintly when he first appeared in Mack's infield in Chicago, September 17; but he was to grow in luster with the years until he became the brightest diamond in Mack's array of stars, and among baseball's all-time second basemen, many believe Collins outshines even Napoleon Lajoie, Mack's first Athletic second baseman. Both have plaques at Cooperstown's baseball Hall of Fame.

Much has been said about how Connie found Eddie and snared him into his Athletic fold, but there was nothing mysterious about it. Eddie didn't hide his light under a bushel; as Columbia's quarterback and shortstop, he was one of the foremost college athletes in the East and was there for all to see. If Connie got the jump on John McGraw and Clark Griffith, the New York managers, it was because he "got there fustest," and maybe with the "mostest men." He had Eddie tied up at the end of his sophomore year.

Billy Lush, a former big-time outfielder who managed semipro clubs in Plattsburg, New York, and Rockville, Connecticut, gave Connie the first tip that Eddie was a natural. Collins played for Lush during summer vacations. Mack sent Jim Byrnes, a former Athletic player to look him over, and Jim sent a rosy report. Connie, Lush, and Byrnes then got the youngster into Mack's room, and Eddie put his signature on a contract. Collins, though a bundle of nerves and as fast as lightning, was inclined to be frail, and at the time weighed only 135 pounds. Perhaps some thought Eddie was too light, and that gave Connie a chance to move in on the inside track.

College athletic associations were fairly tolerant in those days and usually looked the other way when star athletes picked up a few vacation dollars from resort teams. Not only did Eddie play for Plattsburg and Rockville, but also for Rutland, Vermont, during summer vacations.

Collins had been elected baseball captain at Columbia for his senior year. After Eddie had had a busy baseball summer in 1906, Mack invited him to make the Athletics' last western trip, as the youthful shortstop's Columbia classes did not begin until October 1. "If you want to be a ball player, it'll be good experience for you," said Mack. "I may work you into a few games, but I'll not play you under your real name. I'll give you another—a good Irish name, too—how about Sullivan?"

So one looks in vain for the name of Collins in Eddie's first major-league box score, but tucked away between Second Baseman Sheehan, another rookie, and Third Sacker Rube Oldring in Mack's September 17, 1906, line-up was one Sullivan. What's more, Eddie crashed the big leagues in a real ball game. The White Sox were on a sensational winning streak, which gave them the 1906 pennant, and the great Ed Walsh vanquished Waddell in 11 innings, 5 to 4. Walsh fanned 12, and Rube 11. Eddie Sullivan started in well, getting one hit off the spitball king in 4 times up, handling 7 chances at shortstop without a slip, and stealing a base.

Eddie played only 6 games for Mack that fall, then he returned to the university. All went well until someone in the Columbia Athletic Association learned that Mack's Sullivan and Columbia's Collins were the same person. They could wink at Plattsburg and Rutland, but playing with the Philadelphia A's was too much. Eddie was declared ineligible for further participation in Columbia's athletics, and in the Blue and White's 1907 baseball season he was the team's nonplaying captain.

5

In the meantime, Connie had a pair of young ball players of his own. Both Roy and Earle made good in Philadelphia scholastic baseball, and Earle captained Central High when they won the city championship from their old rival, Central Manual. Roy then played second base for Central Manual. He, too, had started at Central High, but shifted to the latter school.

Earle, the younger, was the better player of the two. He caught and played first and wanted to be a catcher like his dad, and when he was only a kid Connie had the Shibe factory make him a small-sized duplicate of Ossie Schreck's glove. Ossie then took Earle under his personal wing and taught him all he knew about the fine points of catching. Connie got many laughs as Earle tried to copy Schreck's system of catching one-handed. Both of the Mack boys were short like their Uncle Mike; neither grew tall like Connie.

Earle went into professional ball as a catcher and first baseman at the end of his high-school career. Except for a few games with the A's, he never got out of the minors, though once he had a chance to go with McGraw on the Giants. Roy confined himself more to the business side of baseball.

Earle managed in the minors and has been coach on the Athletics ever since 1924, and frequently has filled in for his dad as team director. Slated as Connie's eventual successor as team manager, Earle has tried to relieve him of some of his more unpleasant duties. "I have tried in recent years to make myself useful by handling matters which might upset him," said Earle. "But he's pretty hard to fool. He always knows what's going on."

One also is touched by the genuine respect and admiration with which the son speaks of "Dad," much as Earle might have used the term when he was fooling with Schreck back there in 1906. No one on the Athletic team ever speaks of Mack as "the old man." To the sons he is "Dad"; to old players like Thomas and Simmons he is "Connie"; with younger present-day Athletics it is a respectful "Mr. Mack."

CHAPTER XVI

SILK'S DECISION COSTS A FLAG

1

IN ENUMERATING his pennants on the Giants, John McGraw always spoke of the ten he won and an eleventh that "they stole from me in the meeting room." That was the flag he lost on a technicality on Fred Merkle's failure to touch second base in 1908. Connie Mack has won nine American League championships, but the loss of the 1907 flag on an umpire's decision rankled for years in the mind of the man who universally is regarded as baseball's No. 1 sportsman. Even today the loss of that 1907 bunting stirs up unpleasant memories.

"I really think we should have won that year, even though my pitching was badly shot in the last month of the race, and we would have had a difficult time of it with the Cubs in the World's Series," he remarked. While Chicago led most of the season, the Athletics and Tigers always were close, and the A's took the lead on August 12 and then held it most of the time until they were nosed out by Detroit on the home stretch.

"We were several games ahead in mid-September and closing at home, while Detroit had to make an eastern trip, so things were all in our favor," he continued. "However, I was having a lot of trouble with my pitching. Coombs injured his arm early, but what hurt us most was that Bender's arm went absolutely lame at a time when we needed him most. Waddell had become unreliable, and I had to depend almost entirely on

Plank and young Dygert, my little spitball pitcher. Even so, we could have won if Silk O'Loughlin hadn't called that decision against us in that seventeen-inning tie game with Detroit.

That 9-to-9 deadlock of September 30, 1907, which started out to be a double-header, probably is more indelibly impressed in Mack's mind than some 8,000 major-league games that he has seen. A decision by Silk O'Loughlin calling out Harry Davis for interference cost Mack the game and the pennant.

2

It was a year of unpleasant situations. A feud developed between the Giants and Athletics in the latter part of the 1907 training trip, though Mack was no party to it. In fact, he was in Texas with the Athletics' second team when the brawls took place in New Orleans. But he resented McGraw's conduct at the time, especially the Giant leader's verbal assault on Tom Shibe. In addition to Mack's close business association with Tom, he felt a strong personal friendship for Uncle Ben's oldest son.

There was some talk of a "second World's Series" between the contenders of the 1905 series, Mack's A's and McGraw's Giants, in New Orleans in the spring of 1906. It wasn't held, as Mathewson contracted diphtheria, but was then scheduled for March, 1907. The series was well ballyhooed, and promised to draw well. In Mack's absence Captain Harry Davis and Business Manager Shibe looked after the Athletics' interests.

The Giants won the first game, March 27, with McGinnity defeating Jack Coombs, 4 to 3. In the second game, on the twenty-eighth, Roger Bresnahan, the New York catcher, claimed Eddie Plank had balked, and McGraw strongly backed him up. They made themselves so obnoxious that Charley Zimmer, the umpire, a former big-league catcher, requested the New Orleans police to oust the pair from the park. McGraw then took his club off the field, and Zimmer forfeited the game to the Athletics.

The next day McGraw wouldn't play if Zimmer umpired, and the game again was forfeited to the Athletics. Then, so as not to disappoint a good crowd, a game was played with Rickert, a New Orleans player, serving as umpire. In this contest, a farcical exhibition, the Athletics, with Vickers and Plank pitching, shut out the Giants, 7 to 0, defeating Wiltse and Mathewson. The Giants then forfeited the remaining games of the series and later in a hotel-lobby altercation McGraw allegedly insulted John Shibe. New Orleans newspapers called the Giants the "New York Brawlers" and "Hoodlums," and spoke warmly of the fine sportsmanship of Davis, Shibe, and the Athletics.

Connie got the entire affair over long-distance, and Shibe was much exercised over the matter. "It was one of those regrettable things, when the game was younger," said Mack. "McGraw was a firebrand then, and I know Tom Shibe never forgot it. It shows how much better the game is run today, as such a thing couldn't have happened under the able rule of Judge Landis. It left considerable feeling between the Giants and ourselves, and made victory over them in the 1911 World's Series that much sweeter."

3

Connie felt he had a pretty good team that year, stronger than the Athletic champions of 1905. He had acquired a hard-hitting shortstop, Simon Nichols, from the Memphis club, made a center fielder out of the Bronx infielder, Rube Oldring, and started out with the Central High School boy, Jack Knight, on third. Late in the summer the tall manager felt he had made the move which assured him of the pennant by trading Knight to the Red Sox for Jimmy Collins, generally regarded as the top third baseman of all time, but then well past his prime.

"Jimmy had a lot of good baseball left in him," said Mack. "A great third baseman for the Boston Nationals in the nineties, he was a most successful playing manager for us in Boston in the early years of the American League. He won two pennants with veteran players, but his club aged, and in 1906 the Bostons lost twenty straight games. The club soured on Jimmy and changed managers, and I knew he no longer was happy there. I gave up a good young player in Knight, but I wanted to win that 1907 championship, and getting Collins was a good trade for me."

4

When Detroit came to Philadelphia for its last series, September 27, Connie read his morning paper and saw his club still was three points ahead. "If we can beat them two out of three games, that should win for us," he remarked to Mother Mack and the boys at breakfast.

The overworked Eddie Plank was hit pretty hard in the first game, and George Mullin won a close decision for Detroit, 5 to 4. Connie was a little disappointed, as he had expected Eddie to stop Jennings's hard-hitting left-handed hitters, Cobb and Crawford. The A's had hit Mullin sharply, and four runs usually were enough for Eddie to win. All reserved seats were sold for the scheduled Saturday game, September 28, but it rained hard all day, and no game was possible. Connie didn't feel badly about the rain; with the Sunday off-day which followed, it gave his hard-pressed pitchers two days of rest.

It meant a double-header for Monday, September 30, and early in the morning the Philadelphia crowd bore down on Columbia Park from all sections of the city and surrounding districts. "Where are they all coming from?" asked Mack, as trolley after trolley emptied its load of human freight at their doors. Long before the start of the first game, the stands were jammed; the crowd packed the aisles and stood fifteen deep behind the outfield ropes. The police even lost control of the situation, as many fans climbed over the high outfield fence and dropped dangerously into the already packed ball yard.

That crowd saw baseball history—vital, nerve-racking, soul-gripping, everything-happening history, made and written!

The fans started off the afternoon in a carnival mood, which was felt and reflected by Mack and the White Elephants on the bench. Everyone was beaming and in good humor. At the end of five innings of the first game, the Athletics, having slammed Bill Donovan all over the field, led by a score of 7 to 1. The game seemed absolutely in the bag; and, with Plank groomed for the second game, it looked like the pennant. But then Donovan, who won twenty-five games and lost only four that season, suddenly braced, while Detroit started to get to Waddell, who had succeeded Jimmy Dygert in the second inning. "Dygert made two errors, and made a stupid play in the second inning, chasing Rossman almost over the plate," explained Mack. "He seemed nervous; I had to get him out of there and called in Rube."

"Umpire O'Loughlin's decision finally cost us the game, but I still think we could have won two games that day except for Hughie Jennings' sentimentality. We hit Donovan hard enough in the early innings to drive two pitchers out of the box. But Bill was a Philadelphian, and whenever he worked at Columbia Park, his father, brothers, a lot of relatives and friends came out to see him pitch. And if we had made twenty runs off him that day, Hughie wouldn't have taken Bill out; he wouldn't hurt Donovan's feelings before his people."

The Tigers were a tough fighting outfit that year, and Ty Cobb, then twenty-one, was gunning for his first batting championship. Detroit got into the ball game in the seventh inning when the Tigers scored four runs on Waddell. Rube was only partly to blame. A walk, a fumble by Nichols, and a glaring muff by Oldring filled the bases; Crawford's double scored two; Cobb's out let in a third run, and Crawford scored a fourth as Murphy threw out Rossman. The Athletics came back with a run, giving Waddell a three-run lead to hold for two innings. But Rube was tottering; he yielded a run in the eighth and then was blown out in the ninth in a Tiger rally which practically was Waddell's swan song as a Philadelphia pitcher and idol.

Cobb calls that ninth inning one of his brightest memories; the thrill of a twenty-five-year baseball career. The inning is just as vivid for Mack, but the memories are only distressing. Crawford singled; and Cobb, with little reputation as a home-run hitter, knocked a homer over the right-field fence, tying the score at 8-to-8 and knocking Connie off the bench. In Mack's excitement, as Cobb's homer cleared the fence, he slid off the bench and sprawled out among the bats which were strewn along the ground.

Connie got up quickly and motioned forcibly to Waddell to get off the rubber, while he beckoned to Plank, whom he had expected to pitch in the second game, to take over. But there was no second game. From there on, Plank and Donovan fought a stiff pitching duel until night engulfed the ball park.

Each side picked up a run in the eleventh, after which both Donovan and Plank hurled six scoreless innings.

In the fourteenth inning came O'Loughlin's decision, which stirred Mack more than any ruling which has been called against him in his long career in baseball, and which resulted in a feud between Mack and the umpire which lasted almost to the day of Silk's death.

Captain Harry Davis hit a long drive into the overflow crowd in left center field. From all appearances, it was a ground-rule double. As Sam Crawford, playing center, went back to the edge of the crowd, a Philadelphia policeman, sitting on a soft-drinks box, suddenly arose. According to the Detroit players and the umpires, the copper interfered with Wahoo Sam; the version of Mack, the Athletics, and the Philadelphia crowd was the flatfoot tried to get out of Crawford's way.

There was a lot of commotion, players of both teams milling around, with Silk O'Loughlin, umpiring behind the plate, giving no decision. Silk at first told Athletic players he saw no interference, and then, getting the "office" from Tommy Connolly, the base umpire, that he had seen interference, Silk suddenly called Davis out.

Connie blew a fuse. He didn't get vulgar or profane, but he poured as much vitriol into O'Loughlin's ears as his vocabulary would permit. Mack says today that when Detroit first started its complaint, O'Loughlin remarked to the late Topsy Hartsel, who was standing near by: "What are they arguing about? I saw no interference." Mack later procured affidavits from the policeman and persons in center field that there was no interference, which he sent to Ban Johnson.

During the general argument, Monte Cross, then Mack's reserve infielder, and Claude Rossman, Tiger first baseman, started throwing punches at each other. Both were tossed out of the game, but it hurt Detroit more than the A's, as Jennings had to play Killian, a pitcher, at first.

When play finally got started again, Danny Murphy made matters worse for O'Loughlin by hitting a long single, which would have scored Davis standing up. And shortly before the game was called on account of darkness, Eddie Collins, the little Columbian, batted for Oldring in the seventeenth and beat out a bunt.

After the game, Connie, still seething with anger and emotion, did something he rarely has done in his career: he invaded the umpire's dressing room. Poking one of those bony fingers at O'Loughlin, he said: "Silk, if you will tell me why you told Hartsel you saw no interference, and then changed your mind, I will take back everything I said."

Silk made no reply. For many years Connie was unforgiving and refused to speak to O'Loughlin. Oddly enough, Tommy Connolly, the man who changed Silk's mind and who now is supervisor of American League umpires, escaped much of Mack's wrath.

The tie enabled Detroit to leave Philadelphia half a game ahead. Each team had only a week to go, and at the finish the Tigers were nine points ahead. Plank and Dygert did most of the Athletics' pitching in that final week; they toiled valiantly and went down fighting, the little spitballer pitching three shutouts. Rube Vickers, a right-handed rookie from Williamsport, worked a final double-header against Washington. Mack pitched Waddell only once more after his fiasco against Detroit in the famous tie game, and Rube was removed in the first inning of a game with the Senators. Between Rube's three walks of that inning and blowing the six-run lead to Detroit, Mack decided Waddell was through with his ball club. He could tolerate Rube's antics while he was winning, but not when he cost Mack pennants. In the following winter he disposed of the most colorful player who ever has worn the big "A" of the Athletics to the St. Louis Browns.

5

But for a technicality late in the season of 1906, Mack never would have run into that fall pitching shortage which helped lose him the 1907 flag, and he immediately would have had another great left-hander to replace Waddell on his staff. As Connie Mack once almost had Christy Mathewson, the famous National League right-hander, so he had Nap Rucker, the great Brooklyn southpaw, on his hook, but just couldn't bring him in.

On October 5, 1906, Connie purchased Rucker from the Augusta, Georgia, club of the Sally League. "However, the draft rule was changed that year, and the new drafting period started October 1," said Mack. "The old National Commission set aside our sale, ruling that Rucker was subject to draft, and he subsequently was drafted by Charley Ebbets of the Brooklyn club."

The Athletics then took an Augusta right-handed pitcher named Holmes, who never helped much. Rucker, though handicapped with inferior teams, was a star almost the moment he arrived in Brooklyn. What a winner he would have become with subsequent great Athletic teams!

CHAPTER XVII

COLUMBIA EDDIE GOES TO SECOND

1

FOLLOWING the near-pennant of 1907, the A's went into a sharp tailspin in 1908. Socks Seybold, the right-fielder slugger, broke a leg early in the season; it practically terminated the fat boy's career. Rube Oldring was sick a good part of the time, and Bender's arm again was slow coming around. However, it was a close race, and for several months Connie's pitchers kept him in the pennant fight; he even nosed his way into the lead on several occasions.

Then the league race took an odd form: all the competition was among the four western clubs, with the eastern teams settling into the second division. That being so, Connie devoted the latter part of the season to experimentation; and, though the club finished sixth, Mack's lowest position up to that time, he was laying the framework of what he since has called his greatest club, which unquestionably was one of the top teams of all time. Even Connie did not dream then of the team he had in the making.

"I found out that I had to find a place for Eddie Collins," he remarked. "Eddie was very fast and showed me he was a real ball player. He had been a shortstop at Columbia, and I used him in that position in some games. However, I never was quite satisfied with his shortstop play, so I tried him at third base, and in a few games, even in right field." Then Connie enjoyed a little laugh, as he added: "I soon had to get him out of there; a couple of fly balls almost hit him on the head.

"So I got another idea. I thought, why not put my second baseman, Danny Murphy, in right field, and see what Eddie could do at second base? Though Danny had been my second baseman since my first pennant winner in 1902, he never was a really great second baseman. He didn't pivot too well on double plays, but Murphy always was a sweet hitter."

The shift of Danny to the outfield didn't win the immediate acclaim of the Philadelphia fans. Murphy had his friends—many of them. "Why push Danny out in the outfield, just to make room for some kid just out of college?" they asked. But it proved one of the smartest moves of Mack's entire career, and Eddie soon gave the fans their answer. Collins developed into one of the second-base wizards of all time, a hitter who soon was challenging Cobb, and a base-runner capable of stealing 81 bags a season. As for Murphy, he quickly mastered the right-field position and did a better job there than he ever had done at second base.

Connie also tried to find a place for Coombs, who up to then had failed to follow up the great pitching he flashed when he first came into the league from Colby two years before. He also gave Jack quite a tryout in right field, Seybold's old domain; Coombs played 78 games, hit .255, and showed a lot of speed.

2

Rube Vickers, the chap who had pitched the closing doubleheader with Washington the year before, looked great that year. He was a long, lean right-hander, well over six feet tall, with a world of smoke and plenty of guts. He was Mack's hardest-worked boxman in 1908, pitching 300 innings, while he won 18 games and lost 19. "I thought I had a pitcher in Vickers who would help us for a long time," said Connie, "but that was his one big season with us."

However, as the summer wore on, brilliant rookies, men who were to write diamond history, just tumbled over each other at Columbia Park. Mack gave Philadelphia a peep at his new shortstop, black-haired Jack Barry, a former star infielder at Holy Cross. He came from Meriden, Connecticut, where Connie broke in twenty-four years before, and had played some summer ball at South Manchester and Rockville. Connie's brother, Tom, the Worcester innkeeper, signed Black Jack to an Athletic contract. Barry proved a fielding acrobat, worked nicely with young Collins, the Columbia kid, at second base, and hit .222 in 40 games. But all during Jack Barry's baseball career, his batting averages lied. He saved his bingles for vital moments when a hit was needed to win a 2-to-1 or 3-to-2 game.

And late in the season two of the greatest left-handed hitters in American League history, Shoeless Joe Jackson and John Franklin "Home Run" Baker, broke into their first major-league box scores with the Athletics. Jackson, one of the foremost natural hitters of all time—the man after whom Babe Ruth patterned his famous home-run swing—was purchased from the Greenville, South Carolina, club of the Carolina Association for $325 on August 22.

Jackson's hitting reputation in the deep Southland apparently preceded him, as one of the most remarkable bits of baseball crystal-gazing appeared in Horace Fogel's Philadelphia letter to the *Sporting News* in the issue of August 27. In discussing rookies Mack was bringing in, Horace wrote: "Joe Jackson, the Southern whirlwind, who is to be Ty Cobbs's rival of the future, was to have been here before now, and will likely get in this week."

Only three years later that same $325 whirlwind was to hit .408 in the American League and drive Ty Cobb up to .420 to beat him. But that's getting ahead of the story. Joe was a backward South Carolina mill hand, almost illiterate when Mack first purchased him. He got his nickname, "Shoeless Joe," by playing in his stocking feet in Carolina. Shoes hurt his feet. But he surely could lay into a baseball!

Jackson was late in reporting, as Fogel indicated. When he finally did show up in early September, Mack played him in center field in one game. Joe made one hit in four times at bat and then disappeared.

"I learned he had returned to his home in Greenville," said Mack. "It was difficult for him to adjust himself to a big town like Philadelphia. I recognized that Jackson had great potentialities as a hitter, and I sent Socks Seybold down to Greenville to bring him back. Socks got him on the train, bought Jackson's dinner for him, spent the early evening with him, saw Joe was in his berth, and then retired. But when Socks got up in the morning there was no Joe. During the night he had slipped out of his berth, got off the train at one of the stops, and worked his way down to Greenville. We finally brought him back, and he played a few games with me that fall."

The Athletics owned a big chunk of the Reading Tri-State League club that same season, and in September Mack brought up the club's third baseman and cleanup hitter, Frank Baker. He was a farm boy from Trappe, Maryland, strong as a bull, and he packed a terrific wallop at the plate. In nine games that fall, he hit .290. "And don't let anyone tell you that Frank Baker was just a hitter," said Connie. "I get a little impatient with persons who think Frank was an awkward fellow around the third-base bag. He was really a great third baseman. Look it up in the records; year after year he handled more chances than any other third baseman in the league. He had to move around to get all those total chances. People remember Baker as a home-run leader; they may be surprised to hear he also was a fielding leader."

3

The big event of the 1908 season at Columbia Park was Waddell's first game against the Athletics in his new Brown regalia. All Philadelphia had marked that day off on its calendar, and when Rube was advertised to pitch for the Browns, May 19, a crowd estimated at 28,000 stormed into the little ball yard and sprawled along the foul lines and the outfield grass. With this setting, Waddell took partial revenge on Connie for selling him down the river by defeating the A's, 5 to 2. In this game the great strike-out man fanned only four of the Mackmen; while Bender and Vickers, who shared the defeat, had twelve between them.

However, on a hot summer day in St. Louis, July 29, with the sweat dripping from the tip of his nose and his left arm well lubricated, Rube really put on a show against his former mates. Mack could not help but sit back in admiration as Waddell whiffed sixteen of his players, tying a modern strike-out record, but a mark which since has been surpassed by the spectacular Bobbie Feller and Dizzy Dean.

"There was the usual banter between Rube and my players before the game," recalled Connie Mack. "They told him they would pin his big ears back. In reply, he openly boasted he would hang up a new strike-out record. We all laughed but, by goodness, he did it. Tommy Connolly, who umpired the game all by himself, has since told me that in all the time he umpired behind Rube, he never saw him with greater speed and more stuff than he had that day."

Waddell fanned Topsy Hartsel and Rube Oldring three times each; then he got Eddie Collins, Danny Murphy, Si Nichols, and Rube Vickers twice each, and Jimmy Collins and his old battery sidekick, Ossie Schreck, once. Even so, Rube almost lost the game. The A's went into the ninth inning, leading 4 to 1. The right-handed Rube Vickers was just as anxious to win as the left-handed Rube he had succeeded on the Athletic staff. He probably tried too hard in the ninth, or the St. Louis heat got him. In a jiffy the Browns got a rally going and poured three runs over the plate to tie the score. Mack rushed in Dygert, but little Jimmy promptly was belted for another run, and Waddell and St. Louis won, 5 to 4.

When Mack saw that he was getting nowhere late in the season, he released Schreck to the Chicago White Sox on waivers. Without Waddell, Ossie was like a kid who had lost his dog. What was the use of eating Pizzazza sandwiches in bed if it didn't get a rise out of Rube? Ossie, too, burned the candle at both ends. He didn't last long in the majors after that, and preceded Waddell into the game's Valhalla.

Both members of the great battery died of the same dread malady, tuberculosis, at the same age, thirty-nine, and in the same year, 1914—Schreck in Philadelphia and Waddell in San Antonio. While the Giants were training in San Antonio in 1923, John McGraw learned that Rube's grave was marked with nothing but a weather-beaten wooden board, from which the name was almost obliterated. He advised Connie Mack of it, and the two managers raised a fund of $500 from among Waddell's old friends, and there now is a granite monument with a baseball chiseled on it, over the earthly remains of baseball's greatest left-handed pitcher and, next to Babe Ruth, the game's most colorful character.

CHAPTER XVIII

MACK OPENS A NEW TEMPLE

1

EVENTS MOVED thick and fast ror Connie Mack and the Athletics in 1909. It was a hectic year, with many things happening. Foremost was the opening of the new ball park, Shibe Park, at Twenty-first Street and Allegheny Avenue, a site Mack had favored when he, Johnson, Ben Shibe, and Charley Somers looked for a place for the White Elephant to alight in 1901. The park naturally was named after kindly old Uncle Ben; later the words "Connie Mack Stadium" were added under the inscription "Shibe Park." Columbia Park had been built on leased land; the Shibes and Mack wanted a home of their own; and, when the park was opened to the public, April 12, 1909, it was one of baseball's show places and was termed a monument to the enterprise of Mack and the Shibes and evidence of their great belief in the future of baseball.

"We certainly were mighty proud of our park," said Connie. "Baseball still was in the wooden grandstand stage, and our plant was the first that was built entirely of steel and concrete. We wondered whether we could ever fill those long rows of seats."

As we look at ball parks of today, with their extensive grandstands and long rows of boxes, the original Shibe Park was a paradise for the two-bit fan. Of its 20,000 seating capacity, there were only 8,000 grandstand seats, but there were extensive concrete bleachers in right and left field. One could sit directly behind either the third baseman or first baseman for a quarter. The lower grandstand still was 50 cents; later the upper stand was reserved at a dollar.

The opening game with the Red Sox was a momentous occasion and the Philadelphia newspapers of April 13, 1909, as well as *Reach's Guide* for 1910, give the paid attendance at 30,162, without counting several thousand guests. At the very opening it was demonstrated that the Shibes and Mack had not built their park big enough. The crowd wedged into the aisles, hung to new steel rafters, stood behind the grandstand, and trampled over the newly sodded outfield.

Bigwigs from baseball and politics, including many of the pioneers of the game, were present at Connie's opening party, and Mr. Mack was all smiles when he left the field. With his veteran battery, Plank and Powers, in the points, the A's initiated the new park with an 8-to-1 victory over the Boston Red Sox. Connie's line-up that day was Hartsel, left field; Nichols, third base; Collins, second base; Murphy, right field; Davis, first base; Strunk, center field; McInnis, shortstop; Powers, catcher; Plank, pitcher.

Jack McInnis was an eighteen-year-old boy, who less than a year before had played shortstop for the Gloucester, Massachusetts, high school. He was to become another of the big stars in the Athletic firmament. Stuffy, as he was called, filled in for Jack Barry, who was hurt. Amos Strunk, like Jack Knight, had been a Philadelphia scholastic baseball star and was as fleet as Ty Cobb without having Ty's dynamic energy.

2

Exactly a fortnight after the merrymaking and celebration attending the opening of Shibe Park, Mack's clubhouse was shrouded with grief. Catcher Maurice (Doc) Powers, with Connie ever since he came to Philadelphia, died after three intestinal operations. It was one of the saddest deaths in baseball and affected the warmhearted Mack to the very core of his soul.

Whether it resulted from crouching behind the plate, Mike's small intestines became locked, so that nutrition could not reach his vital organs. Physicians at Philadelphia's Northwestern Hospital said the popular catcher literally starved to death. Despite the fact that the best surgeons in the East became interested and difficult operations were attempted, Mike's sad end came April 26, exactly two weeks after he had caught the opening game at new Shibe Park. Mack spent much of his time at the hospital during that trying week, and tears rolled down his cheeks when he was told the dire news. Poor Mike was only thirty-three, and all Philadelphia went into mourning. What made it even more difficult for Mack and Philadelphia fans to understand, was that Powers himself was a young physician, having studied medicine at Holy Cross and Notre Dame.

With the release of Schreck the previous fall and the sudden death of Powers, Connie had to build up an entirely new catching department. With considerable forethought, he had acquired Ira Thomas and Paddy Livingstone the winter before. Both men had previous major-league experience. Thomas had been with the Yankees and in 1908 was second-string catcher on the champion Tigers. Livingstone had caught for Cleveland and the Cincinnati Reds. Thomas soon became one of Connie's favorite players and a trusted lieutenant. He never has left Connie's employ, serving as catcher, coach, manager of affiliated minor-league clubs, or head of the Athletic scouting department, a post he holds today.

3

The kids Mack brought up in the fag end of the 1908 season started to go places even on the training trip of 1909. Mack had some of his crack youngsters, including Collins, Joe Jackson, Strunk, and McInnis on his second team as he came up from the South. Arriving in Louisville, he met an irate "Cap" Neale, general manager of the Colonels and later scout for the Phillies. Cap bawled out Mack, saying: "We expected to see your best club, and you bring a team of scrubs. That isn't fair. Why, we'll murder those kids."

Connie repeated Neale's remarks to his youngsters, and the "A" junior varsity got sore. They went to town! With young Jackson battering down the fences, the Athletic kids won by a score of 21 to 2.

However, Jackson remained difficult to handle and was

© Sporting News

Gettysburg Eddie Plank

He collected over 300 Major League scalps.

© Charles M. Conlon

Chief Albert Bender

He won six World's Series games for Mack.

© Sporting News

Jack "Stuffy" McInnis

Artistic first baseman.

© *Sporting News*

MR. AND MRS. CONNIE MACK AT YANKEE STADIUM, 1938
The Macks were married after 1910 World's Series.

Mack's problem on the trip. After an exhibition game in Reading, the players were on the station platform, awaiting a train for Philadelphia. There was a row of milk cans, with red labels attached to them, on the platform.

"I wish I had one of those labels on me, and that I would be sent away somewhere," said Joe.

Mack overheard the remark and asked: "Do you mean that, Joe?"

"Yes, I do," he replied.

"All right," said Connie, "we'll see whether we can oblige you." He farmed Jackson to the Savannah club, where he hit .358 in 1909.

"Joe got married that season, and we brought him and his Mrs. up in the latter part of the 1909 season. We tried to teach them our way of doing things, but it still was difficult for them to get adjusted. Our players played pranks on Joe, and he regarded them with suspicion.

"My players didn't seem to like him, though I told them at the time he was going to make one of the great hitters of baseball. In 1910 I again farmed him out, this time to New Orleans."

Another great youngster with the Athletics in the spring of 1909 was a college left-hander from St. Mary's College of California, Harry (Lefty) Krause. Harry made one of the most amazing debuts ever recorded in the big leagues. The young coast lefty burst on the American League stage with ten straight victories, all complete games, in which he gave up only five runs. They still speak of it in the major leagues today. He finally was stopped by the Browns in a tough eleven-inning decision. In his ten winning games, Krause pitched six shutouts, three games in which only one run was scored, and a tenth in which he gave up two runs. His main victims were the Red Sox and the champion Tigers; he defeated Boston four times during the streak and Detroit thrice. He was death to left-handed hitters and throttled the great Cobb and Crawford.

Chief Bender's arm came back that same spring; Mack acquired another winning pitcher, a wild but effective spitballer, Cy Morgan, from the Red Sox, and Jack Coombs again began to live up to his fine promise of 1906.

Speaking of Coombs's conversion to stardom, Connie remarked: "Jack had a lot of arm trouble after his first fine season with us. Then, about the middle of the 1909 season, I had him finish a game; he worked six beautiful innings as I recall it, and showed a little curve ball. It didn't break much, but I saw it could be developed into a most effective delivery.

"Coombs was staying with Monte Cross, who lived near the ball park. I called on him after the game and said, 'Jack, if you'll pitch that curve, you can be a great pitcher. Just work on it a while and practice it whenever you can." Well, before long Jack had developed that curve so that he could get it over the plate and break it until it almost reached the ground when the catcher caught it. I'll tell you it was a mighty hard ball to hit, and was Jack's best delivery in his later big years."

4

As the season advanced, Connie's young infielders, Baker, Collins, and Barry, steadied at first base by the veteran Davis, began to click. The college kids, Black Jack Barry and Cocky Collins, functioned beautifully as the new keystone pair; and young Baker, inserted into the line-up at third base after a week's play, began crashing balls to all fields. Ira Thomas was catching great ball, and a young coast slugger, Heinie Heitmuller, was working well in the outfield with Oldring and Danny Murphy. Young Strunk had been sent out for more experience.

With the big Tiger right-hander, George Mullin, enjoying an early winning streak of eleven straight, Detroit started to make a runaway race of it; but Mack's young team, to the delight of the nation's fans, got better and better as it went along; and by September Connie and his old rival, Hughie Jennings, were at it again, hammer and tongs. The big September, 1907, Tiger series at Columbia Park had a 1909 return engagement at new Shibe Park.

When Jennings brought his veteran team, league champions of 1907 and 1908, to Philadelphia, September 16, the Tigers were three and a half games to the good. To take first place, the Athletics had to win four straight. "I never wanted to sweep a series so badly in my life," said Connie. "The bitterness of the hot fight of 1907 still was in our memories, and Detroit had a hard-fighting club. There also was much feeling and a strong rivalry between the two clubs. We almost did it—but not quite, as Jennings got one game of the four."

The series, drawing over 120,000 paid, was the best attended in Philadelphia up to that time—and one of the best anywhere. In every game the crowd spilled onto the field, and in the Saturday game 35,409 crammed their way into Shibe Park before the police ordered the gates closed. Gallant Eddie Plank beat Summers in the first game, 2 to 1. On September 17 Detroit won its only victory of the series, Mullin defeating Krause, the early-season Tiger jinx, 5 to 3. Cobb outsprinted an important bunt, and Detroit stole seven bases by as many different players—Cobb, Crawford, Delehanty, Moriarty, Jones, McIntyre, and Bush.

"Harry just couldn't hold runners on base that day, and they were off before Ira had a chance to shoot them down," said Mack. "Those steals were very costly."

Before that great Saturday crowd, with fly balls in back of the infield going as ground-rule doubles, Bender and Bill Donovan pitched a remarkable exhibition, the Chief winning, 2 to 0, as he gave up only three hits and Wild Bill four. In the Monday game, September 20, Plank again won over Summers, 4 to 3. The series left the Athletics only a game and a half behind.

5

That final Detroit series was filled with vitriol, acrimony, and rancor. In the first game, Donie Bush, Tiger shortstop, crashed hard into Eddie Collins in a play at second base. Overnight Eddie's ankle swelled to the size of a balloon. Connie was over at Harry Davis's house, where Eddie lived, as Trainer Lawler worked on the ankle much of the night to reduce the swelling. He taped it up, and Eddie played, but he was handicapped in his play, both in hitting and in fielding.

During the early games of the series, Ty Cobb, who was always demanding his full right of way on the base lines, spiked both Jack Barry and Frank Baker. Both had their uniforms slit and suffered cursory spike wounds. Neither was forced out of the line-up, but Philadelphia fandom went wild with rage.

Cobb received letters, telegrams, and telephone calls threatening him with bodily harm. Several wrote unsigned letters saying they would shoot him if he again showed up at the ball park.

Cobb gave the letters to Jennings, and Hughie called Mack on the telephone. There was no love lost between the pair at the time, but when Jennings requested police protection for Cobb, Mack replied icily: "I'll see no harm befalls him." Connie telephoned headquarters, and they certainly gave Ty protection. He was escorted to and from the park by a motorcycle squad; there was a solid wall of Philadelphia bluecoats between Cobb, playing right field, and the right-field overflow crowd; while several dozen plain-clothes men were scattered through the stands. Cobb was booed but not molested; but there was no more spiking.

The Tiger series had an unhappy aftermath for Mack. The seventh-place Browns came to Philly immediately afterward, and in the first game the A's were beaten by a little left-hander, Bill Bailey, 2 to 1. "It was an awful tough one to lose, as the scoreboard showed Detroit was beating Washington," the A's director confided. "Here we had planned, schemed, worked, and sweated to cut two games off Detroit's lead, and little Bailey put us two and a half games behind again. We never could make it up, and that was the margin by which we lost the 1909 pennant."

CHAPTER XIX

A GREAT CHAMPION

1

MANY THOUGHT Connie's team was too young—still too much in the experimental stage, too uncertain in the outfield—to figure strongly for the 1910 pennant. The Detroit Tigers were favored to make it four straight. Others thought Boston, the strong third-place club of 1909, had been sufficiently strengthened to make them the club to beat. As for Sir Cornelius, he was sanguine. "I had a feeling what our club could do," he said. "From the time we reported at Virginia Hot Springs for training, I felt we were pennant-winning material."

Even defeat in the opening game of the season, when Walter Johnson held the A's to one hit while defeating Plank, 3 to 0, failed to dampen his enthusiasm for this new team of destiny. Perhaps even he did not realize the heights to which Eddie Collins, Frank Baker, and Jack Barry would go; but he had seen enough to know he had the makings of one of the great infields of baseball. Harry Davis now was thirty-seven, but still a dependable player and a steadying influence on the three great youngsters in the other infield positions.

When pennant lightning struck again for the A's, Mack's third flag came fairly easily. Detroit fought well for half the season, but the famous Tigers were breaking up, and the Philadelphia pace was too severe. George Stallings had the Yankees up in the race, as he built up a superb pitching staff around Russell Ford, Jim Vaughn, Jack Quinn, Ray Fisher, and Jack

Warhop. They clung pretty close until August, when dissension broke out on the New York club; and Hal Chase, the brilliant first baseman, replaced Stallings as manager. That made the Athletic task easier, with Mack's club rolling up 102 victories, the first American League club to get into the century-victory class; their percentage of .680 was the highest in the 10 years of Johnson's league as a major. After the tight nip-and-tuck races of 1907 and 1909, Connie had a chance to sit serenely on his bench during September as his team breezed in 14½ games ahead of New York.

Perhaps the biggest difference between the Athletics runner-up of 1909 and Mack's third championship team in '10 was the big son of Colby, Jack Coombs. That fast curve really was dipping by this time. "Jack was magnificent that season," said Connie. "No pitcher ever did more for a manager."

Young Krause failed to follow up his brilliant promise of 1909—he broke even in 12 games; but Coombs did much more than take up the slack. He was to Connie Mack what that former iron man of New York, Joe McGinnity, had been to McGraw of the Giants. Jack pitched 353 innings, was credited with 31 victories while losing only 9 games. Coombs's 13 shutouts that year still constitute an American League record. One of those shutouts was a brilliant 16-inning 0-0 tie with Ed Walsh of the White Sox in which Jack yielded only 3 hits; he since has called it the best game he ever pitched.

Chief Bender was right with him, leading the American League pitching parade with 23 victories against 5 defeats. Eddie Plank, bothered at times with a sore arm, won 16 games while losing 10; while Cy Morgan completed Mack's "Big Four" with an 18-to-10 performance. Jack Lapp, a Frazer, Pennsylvania, lad, procured by Connie from Hazleton in 1908 and then farmed to Newark, was an energetic, strong-armed newcomer on the catching corps, and soon became Coombs's favorite receiver.

The club took the batting leadership from the slugging Tigers, though Eddie Collins, the team leader, dropped a little from his .346 of 1909, hitting .322. However, Connie got many a thrill out of the speed of his Columbia courser. In 1909 Mack and all the Athletics were pulling for Cocky, as his teammates called Collins, to beat out the great Cobb in steals, but Ty led at the finish, 76 to 67. It therefore was as big a kick for Connie as it was for Eddie when the Columbian reversed the order in 1910, filching 81 bags to 65 for the Georgia Peach.

"Eddie surely ran for me that season," chuckled Mack. "We still were playing for that one run, and if Collins got on and stole second or third, we had good men in Baker, Davis, and Murphy to drive him home. It was the kind of game I liked best; when the home-run era came in I adjusted myself to that kind of an attack, but I derived much more personal pleasure out of directing a base-running offensive, as when Collins was stealing all those bases."

In the meantime, those youngsters were pulling all kinds of spectacular plays: the double squeeze—two men scoring on a bunt—while several times the daring Collins and the fleet-footed Oldring scored from second on outfield flies. And on the defense Collins and Barry became baseball's foremost pair in breaking up the double steal. One would move into the infield; if the runner on third tried to come in, he would take the throw and whip it back to the plate; if not, he would let the catcher's throw go through to his mate, covering the bag.

"We learned our baseball at Connie's knee," said Collins. "He suggested most of the plays we pulled off. We thought up a few ourselves, being always together and talking baseball when we were off the field. But we always let Connie in on our schemes and got his approval before we tried them out."

2

The little towhead, Topsy Hartsel, started to slip perceptibly in midseason. One couldn't tell that Topsy was growing old by the tint of his hair, but balls which he once ate up were getting away from him. On July 25 Connie made a trade with Cleveland, which braced his outfield for that season but cost him his clouting rookie, Joe Jackson, then on option to New Orleans. To regain the services of Bris Lord, the Upland boy, then with the Indians, Mack gave up Morris Rath, utility infielder and a product of Philadelphia's Central Manual High, and his title to Jackson.

"I knew exactly what I was doing when I let Jackson go to Cleveland," said Mack. "Lord, of course, helped me at the time. I said our players didn't like Jackson, but that isn't why I traded him. I also knew Joe had great possibilities as a hitter. At the time, things were going none too well for Charley Somers in Cleveland, and I was anxious to do him a good turn in appreciation for the way he had helped us out in Philadelphia in the early days of the league. So I let him have Jackson."

For those who admired Joe Jackson as a ball player and knew his background, this deal always has been looked upon with regret. Not because Connie Mack lost this really great hitter, for in the next four years his teams were strong enough to turn the American League inside out. However, had Jackson, the former illiterate mill hand, remained under the steadying and wholesome influence of Mack, he might have avoided the tragedy and disgrace which befell him nine years later, when Joe, tempted by more worldly-wise associates on Comiskey's White Sox, was one of the unholy octet which participated in baseball's worst offense—the sellout of the 1919 White Sox–Cincinnati World's Series.

When Lord joined the club in late July, he was placed in center field, and Rube Oldring moved to left, where the Bronx boy was to play during much of his remaining stay with the club. In late September Rube suffered a broken leg, but the injury was offset a few days later, when Johnny Evers, keystone king of Mack's World's Series opponents, the Chicago Cubs, suffered a similar fate. Mack sent his former Philadelphia sandlotter, Amos Strunk, to Rube's vacant spot in the outfield. Amos was out a good part of the season, but in 16 games he managed to hit .333, and he was as fleet as a deer.

Amos was injured early that year, when Connie used him as a guinea pig trying to correct Harry Krause's former weakness—inability to hold runners on the bases. With the infield in the field, Mack put his speed-boy, Strunk, on second as a base-runner. The game was to see how far Amos could roam off his base of supplies before Krause, turning about in the box, could nail him. It was a game which went on by the hour and had an unfortunate ending. In skipping back to the bag, Strunk's spikes caught in the ground and severely wrenched his left leg at the ankle. It was months before Amos again could run.

3

On October 5, several days before the end of the season, Connie had a great day. It was difficult to keep any Athletic clubhouse secrets away from Connie, but Captain Davis did a great job on this one. He had the players chip in from their anticipated World's Series returns to buy Mack his first car. Shortly before game time, an outfield gate opened, and one of the early stem-winder models chug-chugged into the park and was brought to a stop at the home plate. The happy players gathered around it, and Harry said proudly: "Connie, it's just a little gift to you from the boys; an appreciation of what you have done for us."

If that wasn't enough for one day, Connie let his second son, Earle, back with the Athletics from Utica in the New York State league, catch Eddie Plank and Jack Coombs. The Yankees, with Ray Fisher in the box, won by a 7 to 4 score, but that meant little with the pennant long since stowed away; what mattered was that Earle hit a triple and a single. Connie was as happy as a proud hen; it was difficult to say which gave him greater pleasure as he sat down to dinner, the new car or Earle's two hits.

The National League in 1910 adopted the crazy "Columbus Day schedule," the brain child of Squire Ebbets, former Brooklyn president, and did not close its season until October 15. Ebbets used to insist that, with proper promotion, Columbus Day could rival Fourth of July as a baseball holiday. He couldn't sell his idea to Ban Johnson, and the American League shut up a week earlier, October 9.

Connie Mack conceived the idea of using this idle week to brush up his team for the World's Series by playing his Athletics against the crack stars of the American League. Ban Johnson readily fell in with the idea and encouraged his club owners to contribute their best players to this star aggregation. Some of the later-day American League All-Stars must blush when they are contrasted with the team which served as a tuning fork for the 1910 A's. The outfield was made up of Clyde Milan, Tris Speaker, and Ty Cobb. The infield was Harry Lord, third base; George McBride, shortstop; Germany Schaefer and Kid Elderfeld, second base; and Jake Stahl, first base. The catchers were Billy Sullivan and Gabby Street, and the pitchers, Walter Johnson, Ed Walsh, and Doc White. The series was played in Philadelphia and Washington, with Mack employing his pitchers in three-inning shifts. The All-Stars won the series, four games to one.

4

The general opinion among the nation's sports writers was that the Cubs—easy victors over Jennings' Detroiters in 1907 and 1908—would win the 1910 World's Series. Some loyal chaps in Philadelphia such as Billy Weart, Jimmy Isaminger, Stoney McLinn, and Gordon Mackay strung along with Mack's young team, but they bucked the consensus. Hughie Fullerton, the baseball oracle, especially went out on the far end of a limb by predicting that Mack's youngsters would be no match for the experienced and battle-scarred Cubs. And Hugh had won considerable distinction as a seer by prophesying the surprising 1906 Hitless Wonder White Sox victory over Chance's 116-game winner, and the easy Cub successes over Detroit the next two years.

But this time Hughie was wrong—dead wrong. Instead of Connie's young charges getting buck fever when they met the renowned Chicago machine—unquestionably one of the great teams of all time—they played "ring-around-a-rosy" with the crack Chicago infield and "tit-tat-toe" on Chance's renowned pitching staff. As for Cub catchers Johnny Kling and Jimmy Archer, they became dizzy as the Athletic merry-go-round cashed brass rings at the plate.

Connie expected victory—had a deep conviction his team would win; but he had much respect for Chance's team and expected a furious struggle. In his fondest expectations he didn't anticipate the joy-ride he was to enjoy. When the series ended, with the Athletics victorious in four out of five games, Connie felt that the stigma of those four shutouts and a club batting average of .162 in 1905 was thoroughly effaced from the club's books. Not even in the later Ruthian era and the period of the Jackrabbit ball has any World's Series team excelled the .316 batting average which Connie's brash kids compiled against Chance's pitchers. In sharp contrast, the Cubs hit only .221 against Mack's two right-handed aces, Bender and Coombs, the only pitchers employed by the tall Philadelphian.

5

Mack's second World's Series opened in Shibe Park on a crisp cold fall day, October 17, the latest date any of the American-National League championship series has gotten under way. Looking from an office window, three hours before game time, Connie smiled as the big bleachers in left and right fields already were jammed and hundreds stood behind outfield ropes. The Cubs had played their last National League game in Chicago on Sunday, October 15; they spent Monday getting to Philadelphia; and few of them had seen the comparatively new Shibe Park until around noon when they came swaggering onto the Philadelphia field for their early practice. "So you're the guys who think you can beat the Cubs," jabbered Johnny Kling, their great catcher, at some of the young A's who were bunting on the side lines.

"Think it!" snapped Jack Barry. "We will."

Two days before Connie had spoken simply to Bender: "I'm looking for you to take care of the first one, Albert."

"I'll be ready," replied the great Chippewa.

Chance's opening pitcher was big Orval Overall, husky right-hander, now a banker in California. Big Orvie had not been worked as hard by Chance that season as in former years, but he had the second-best earned-run record in his league, and he had made monkeys of the Tigers in 1907 and 1908.

Connie Mack was much annoyed when the start of the game was delayed over a prolonged argument as to whether motion-picture men could remain on the field with their cameras. It was the first World's Series to be put on celluloid. Hank O'Day, Mack's old pitcher in Washington, was the base umpire; a great arbiter, Hank was inclined to be touchy and officious. He tried to shoo the men off the field. Instead of leaving, they went over to Ban Johnson's box and staged an indignation meeting. Ban had given them permission to take the pictures. Johnson called over his umpire, Tommy Connolly, and told him the movie men had a right to stay on the field. Then Frank Chance, the Cub manager, came up with a long beef.

He didn't want any photographers standing in back of the plate.

"Get on with the game! Get the game started!" Connie yelled impatiently from his bench. His pitcher, Bender, had been warmed up since three o'clock. The sun was shining, but it was a cool day—around 50°, and he didn't want the Chief to cool off.

The arguments finally ended with the cameramen on the field. With Sheckard disposed of in the first inning, Schulte, hard-hitting Chicago right-fielder, stung a hard single to right field. "All that wrangling didn't do the Chief any good," Mack thought to himself. But he had no occasion to worry. Not until the ninth inning was he again to hear the ring of a second Cub base-hit.

Overall's old World's Series charm got him through the first inning, but the second frame gave a foretaste of what was in store for the famous but faltering Cubs. Roping and tying down Mack's White Elephants was to be a different matter from their successful Tiger hunting of former years. Overall was pitching on the outside to Baker, a right-field hitter; but Baker got his Maryland power behind a swing, and a shriek of joy went up from the crowd as Frank's line fly landed in the left-field crowd for a ground-rule double. Mack smiled as he gave Davis the sign to sacrifice J. Franklin to third.

There were shrill cries on Mack's bench of "Bring 'im in, Danny," to Murphy, and Danny obliged. A thrill went down the full length of Connie's spine as Murphy rifled a hot single down the third-base foul line, and Baker cashed a precious run at the plate. That wasn't all. Aided by a high pitch to Barry, which Kling barely held, Murphy stole second. Jack's out then advanced Murphy to third. Chance played it cagey; he ordered Overall to give Ira Thomas four balls, expecting to make Bender the fall guy. It was difficult to say who got a greater kick out of the Chippewa's stinging single to center—a hit through Zimmerman which scored Murphy—the hat-throwing crowd, the stolid-faced Bender, or the happy Mack.

Another run scored on Overall before Chance took him out at the end of the third inning. With one down in that frame, Bris Lord doubled to center, was pushed to third on

Collins' bunt, and scored when Baker again crossed the Cubs by hitting safely to left.

Baker also brought in the fourth Athletic run off Harry McIntyre in the eighth. Collins worked Overall's successor for a pass and vexed Harry as he took long leads off first. Twice he threw over to Chance to get the speed-boy, and the second time almost nipped Eddie. He tried it again, and Mack joined in the laugh on the bench when he threw into right field, while Cocky joyfully scampered around to third base. Baker's double which brought him in was a more orthodox hit for Frank—a drive into the right-field crowd.

"That's right, mix 'em up, Frank," congratulated Mack. "They won't know how to play you."

Two errors in the ninth marred Mack's otherwise perfect day. It didn't prevent victory, but after Bender's masterful exhibition, Connie was sorry to see the boots cost Albert a merited shutout. Up to the ninth, Schulte was the only Cub to reach base on him—on that first-inning single and later on a walk. Each time Ira Thomas shot him down stealing. In eight innings, only 24 Cubs faced the Chief.

The spell was broken when Thomas muffed a foul by Joe Tinker, first Chicago batsman, in the ninth. "Gosh, I thought Ira had that!" said Mack. His batting life saved, Tinker shot a single to center and young Strunk fumbled it into an extra base. Kling scored Joe with another single. "One run in—and none out: are the Cubs at last to show their claws?" thought Mack. His face was grim, but he had full faith in Bender.

Ginger Beaumont batted for McIntyre and rolled weakly to Collins. A shout of joy went up as Bender struck out Sheckard for his eighth victim. Again the troublesome Schulte walked, but the game came to a happy end when Baker gobbled up Artie Hofman's grounder and stepped on his bag, forcing Kling at third.

6

If Mack had an easy day in the first game, he did a lot of bench-wiggling before Jack Coombs, his 1910 shutout king, came out victor in the second tussle by a score of 9 to 3. The game was much closer than that final score indicates, and Coombs was in enough hot water to parboil a bucketful of his Maine lobsters. The Cubs put droves of runners on the bases; Mack suffered as Jack walked nine, gave up eight hits, and was guilty of two errors. However, with this mess of scoring ingredients, the Cubs concocted only three runs. Fourteen of the Chicago bears were left on base, and three fancy double plays, two started by Collins, helped the Colby man out of difficulties as Connie gave thankful sighs of relief.

The great Mordecai Brown, known also as Miner Brown and Three-Fingered Brown, was Chance's pitcher. He had slipped a bit from his prime, but still was rated next to Mathewson, the king pitcher of the National League. Brownie, who had lost two fingers as a boy and learned to pitch a defective fork ball from his three remaining right fingers, had better control than Coombs. The Athletics, however, were hitting him solidly, but for six innings not too successfully in the pinches.

The A's led by the slim margin of 3 to 2 when the big blow-off came in the seventh; they wrecked the great Brown with the heaviest barrage fired against a National League pitcher in World's Series competition up to that time. What's more, Chance made Brown take it, as there was no relief for the Miner until after the side was retired. Connie's heart danced with excitement as the big rally raged; this was really cleaning those 1905 shutout defeats off the ledger.

Eddie Collins, who was a thorn for Chance all day with two doubles, a single, and two steals, started it with a walk. That dangerous Baker man followed with a single, and doubles by Davis and Murphy into the overflow crowd were good for three runs. But the scoring merry-go-round kept spinning! Barry sacrificed Murphy to third, and Thomas' single sent Danny home. There was a lull when Chance retired Coombs; but the kid, Strunk, lined out a two-bagger, driving in Thomas. Amos then romped home when Hofman muffed Lord's line drive. With Collins up for a second time, perhaps Mack's spirit of humanitarianism got the better of him. He thought Brownie had taken enough. He gave Lord the signal to go down on a steal, and Bris was an easy victim of Kling's strong arm.

7

There was an off day after the second game, October 19, as the two clubs took fast-moving trains to Chicago, the home lair of the Cubs. In several of the larger cities on the route, the Athletic Special still was standing in the station when the Cub caravan rolled in on an adjoining track. Quips and wisecracks passed between the two clubs. "You lucky stiffs; we'll get you in Chicago," yelled the Cubs. "How did you ever win in the National League? You're a bunch of has-beens," shot back the young Athletics.

Reporters knocked at Connie's drawing room and asked: "Who are you going to pitch in the third game tomorrow, Mr. Mack?"

Without blinking those blue eyes, Connie replied: "Well, Coombs did a real good job in Philadelphia yesterday, so I think I'll come right back with Jack."

Many of the boys thought Connie was spoofing and having a little fun at their expense. In their stories they already had said Plank would pitch the third game against Reulbach. "How about Plank; what's the matter with him?" they asked.

"Why, I just think I'll pitch Coombs again," Mack reiterated.

In the race of the Specials, the Athletics pulled into Chicago ten minutes ahead of the Cubs. "That's a good omen," said Connie; "let's stay ahead of them." Chicago had not weakened on the Cubs; the fans felt that back in their West Side Park they would put these young Philadelphia upstarts in their place. A crowd of 5,000 was at the station. They received the Athletics with a curious but respectful silence as Connie edged his tall frame through the crowd, saving their plaudits for Chance's twice defeated gladiators. It was a nice display of loyalty to the home team.

However, the next day a depressed, dejected Chicago crowd of 26,242 realized that the old baseball monarch was dying, and the nation was preparing to yell: "Long live the king," to the new monarch. Sure enough, Mack had not been kidding the boys. Coombs was back on the mound for his team, after only one day of rest, and that spent on a railroad train. His starting opponent was Reulbach, but McIntyre and Pfiester were in before the 12-to-5 slaughter was over.

It was a ball game for two innings, with the Cubs matching the one run scored by the A's in the first, and the two hung on the scoreboard in the second. Reulbach went out for a pinch-hitter, and Mack's kids went to work on McIntyre in the third. That bear-baiting pair, Collins and Baker, both singled; and, when Schulte fumbled Frank's hit, Cocky never stopped running until he scored. Davis was hit by a pitched ball, and Murphy cleared the bases with a terrific drive which hit a distant fence for what Patrol Umpire Connolly ruled was a home run. Chance argued until he was blue in the face that it was a ground-rule double. Tommy insisted just as vehemently that, as the ball had hit a portion of the field free of spectators, the two-base ground rule did not apply, and that it was a legitimate Murphy home run.

"My goodness, what is he arguing about?" said Connie on his bench. "Any fool could see that was a home run."

Chance continued his protest until he kicked himself out of the game. Pfiester relieved McIntyre at the same time that Archer went to first base in place of Chance. A fifth Athletic run was scored that inning on Barry's double and Tinker's wild throw on Thomas.

Connie had another picnic as the A's had a final four-run explosion in the seventh, the entire team batting against Pfiester, the left-hander. It all started with two out, when Steinfeldt messed up Baker's bunt. Davis then singled, and Tinker fumbled Murphy's grounder. Barry's infield hit, a pass to Thomas, and singles by Coombs and Strunk kept the runs rolling over the plate. Of the fifteen Athletic hits on that merry day, the veteran Davis, young Barry, and Coombs each collected three.

8

Rain prevented a game on October 21 and gave the Cubs and Chance a chance to pull themselves together, but Mack since has reproached himself for not making it four straight and feels he blew the fourth game over a touch of sentiment. He saw his boys lose in ten innings by a score of 4 to 3. With his back to the wall, Chance pitched a first-year man, King Cole, who had enjoyed a splendid season, but his manager had held him back because of lack of experience. Chance also benched his crack veteran catcher, Kling, and called on Jimmy Archer to catch the youngster. Connie returned to his first-game pitching selection, the crafty, cool Bender.

The Athletics went into the eighth inning leading by a score of 3 to 2. And here is where Connie blames himself for losing the game. He feels he tossed away another big scoring inning by disregarding his own hunch. Baker led off with a safe bunt to Chance; he got the hit when Cole neglected to cover first base. Chance gave the kid pitcher a black look. The King was flustered—he passed Davis; and, after Murphy sacrificed, Cole hit Barry, filling the bases. The youngster was visibly unsettled and needed just a light shove to take a trip into the clouds.

Mack's hunch was to send little Topsy Hartsel to bat for Thomas. He thought the little towhead could easily work Cole for a pass, force in a run, leave the bases still full and Cole and Chance higher up in the air. Then, the counter thought came: "But we're a run to the good, and Ira would feel badly if I took him out." He let Thomas bat, and the catcher spoiled the big opening by hitting into a double play, retiring the side.

The Cubs tied amid a pandemonium of noise in the ninth and just missed winning in that inning. Schulte, first up, cracked a double to right and Hofman sacrificed him to third. Chance was hit by a pitched ball and started to run to first. He growled like a wounded bear when Connolly, the plate umpire, called him back, charging he had made no real effort to get out of the way of the pitch. It proved a good break for the fire-spitting Husk. Muttering through his clenched teeth, he took a furious swing and rammed out a triple, scoring Schulte with the tying run. The partisan, shouting crowd scented victory and appealed to the next two batters, Zimmerman and Steinfeldt, to bring in their manager. But the imperturbable Bender staved off defeat for one inning. Mack thought the jig was up when Zimm hit a difficult fly to short center. For a few minutes it looked as though it would fall safe, when Eddie Collins, coming from nowhere, reached out and grabbed it. A moment later Steinfeldt fouled to Baker.

Mordecai Brown had succeeded King Cole in the ninth, and Harry Davis made a bid for victory in the first half of the tenth when he drove a solid double to right; but Murphy hit hard to Tinker, and Harry was nailed at third; then Brownie whizzed a third strike over on Barry.

The Cubs then won in their half, a game which Connie always felt he let slip through his fingers. After Barry back-pedaled into left for a difficult catch on Tinker, Archer hit a long double down the left-field foul line. Brown grounded to Barry, but Jimmy Sheckard rifled the Chief's first pitch into center field, bringing in Archer with the winning marker.

9

The victory gave Cub fans fresh heart—their great team at last had found itself; perhaps it still could pull out the series by turning back these fresh Philadelphia kids four straight. Though the date now was October 23, the Chicago Sunday was clear and warm and drew the best crowd of the series—27,371. For the third time Mack called on his tall Colby collegian, Friday's postponement having given Coombs two days of rest since he won the third game. Connie also made two changes in his line-up—he sent in Jack Lapp to catch Coombs in place of Thomas, who had worked all four games, and little Hartsel to his old pasture in left field. Bris Lord moved over to center. Amos Strunk had hit well, but Connie preferred to take advantage of Hartsel's greater experience before the big frenzied Sunday Chicago crowd.

Despite the two innings he worked on Saturday, Brown was Chance's last hope, and his game paralleled his defeat in the second game at Shibe Park. For seven innings it was nip and tuck, and Connie slid nervously up and down the bench. He then sat on a small box near the bench, only to have his enthusiastic youngsters push him off the box and roll him on the ground during the fourth inning excitement as Coombs fanned Tinker and Archer with the bases full. As Coombs returned to the bench, Mack was picking himself up and brushing away the dirt, but his face was one broad grin as he said: "It's all right, boys; I have another suit at the hotel."

Coombs continued to go well, and after seven innings he had a 2-to-1 edge, but that was too close for Connie's comfort. Then in the eighth the A's exploded another bomb under Brownie similar to that six-run seventh at Shibe Park. Coombs started it himself with a single to right and was forced by Hartsel. Topsy just missed being the victim of a double play. That half a step made the subsequent rally possible. Driving his attack, Connie flashed a signal for Hartsel to steal second. Topsy got the decision on another close play, the Cubs setting up a terrible beef at Base Umpire Sheridan's second unfavorable decision. "Is there any law about calling that white-haired monkey out?" roared Chance as Connie enjoyed his discomfiture. Bris Lord drove in Topsy with a double, and the Upland boy followed on another two-bagger by Eddie Collins.

Brownie was weakening visibly, and Cocky, taking a long lead, stole third. There was a brief pause in the spirited Philadelphia attack when Baker poked a hot one down to Zimmerman, and Heinie's throw nipped Collins at the plate. Davis drew his base on balls, and the Cub fans then saw their great machine fall apart on the next two plays. Murphy hit a slow ball past second base, which Zimmerman chased, recovered, and then pegged wildly to the plate to head off Baker. Frank scored, as did Davis, and Murphy pulled up at third. From there Brown wild-pitched Danny home. The flustered Mordecai next walked Barry; but Lapp, ninth man up in the inning, kindly ended the assault with a tap to Brown.

The Cubs got one run back in their half of the eighth, making the score 7 to 2. Brownie had tears in his eyes when he came out for the ninth inning. He was in further trouble; for, with two out, Lord walked and Collins doubled, but Mordecai clamped down on Baker, who failed to get a hit in this fifth game.

One-half inning is all that stood between Mack and his first coveted World's Championship. Nervously he leaned forward and motioned for Lord to move over a few feet for Steinfeldt. Steinie's lazy fly fell into Lord's maw, and Bris also grabbed Tinker's lift. A flicker of hope remained in the Cubs as Archer singled, but the game came to a sudden end as Johnny Kling, serving as a pinch-hitter, grounded to Shortstop Barry. Jack ran over to second base, happily toed the bag for a force play on Archer, ending the game, and then joined the happy throng of Athletics who gathered around Coombs.

Everybody wanted to slap the big Maine man on the back at the same time. There was singing, shouting, rejoicing, skylarking in the Athletics' clubhouse. Bender gave a few Chippewa war whoops. Connie, beaming like a Cheshire cat, congratulated all hands and was especially appreciative of Coombs's work. "You were great, John," he said, "simply great."

Portly Ban Johnson shouldered his way into the clubhouse, his round face radiant with joy. He embraced Mack, the man to whom he had awarded the Philadelphia American League franchise ten years before. Ban was prouder than an oriental potentate. "They'll not speak disparagingly about the American League after the licking you gave them," he said.

In Philadelphia the interest and rejoicing was such that the *Philadelphia Times,* an evening newspaper, put out a special Sunday World's Series edition and sold 300,000 copies.

10

When Mack brought his new World's Champion Athletics back from Chicago, they were given a tremendous reception. A crowd estimated at 50,000 packed the streets around Broad Street Station at Broad and Market streets, with the police having difficulty in opening a lane for the players through the cheering multitude. One of the 50,000 was a lantern-jawed, square-shouldered former sandlotter from Philadelphia's Germantown section. He already had played a little professional ball but still was a strong Athletic fan and a Connie Mack hero-worshipper. His name was Joe McCarthy. Nineteen years later he was to lead another Cub team against his boyhood idol, Connie Mack, and also lose four games to one.

Mayor Reyburn, other city officials, Ben and Tom Shibe warmly greeted Connie and his kids; the First Regiment Band played "Hail, the Conquering Hero Comes," and "Home Sweet Home," and Reyburn gave Mack the city's key.

Connie Mack had another reason for wanting to get the series over with in Chicago and do no more ball playing in Philadelphia that fall. Late in that summer, Miss Katherine Hallahan had answered "yes" to Connie's proposal, and added, "But not until after the World's Series." So Mr. McGillicuddy contracted his second marriage on October 27, four days after the last game of the series, and the couple went on their honeymoon to Atlantic City.

It has proved a full and happy marriage, and five fine children have sprung from it—Mary, born in 1911; Connie, Jr., who came in 1912; and three other girls, Ruth, Rita, and Elizabeth, born in 1915, 1917, and 1920, respectively.

On Mack's return from his honeymoon, the city held a civic parade for the new World's Champions, November 5, followed by a municipal dinner at the Bellevue-Stratford to Philadelphia's baseball heroes, where loving cups were presented to Connie Mack, President Ben Shibe, and Captain Harry Davis. Numerous persons spoke, Mayor Reyburn, Ban Johnson, and other bigwigs; but a news story of the event says that "the most impressive speech—in which in simple sincere language he lauded the Athletics and paid tribute to Philadelphia as a great baseball city—was made by Connie Mack."

CHAPTER XX

ANOTHER JOYFUL YEAR

1

CONNIE HAD been unable to follow through after his winners of 1902 and 1905, but this time he had a feeling he had a club which would stay up a while, maybe win a string of pennants. "Occasionally you'll find a club which goes wild in one year and crashes through to a pennant," once remarked John McGraw, Connie's great managerial rival in New York; "but it isn't a really good club unless it can repeat, and it isn't a great club until it can win three years in succession." Mack's inner conviction was that he now had such a club. He didn't win three straight, but he won four flags in five years.

He stuck pretty well to his 1910 team at his 1911 Savannah training camp and didn't overwork his new World's Champions. A remark he made to Billy Weart, the former well-known Philadelphia sports scribe, in Savannah is well worth repeating; it is a lesson in the philosophy and science of training a big-league club for a hard 154-game grind, and applies especially to managers who fret and fume when they lose a few days' work because of inclement weather.

"There is no good in putting a team of ball players right on edge for the opening of the season," said Mack. "The players should be conditioned slowly. The race is so long that, no matter how carefully the men are worked, the players individually and collectively are certain to go stale at some stage of the campaign. For this reason I do not believe in working players too hard down south. A complete rest of a day or two does them more good than harm, for when they return to the field they go at their work with more zest than if they had to do many hours exercise each day."

A disappointment in the rookie crop of that Savannah camp was Clarence (Lefty) Russell, purchased from the Baltimore club late in the previous season for $12,000. That topped the price of Rube Marquard, the Giants' $11,000 lemon—who developed into a prize and was quite a story. But Russell developed early arm trouble, and Mack and the Shibes got back little on their investment.

Mack permitted a lively youngster, later one of the great catchers of this century, to slip through his fingers that spring. The kid was Steve O'Neill, of Minooka, Pennsylvania, present manager of the Detroit Tigers. Mack drafted Steve, kid brother of the former O'Neill battery of the Cardinals, from the Elmira club of the New York State League.

Connie had the Minooka youngster at the 1911 Savannah camp. Steve reported with shoes three sizes too big and a big clumsy glove he had purchased in Scranton. "Here, you can't play ball with that kind of equipment," said Mack. He wired up to the Shibe factory in Philadelphia for new shoes and a glove for O'Neill; it was a gift from Connie, and Steve is grateful for that bit of consideration to this day.

Mack saw plenty in the kid, but at the end of the training season he sent O'Neill to Jesse Burkett's Worcester club. Connie's son, Earle, was also a catching rookie at Savannah, and his dad sent him to Scranton.

Steve, never a backward lad, spoke up and asked Connie why he had to go to Worcester. "Why don't you send me to Scranton?" he said. "That's just outside of my home town. Then you can send Earle to Worcester. He has an uncle up there and would feel at home."

"I'm sending you to Worcester, Steve, because I'd rather have you be a big fish in a little pond than a little fish in a bigger pond," Connie replied.

Recalling O'Neill late that season, Mack released him to Cleveland. "I want you to know, Steve, I'm not releasing you because I don't think you're a good catcher. In fact, I think you have very good prospects. But Harry Davis will be in Cleveland next season as manager; he needs young catchers and can give you lots of work."

Mack explained that he sent O'Neill to Cleveland not only to help Davis in 1912, but further to help out the early benefactor of the Athletics, Charley Somers.

There was another interesting development on the Athletic team early in that season. Ben Houser, a former Baltimore player, had been used in 1910 as an extra first baseman to help out Harry Davis, and by most of the Athletics and Philadelphia fans it was felt that Houser would be the popular veteran's eventual first base successor. Certainly Ben thought so himself.

However, Mack knew he had to find a place for Stuffy McInnis, carried ever since the Gloucester kid served as substitute shortstop when Shibe Park opened its doors in 1909. Baker, Barry, and Collins were all young players, likely to go on for years. Stuffy was rather short for a first baseman, but he had a good pair of hands and was a natural fielder, and Connie got the idea he might make a pretty good first baseman. He also regarded McInnis as a much better potential hitter and all-around player than Houser.

"Get yourself a first baseman's mitt, Jack," Connie told the former Gloucester scholastic star. "Work around the bag at every opportunity. I want to see how you look around there."

"It was funny," recalled Mack years later, "how Ben took it. Every time Stuffy would go to the bag, Houser would come out from the bench and try to shove him away. Ben was much taller and had a good reach, and at times when both were around the bag Houser would outreach Jack for thrown balls."

However, when Mack noticed that the years were creeping up on Davis and decided to make a change, he named McInnis, not Houser, as Harry's successor. The change was made in June and completed Connie's famed $100,000 infield. At prewar baseball values, the quartet would have been rated nearer $1,000,000. McInnis fully vindicated Mack's judgment and hit .321 in 126 games in his first season as a regular.

Unfortunately for Stuffy, he suffered a broken bone in his right hand when hit by an inside pitch thrown by George Mullin, the Tiger pitcher, in the last week of the season. It put McInnis out of the World's Series with the Giants, but enabled

Davis to wind up his Athletic career in a blaze of glory. Captain Harry returned to his old post for the second series with McGraw's team, after which Connie released his favorite player so that he could take over the management of Somers' Cleveland club.

2

The 1911 Athletic team struck a discouraging note for Mack in the first fortnight of the race. After Bender lost the opener, 2 to 1, to Big Jim Vaughn, known as "Hippo" Vaughn, of the Yanks, the Athletics dropped six games of their first eight, and after two weeks of play they were in the cellar. They started to do better after that, but Detroit, the former chronic pennant winner, threatened to make a strong comeback and won 21 of its first 23 games. That early reservoir of victories propped Hughie Jennings in first place until August 4, with the exception of July 4, when Connie dislodged him for a day. Cobb was a veritable ball of fire that season, hitting .420, scoring 147 runs and stealing 83 bases.

But Mack's training philosophy, expressed on the Savannah trip, worked itself out in practice during the season. The Tigers were on edge for the opening of the season, but they staled in August, when the White Elephants trumpeted past them and soon left the Tigers far behind. The happy A's came down the home stretch all by themselves, winning by 13½ games.

3

As the 1911 season drew to a close, it became evident that the Athletics' World's Series opponents would be the New York Giants. Connie relished the opportunity to get back at John McGraw. He still felt the smart of that whitewash dousing which McGraw, Mathewson, and McGinnity had given him six years before, and there were reverberations of the New Orleans feud of 1907. Tom Shibe's wounds in that brush with McGraw had never healed. Bender, Plank, Davis, and Danny Murphy, survivors of the 1905 team, also were keen to do battle again with McGraw's scrappy warriors.

"Matty still is a great pitcher," Connie confided to Captain Davis. "But he's six years older than he was in 1905, and I'm sure he's not as fast. And I think we have better hitters than we had in that earlier series."

Connie guessed correctly. Unfortunately, the *Philadelphia North American* did not put up its gong at Broad and Market streets for this series. If it had, it could have smote it for three Athletic homers, two by Frank Baker, the slugging Marylander, which were to make history and win him the sobriquet, "Home-Run" Baker, for the remainder of his days.

The American League closed the season on Saturday, October 7, in the East and Sunday, October 8, in the West; but the National League again went in for its Charley Ebbets foolishness and dragged out its schedule until Thursday, October 12, Columbus Day. It gave Connie Mack a second chance to polish his team for the series against the cream of the American League stars—Cobb, Chase, Street, Johnson, Mullin, Joe Wood, etc. Games were played in Washington, Richmond, and Philadelphia, each team winning two. Again Connie felt certain he wouldn't send a stale club against the National League champions.

Ben Shibe lost the flip of the coin for the opening game, and the 1911 World's Series got under way at the Polo Grounds, Saturday, October 14. Perhaps more words were written on that 1911 series than any other, as the winter snows were almost on the grounds when it finally was over. The enterprising baseball writer, Jack Wheeler, of the *New York Herald,* gave birth to the idea of having McGraw, Mathewson, and Chief Meyers "write" the series. The idea spread like wildfire, as Mack, Eddie Collins, Bender, Marquard, Charley Herzog, and other celebrities on both teams broke out as reporters.

The New York and Philadelphia newspapers sent their top staff men and cartoonists to cover the series, along with their baseball writers and sports editors. Brush and McGraw again dressed up their Giants in the 1905 World's Series uniforms of black with white trimmings. The special regalia backfired badly when the tide of the series swung against the Giants. Tom Powers drew the New Yorkers as little black pot-bellied Glooms, with black Napoleonic hats, which the Athletics' grinning Joys chased all over Tom's widely syndicated cartoons.

New York then was more provincial in its baseball rooting than it is today, with the Lambs Club a hotbed of McGraw

© *Sporting News*

FRANK "HOME RUN" BAKER
He wrecked Giants in two World's Series.

© *Sporting News*

CATCHER IRA THOMAS
"Put it there, Chief."

© Ledger Photo

MACK AND FOUR OF HIS GREATEST FINDS

Jack Coombs and Chief Bender (*rear*), Grove and Cochrane (*front*).

rooters. This was the series in which Georgie Cohan, another Brookfield boy who made good, was in Connie Mack's quarter. The old wooden stands at the Polo Grounds had burned down the previous spring, and when the concrete Brush Stadium was erected the New York writers—misled by the club as to the new capacity—gave good Saturday turnouts as 50,000. There was a ticket scandal before the first game, and almost another scandal, when the first-game crowd—with thousands standing in the aisles—was given out officially as 38,281. The Giant players, believing those 50,000-crowd stories, felt they were being gypped, and a committee of indignant players, headed by the Indian catcher, Chief Meyers, waited on Chairman Herrmann of the National Commission. It annoyed and irked the big shots of baseball, as it questioned the honesty of their turnstile count. However, Mack would have no part in it and cautioned his players against participating in the protest.

4

Even though Mack lost the opening game, in which Mathewson, still working some of his 1905 magic, defeated Chief Bender, 2 to 1, he still calls it one of the greatest games Bender ever pitched for him. "The Chief was wonderful that afternoon; I don't think he ever was faster or had more stuff," he remarked. "Of course, Mathewson was good, too, that day, but the breaks gave him the game. One of McGraw's runs came in on a fumble by Collins, but it was on a hard-hit ball."

Giant players who opposed Bender in 1911 and 1913 said it was the Indian's greatest World's Series effort, saying he was better then than in any of his subsequent victories. "His fast ball looked the size of a pea as it came over the plate," said Larry Doyle, the Giants' captain. The Chief fanned 11 of the Giants; he gave up 5 hits. Matty fanned 5 and was tagged for 6 hits.

There was no Sunday ball then in the East, and Connie had a day to think things over. His heart was a little heavy; he knew Bender never was better, and still he lost. Was this to be 1905 again? He told Eddie Plank that he would pitch the second game, which was scheduled for Shibe Park on Monday, October 16. "McGraw will pitch Rube Marquard against you," he told

Eddie. "He's good and has a lot of stuff, but Rube's still young and lacks experience and may give us an opening. I think you can beat him."

Mack's prediction that Rube would be tough was borne out; also that he might give the A's an opening. The Mackmen made only four hits off Marquard and Otey Crandall, who pitched the eighth inning; and the Giants got only one more off the steady left-handed sharpshooting of Plank. But one of the four Athletic hits—Frank Baker's sixth-inning home run—wrote history.

Each club picked up a run early. The A's scored theirs in the first when Bris Lord opened with a single to left and took an extra base on Red Murray's fumble. Oldring advanced Bris to third with a sacrifice, and then McGraw's tall Rube gave Mack one of the openings Mack had predicted. While Eddie Collins was at bat, Marquard uncorked a wild pitch which let in Lord. Mack was annoyed when New York tied in the second. He had placed Oldring with his scorecard for Herzog, but the Bronx boy misjudged Buck's line fly, and it got over his head for a double. Meyers drove in Herzy with a clean single to center.

From then on, both sides went out almost in order until the Athletics' sixth. The A's started off peacefully enough as Marquard set down Lord and Oldring on lazy flies. Then Eddie Collins started the cheering by lining a two-bagger down the left-field foul line, setting the stage for Baker. With the count one ball and one strike, Frank, the Trappe mauler, took a cut at a low fast ball, just above his knees, and lashed it over the right-field fence, the happy Collins prancing in ahead of him. It was five minutes before the crowd, crazy with delight, gave some sense of sanity, while a similar situation of wackiness prevailed on the Athletic bench, with Connie one of the wackiest.

The final score was Athletics, 3, Giants, 1, with Plank striking out eight, half of the whiffs being provided by Josh Devore, McGraw's little lead-off man. "Josh doesn't know yet what Eddie threw at him that day," laughed Connie. "He never did see the ball."

As an aftermath of the game, in the next morning's paper, Christy Mathewson—or his ghost writer—gave Marquard a severe dressing down for pitching the "home-run ball" to Baker. "We had scouted the Athletics, and McGraw carefully went over all the Athletic hitters with us, paying especial attention to Baker and Collins. And Rube was especially warned not to pitch low to Baker."

5

The Athletics got a lot of fun out of Matty's piece, and one of the wits of the club, Cy Morgan, pinned it in the clubhouse with a notation on it, "Don't pitch low to Baker," when the series shifted back to the Polo Grounds for the third game, October 16. "That's one game I'll never forget if I live to be 100," said Connie. "I think I lived a lifetime during it."

Mack pitched Jack Coombs, his third big ace, while McGraw came back with Mathewson. The Athletics won in eleven innings by a score of 3 to 2, and, though Coombs pitched a magnificent game, a three-hitter, the great hero of the game, whose name became a household word, again was Frank Baker. The Giants got away to a one-run lead in the third, when the Giant battery, Meyers and Mathewson, made the only hits off Coombs until the eleventh. With one out, the Chief scratched a hit to Baker and chugged to third on Mathewson's long single to right. Then came a bad break for Coombs and Mack. Jack Barry fumbled Devore's grounder long enough for Meyers to score, but he recovered it in time to force Matty at second.

As the game moved steadily along, that one run loomed as large as the Woolworth Building. The shades of a fall night were creeping over the field and the big crowd was starting to move out of its seats as Charley Herzog tossed out Eddie Collins, first "A" hitter in the ninth. Matty needed only two putouts for a 1-to-0 shutout. Connie was blue; was it to be that same old Mathewson jinx again? His attack had been full of opportunities, and he felt it a crime if Coombs lost.

"Pick out a good one, Frank," he said to Baker as the third baseman left the dugout.

Feeding Baker his sharp-breaking fade-away, Mathewson, the king of control, had two strikes on the Marylander, when, *crash!* a white sphere went hurtling into that lower right-field

Polo Grounds grandstand, now a favorite home-run zone but in 1911 considered almost as far away as New York's Battery. With the exception of a few thousand fans who came over from Philadelphia—who went into paroxysms of joy—the great New York throng sat stunned. No one could do that to their Matty! As for Connie, he gulped a couple of times; had he been a tobacco chewer, he would have swallowed his cud. For a while he was almost speechless with joy and then fought with his players to be the first to grab Baker's hand when Frank returned to the bench after completing his happy jaunt around the bases.

While Baker's home run only tied the game, Mack, his players, the crowd, and the press seemed to sense that it was the doom of the Giants. It was a psychological thing that went through the Polo Grounds, and it must have been felt on McGraw's bench.

Neither team scored in the tenth, but as the late afternoon shadows grew deeper, Mack's team broke out with a pair of runs in the eleventh. Herzog and Fletcher helped derail Big Six with a pair of errors; but Collins, Baker, and Davis reached Matty for hits. The Giants came back with one in their half, also helped by an error; and the big Indian, Meyers, almost undid Baker's work with a powerful drive into the left-field bleachers. Connie had a sinking feeling as the ball started fair, but at the last moment a gust of wind blew it foul by inches. "That gust of wind was one of the great thrills of my baseball life," recalls Coombs.

Jack Lapp recorded the last putout when he shot down Beals Becker, McGraw's pinch-hitter, trying to steal second. Jack gave Mack almost as much of a thrill that day as Baker and Coombs. Though the Giants made only three hits and Coombs walked four in the long game, Lapp nailed five of the New Yorkers stealing. Only one Giant was left as McGraw fumed at Tommy Connolly, the American League umpire, who called 'em on the bases, and charged him with unduly favoring the cause of Mack.

This time Marquard's ghost writer had his chance to go to town. He upbraided the great Matty and asked if Christy was so smart, why didn't he pitch to Baker's weakness? Connie joined in the laugh when Cy Morgan pinned the piece in the clubhouse, Cy adding a postscript: " 'Bake' ain't got a weakness."

6

In the ninth inning of the third game, Fred Snodgrass, McGraw's center-fielder, was hit by a pitched ball, but Umpire Brennan wouldn't let him take his base, saying he hadn't tried to duck the pitch. The Athletic players guyed and poked fun at Snodgrass, a particularly truculent player. Fred eventually walked, reached second on Murray's sacrifice, and, advancing to third on a short passed ball, he went into the bag with one foot high in the air. He ripped Baker's knickers from the crotch to the knee and spiked Frank on the thigh. Earlier in the series, Snodgrass spiked Baker on the arm. It stirred a lot of bitter feeling on the Athletic bench, and Philadelphia writers denounced Snodgrass, saying the spiking was intentional—an effort to put Mack's big gun out of the series.

It vexed Connie Mack; he declined to go as far as his players and made no direct charges against McGraw's Californian, but did say: "There is no excuse for a player going into a bag with his spikes that high; we don't slide like that on the Athletics."

As the Giants came over to Philadelphia for the fourth game, Snodgrass's spiking of Baker was blazoned across the Quaker City sports pages. There were reports that some of the Kensington boys, strong Athletic fans and rabid Baker rooters, would be out to get Snodgrass; and the New York player received a stack of threatening mail when the Giants stopped at the Majestic Hotel on North Broad Street. It was the 1909 Ty Cobb incident all over again, and Connie told friends on the police force they had better throw a little protection around McGraw's outfielder.

If there was any danger of violence against Snodgrass, it cooled off in the longest rain which ever interrupted a World's Series. The fourth game was scheduled for Shibe Park, Wednesday, October 18. Eventually the series was resumed Tuesday, October 24. Like Noah looking out of the ark, day after day Connie stuck his long neck out of the window of his Shibe Park office, scanned the gray, angry horizon, and pulled his head in again, the rain dripping off his face. "Goodness gracious, will this never stop?" he exclaimed. It did stop after five days, but it took another day to partly dry the waterlogged field by burning cans of gasoline, as old Ben Shibe damned the National League's "Charley Ebbets schedule," which had delayed the start of the series to October 14.

When play was resumed, it was the first-game pitchers, Bender and Mathewson, all over again. "I think you're going to win this one, Albert," said Mack as he told the tall Indian he would pitch. "I don't think we'll find Mathewson as effective as in the first game."

Connie, however, had some anxious moments at the very start, as the Giants pushed over two runs in a jiffy. Devore led off with an infield hit, a ball which the Chief deflected just enough to keep it out of Barry's reach. Doyle, the next batter, tripled Josh home with a hit over Oldring's head as Rube had difficulty in moving around on the slushy ground. A moment later, Snodgrass, greeted with a chorus of boos, fetched in Doyle with a long fly to Lord.

The afternoon brightened for Mack in the fourth, as the A's finally got to their old nemesis, Mathewson. Thrills ran up and down Connie's spine, as Baker, Murphy, and Davis put on a real hit parade, hitting successive two-baggers. That tied the score, and the A's went ahead when Barry's out advanced Davis to third and Ira Thomas brought Captain Harry home with a long fly to Murray. Just to make it safer, Eddie Collins singled in the fifth and galloped all the way home when that dangerous Baker boy, still refusing to tip Matty off to his weakness, hit McGraw's ace for a second ringing double.

They were a happy band of Athletics as they rushed to their showers, while Mack beamed from ear to ear as he left the park. This time they really had put it to Matty, reaching him for ten hits in seven innings before McGraw pulled him for a pinch-hitter. The victory gave Mack the big edge—three games to one; he needed only one more game to clinch his second world's title. Before he left the park he told Coombs: "You'll go in New York tomorrow, John. I think you can finish it."

7

It was Coombs against Rube Marquard, October 25, and but for an injury Jack probably would have won easily. For six innings he was as effective as in the third game, and Rube Oldring's three-run homer off McGraw's left-handed Rube in the third gave Jack an early 3-to-0 lead. But in the sixth, while pitching to Fletcher, Coombs's pitching foot failed to come off the rubber; the sole of the shoe and the spikes caught in the space between the rubber and the earth. The ball slipped out of his hand and hit the grandstand near third base, while the pitcher tore some ligaments in his groin. The pain was severe at the time, but neither Jack nor Mack appreciated the severity of the hurt.

After a few pitches, Connie's keen eye noted something was wrong. He sent Ira Thomas out to the mound to ask: "What's wrong, Jack?" "Oh, it's nothing, Ira; I can go on," the big pitcher replied.

Jack was in obvious distress in the seventh, when the Giants scored a run, aided by a muff by the usually reliable Collins. When Doyle hit him for a hard single in the eighth, Thomas and Bender both came out to consult with Jack. "Tell Connie I'm all right; I can make it," he insisted.

However, the heart only was willing, and in the ninth the Giants tied the score in a two-run rally which brought out the most spontaneous outburst of cheering ever heard at the historic Polo Grounds. It went on unabated for ten minutes, while the game Coombs suffered physical and mental pain and the sympathetic Mack suffered with him. And Connie had been within one putout of his second straight World's Championship and sweet revenge of John McGraw for that lambasting of 1905!

New York's tying runs came with two out. After Jack got Herzog on a grounder to Barry, Mack felt annoyed when Fletcher's fly dropped at Lord's feet for a double. Bris sloshed over the ground still wet from the recent rains and couldn't quite get to it. However, when Coombs got the hard-hitting Indian, Meyers, on another grounder to Barry, Connie breathed easier, and the daubers of the crowd sagged to their knees. Thousands started milling for the exits to beat the rush downtown. But with every pitch Coombs was in excruciating pain. Crandall, the hard-hitting relief pitcher, doubled over Oldring's head, scoring Fletcher. The crowd paused; maybe there was still a chance.

Mack had sent Plank to the bull pen. His judgment told him to call in the left-hander, who had fanned little Devore, the next hitter, four times in the second game. His eyes met those of Coombs; Jack wanted so badly to go on and win that game unaided. Connie acceded. Devore hadn't made a hit off Jack, but this time the little guy singled sharply to left, scoring Crandall with the tying run, and the crowd went insane.

Even so, Connie permitted Coombs to bat in the tenth, and he beat out a slow chopper to the infield. Mack saw Jack's face screwed up with pain as he pulled up at first and acted promptly. "Go out there and run for Jack," he said to Amos Strunk.

Strunk was left, and then with night fast falling over Harlem, the Giants pulled out the game in the tenth with a run on Plank. Doyle, who had a big day, opened on Gettysburg Eddie with a double, and on Snodgrass's sacrifice bunt the left-hander threw too late to Baker to get Larry at third. Plank retired Murray, but Fred Merkle sent Murphy back to the concrete wall in right—almost at the foul line—for his fly. Danny was undecided whether or not to make the catch, but eventually did, snaring the ball just inside the line. He let fly a good throw to the plate; but Doyle, running in from third and using the old McGraw "fall away" slide, easily beat the throw. But he fell away to such an extent that he never touched the plate. Lapp, however, believed he had touched it and ran off the field with the other players, Athletics and Giants. Umpire Bill Klem stood at the plate, and made no decision. He later said that if any Athletic had tagged Doyle before he left the playing field, he would have called him out.

Mack and Harry Davis have since said they noted the omission, but the crowd already was on the field, rejoicing over the Giants' snatched-from-the-jaws-of-defeat victory, and Mack feared that, if Doyle had been called out, it would have precipitated a riot. It then was only three years since the Giants had lost their 1908 league pennant on a technicality. McGraw also admitted he had noted Doyle's failure to touch the plate and complimented Mack and Davis on what he termed their "prudence and good sportsmanship."

Coombs was in bad shape that night, and doctors permitted only Mrs. Coombs and Mack to see the big pitcher. The medical men said the big pitcher's condition was not too good, and that the tear could result in serious complications. Ira Thomas succeeded in crashing his old battery mate's room next day. He found Mrs. Coombs crying. While Jack was in bed, with his groin tightly bandaged, she was reading a letter from a fan who had accused Coombs of selling out to the Giants.

8

The White Elephants didn't forget, and next day at Shibe Park, October 26, they were battling for old Colby Jack and literally tore the Giants apart, limb from limb. After Connie's tension through five gripping contests, in which the game hinged on almost every pitch, he had a chance to take a joy ride in the grand finale, as McGraw cursed, fumed, and fretted on the opposite bench.

Bender had an easy task bringing this one home, 13 to 2; and, after the A's had knocked out Red Ames early, the Elephants really became the thundering herd in the "lucky seventh" as they hung seven runs on the scoreboard. The big inning, which had Connie grinning, produced seven hits, most of them off Left-hander Hooks Wiltse. Merkle dropped a throw on a sacrifice bunt by Collins; and, after Marquard relieved Wiltse, Davis and Barry both rode in on the Rube's wild pitch. The Athletics almost fell off the bench with laughter when Marquard and Meyers glared at each other, and the Chief refused to chase the wild pitch, and they later had a heated session in the box. Oddly enough, the Athletics committed five errors, three by Barry, in scoring the one-sided victory.

The entire nation was singing the praises of Frank Baker, who had .375 in the series and smote those two damaging home runs. Failure to get a hit in that last slugfest pulled Cocky Collins's average down to .286; but John McGraw, the defeated manager, said the Columbian was "the greatest player on the field for either team."

A few days after the joyous ending, Philadelphia again officially wined and dined Mack and his two-time World's Champions, with the old National Commission, Garry Herrmann, Ban Johnson, and Tom Lynch assisting in feting the joyous White Elephants. There were some nice tributes to Connie Mack for not protesting the run on which Doyle failed to tag the plate in the fifth game.

When Connie was called on for his speech, he admitted both he and Davis had observed the oversight, and then added: "If any of my players had raised the point about Doyle's run, I would have felt so sore that I believe I would have taken him by the scruff of the neck and thrown him over the grandstand."

After that, Connie and Katherine, with their young infant, Mary, born the previous summer, went down to Atlantic City to enjoy the ocean breezes and relax from the strenuous season. And Connie was as happy as a baseball man possibly could be.

CHAPTER XXI

CONNIE'S "GREATEST" TEAM

1

THE ENTIRE nation—and of course including Connie Mack—expected to see the Athletics, World's Champions of 1910-11, repeat in the American League in 1912. Yet the club finished third, losing the runner-up position to Washington, seventh-place club in 1911, on the last day of the season. The Boston Red Sox, fifth-place team in 1911, with their great outfield trio of Duffy Lewis, Tris Speaker, and Harry Hooper, and Smoky Joe Wood hanging up a 34-to-5 pitching record, won the pennant with 105 victories, the greatest number won by an American League club up to that time. Jack Stahl, the first baseman, was playing manager.

Even today Connie calls his 1912 Athletics "his greatest team," greater than any of the pennant winners which came before or which followed. "That club had speed, hitting power, pitching skill, and more brains than one ordinarily finds on three clubs; but it didn't win," he recalled. "We still had our big pitching three—Bender, Plank, and Coombs—and Eddie had one of his greatest seasons for me, winning 26 games and losing only 6. McInnis came along fast that year, as did Strunk, and in the latter part of the season we acquired Eddie Murphy and Jimmy Walsh from the Baltimore club to give us additional outfield strength.

"There was talk of our having a monopoly on the pennant, like the later-day talk about the Yankees. The whole attitude of the league was that we would win again in a walk. That became so contagious that our players caught it. They became puffed up and believed themselves unbeatable. If ever a club suffered from overconfidence, it was my 1912 team.

"Why, when we got off to a poor start, they laughed it off. Nobody paid much attention to it, and they took the attitude: 'We'll win when we want to.' I began to worry; I didn't like the attitude, but didn't say anything. Maybe I, too, was too complacent, and thought the men would step up their pace when they saw they had a mighty good Boston club to beat. Then May slipped into June, and June into July, and still we weren't playing our game. By this time I was doing a lot of worrying and asked them: 'What's wrong with you fellows?' They still chuckled and replied: 'We'll get going right along.'

"Two weeks later I called them together again, and this time I really sailed into them. They were surprised to hear me talking like that, and I think some of them really thought I was trying to frighten them into a pennant, but if they were impressed it was too late. By August we were playing the Red Sox, and they already were chiding us as the ex-champions, and we could do nothing about it."

2

Under the present system of rewarding second-, third-, and fourth-place clubs with substantial checks for first-division money, Connie no doubt could have finished second in 1912. But when he saw he couldn't win, he did a lot of experimenting, especially with younger pitchers. And it was a big feather for Mack's old friend, Clark Griffith, to finish second in his first season in Washington.

Mack worked two young pitchers in with his Big Three—Carroll Brown and Byron Houck. Carroll was a former Atlantic City High School star, and the latter came from the University of Oregon and was drafted from Spokane. Both had worlds of stuff and natural ability but were wild as young mustangs. Walter Johnson had a phenomenal season that year, winning 32 games and losing 12; and Connie's strategy was to pitch either Brown or Houck against him. Connie figured that the edge was with Johnson anyway, so he held back his own aces for Griffith's lesser pitchers.

During the season Mack also came up with three of the great pitchers of his league—Herb Pennock, Joe Bush, and Stanley Coveleskie—though only Bush did much pitching for his club.

Pennock was only eighteen when Connie Mack signed him in midseason. He came from an opulent Quaker family of Kennett Square, some forty miles outside of Philadelphia. The Pennocks rode to hounds and lived like English manor folk. For years Herb's nickname was "the squire of Kennett Square." He had been a prep-school boy in the Philadelphia suburbs, and Mack snatched him off the Wenonah Military Academy team. Pennock later became one of the great—and perhaps the most graceful of all left-handers. He now is the general manager of the Philadelphia Nationals, tenants of the Athletics at Shibe Park. In a dinner to Herb, shortly after he assumed his National League job, Connie admitted his release of Pennock to the Red Sox in 1915 was his No. 1 managerial blunder.

"I thought Herb didn't care whether he played ball or not, and let him go to Boston," said Mack. "He was young then, and I didn't have much of a team behind him, and I thought he was indifferent. But I never was so wrong in my life; letting him go when he had all that natural ability was the biggest mistake of my career."

Joe Bush was just a year older than Pennock, nineteen, when he joined the Athletics late in the season. His home town of Brainerd, Minnesota, was the same as that of Chief Bender; it was an odd coincidence that this Minnesota hamlet should produce two of Mack's foremost pitchers. Connie plucked his Bush out of baseball's deepest bushes—Missoula, Montana, where the sturdy lad had compiled a formidable record, winning 29 games and leaving a raft of strike-outs in his wake. His name was Leslie Amrose Bush, but his nickname was "Bullet Joe" because of his speed, and everybody started calling him Joe.

Connie saw the early possibilities of Stan Coveleskie, a pickup from Atlantic City and a right-handed brother of the southpaw who used to vex McGraw, Harry the Giant-Killer. Recognizing that Stan wasn't ready and needed experience, Connie sent him to the Spokane club on one of those old "gentlemen's agreements." But Spokane forgot all about it and later sold Stan Coveleskie to Cleveland, where he became the famous battery mate of Mack's catching rookie of 1911, Steve O'Neill.

With the bringing up of his new outfielders from Baltimore, Eddie Murphy and Jimmy Walsh, the public first became conscious of Mack's practice of waving his scorecard to his young outfielders and placing them in position for enemy hitters. He had done it before, but Eddie and Jimmy were new in the league and needed extra instructions. It emphasized the wigwagging, and the fans got a big kick out of it.

Even after such old hands as Ty Cobb and Tris Speaker became members of his team, Connie put them in their "proper positions," just as he did with outfield rookies. The wigwagging doesn't always place the outfielders; Mack often uses it to signal plays to his coaches, and from them to the players.

Of course, the well-laid plans of mice and men go oft astray. Connie admits there have been occasions when wigwagging his scorecard hasn't been a complete success. "We were playing the Yankees in an important game later on, and Babe Ruth was the first hitter of the inning," he recalled. "I waved my outfield around, and the players moved, but still I wasn't satisfied. I gave another wigwag, and a couple of players weren't quite where I wished them to be, so I got up and stepped in front of the dugout.

"Meanwhile, my pitcher was all set, and the Babe was at the plate, patiently waiting. After what seemed like another two minutes of waving, I sat down perfectly satisfied, just as the pitcher let go of the ball. The next moment I heard that *crack,* and you can imagine what had happened. Ruth had hit the first pitch right out of the park!"

Returning to the season of 1912, Connie had a superstition of marking his scorecard daily with the same pencil. It was his winning pencil. Joe Ohl, the Athletic secretary, borrowed it one day before the A's took the field in New York for the first game of a double-header with the Yankees. Mack lost the first game and sent a substitute player to get his pencil back from Joe, but the rookie couldn't find Ohl. Then Connie lost the second game. Meeting Ohl in the hotel lobby that night, Mack reprimanded him sharply: "Don't you ever borrow a pencil from me again; bring your own pencil!"

Having lost the pennant of 1912, largely because they never could arouse themselves, Mack's 1913 team, profiting by the sage counsel of their leader, took on a new psychology as they reported for training in San Antonio. Jack Coombs was at the camp, but early developed typhoid; it settled in his spine and he was on his back for months. There were gloomy forecasts that the big Maine man never would pitch again; but Mack, always optimistic, wouldn't credit them. "They'll have you as good as ever," he told Coombs.

He gave most of his attention that season to his young pitchers, Brown, Houck, Pennock, and Bush, who had come up the year before, and Weldon Wyckoff, from Mathewson's old college, Bucknell. Bob Shawkey, who was to prove another find—but whose best work was in the service of the Yankees—was acquired from Baltimore in midseason. A catching rookie who early captivated the manager's fancy was a rollicking kid from Buffalo, strong as a bull calf, who loved to shoot the ball around—Wally Schang. He had only one year's experience with George Stallings's Buffalo club, but next to Mickey Cochrane, who came some years later, Schang was destined to be Connie's greatest catching discovery.

Near the end of the training season, Danny Murphy, who had succeeded Davis to the captaincy, injudiciously permitted Carroll Brown to pitch the full 18 innings of a 2-to-2 spring-series tie with the Phillies. Mack still was on the road with the Athletics' second team at the time. While Brown was credited with 18 victories that season, the Atlantic City boy always felt the strain of that long early April grind was responsible for the sore arm which shortened a most promising career.

Mack adopted a new and successful winning system that season. He usually started his kid pitchers and then called on his skillful veterans, Plank and Bender, to hold the leads for the young fellows.

The amiable and able Billy Weart, the *Sporting News*'s Philadelphia correspondent for 1913, wrote on July 17: "The manner in which Connie Mack has kept his team on the winning road with a pitching staff which has not been rated very high has been one of the marvels of the career of this truly great baseball general. To the writer's way of thinking, Connie never performed a greater achievement than he has this season, when he has had his team leading the race from the start with only two veteran pitchers, Plank and Bender, and a number of youngsters who have been taken off the rubber more frequently than they have been able to go through an entire contest. Meanwhile the youngsters daily are gaining more experience, and the chances are that before either of the veterans shows signs of a letdown the juvenile hurlers will have rounded into first-class workers."

Harry Davis had not been a managerial success in Cleveland, and was back with Mack as his lieutenant. Harry's Cleveland successor, Joe Birmingham, aided by Joe Jackson's telling wallops, gave Connie quite a bit of contention in the first three months of the 1913 race. But Mack always could spur his team into taking those vital series from the Indians, and a 15-game winning streak put the tall tactician on Easy Street. Cleveland couldn't even hold the runner-up position, the Senators beating them out for second place. Even though Walter Johnson had his greatest year, winning 36 games and losing only 7, Mack's system against Griffith worked so well that his young pitchers won the year's series from Washington, 14 games to 8.

5

The 1913 World's Series was one of Mack's most pleasant experiences. He had a few vexing problems—once in an exciting moment he jutted his head into the concrete top of the Polo Grounds dugout—but most of the time he could sit back and relax and let McGraw, his National League rival for the third time in 8 years, do the worrying. Connie won the series, 4 games to 1, and he still feels a little regret that he wasn't the first manager to win a series in four straight games.

As both McGraw and McGillicuddy had won one series from the other, each Mac was most keen to take the rubber event. If the easy victory gave Connie a pleasant winter, it was a bitter pill for McGraw, as it was his third straight World's Series setback in as many years. Mack had the good luck to catch McGraw's Giants when they were badly battered. Snodgrass, the center fielder, who spiked Frank Baker two years before, suffered from a charley-horse and made only two brief appearances during the series. Jack Meyers, hard-hitting first-string Indian catcher, broke a finger in the first game, though Larry McLean did a fine job as his understudy. First baseman Merkle twisted an ankle in the first contest and, while he missed only the second game (the only one the Giants won), he limped through the remainder of the series.

Before the first game in New York, October 7, a fortune teller managed to get hold of the obliging Connie's hand on his bench and said: "You will win the series, Mr. Mack."

Connie grinned. "Yes, but my men will have to fight for it all the way."

"You will win it easier than you did two years ago; all the signs are favorable," she insisted.

The signs *were* favorable that afternoon, for before a fine opening crowd of 36,291 Connie saw Bender, Baker, and Eddie Collins put on their usual World's Series shows as his boys turned back the Giants, 6 to 4. They knocked out Rube Marquard in five innings. Baker put on the old home-run specialty with Collins on base, and the kid catcher, Schang, inserted a timely triple. The Chief wasn't as effective as when he lost the 1911 opener to Matty, as each side got 11 hits. However, it was a dark, threatening afternoon, with rain falling in the eighth and ninth, when Bender was at his best, snapping his fast ball over the corners in the evening dusk.

As in the 1911 series, play shifted each day between New York and Philadelphia, and the second game was at Shibe Park, October 8. It brought together those Pennsylvania collegians, Plank and Mathewson, who first hooked up in 1905. McGraw started Snodgrass, still riding his charley-horse, at first base in place of the injured Merkle, but Fred withdrew after three innings and turned the bag over to George Wiltse, the southpaw pitcher.

For eight and a half innings, Plank and Matty fought each other to a scoreless duel, and in his half of the ninth Connie thought he had the game in his bat bag. Strunk opened with a single, and Barry beat out an infield chopper between Doyle and Wiltse. In his desperate effort to get Black Jack, Doyle heaved the ball to the grandstand, and Strunk pulled up at third and Barry at second. That was the situation when Matty and Wiltse made one of the heroic stands of World's Series play.

Lapp hit a sharp grounder down to Wiltse, and the deer-footed Strunk, off with the pitch, appeared to have scored before George could shoot the ball to McLean at the plate. The decision was close, but Tommy Connolly waved Strunk "out." "I've always thought Tommy missed that one," said Mack. "Amos had a fine start, and it looked to me as though he had slid into the plate before McLean could put the ball on him."

However, Barry made third, and there still was only one out. Most of the fans thought Connie would send in a pinch-hitter for Plank, as he had Danny Murphy, Schang, and Walsh, all good hitters, on the bench. He let Plank bat, and Eddie also shot down to Wiltse, whose return throw to McLean had Barry caged between third and the plate. The impressive inning flickered out as a dud when Eddie Murphy tapped to Mathewson for an easy out.

Connie was criticized for his failure to use a pinch-hitter for Plank, but, looking back over a perspective of thirty-two years, he has no regrets. "Plank was stinging the ball hard all day; I thought he could bring in Barry from third."

Aroused by that great stand, the Giants were an inspired team in the tenth inning, and they tore into Plank for three runs, Mathewson driving in the first one himself. Eddie lost the game, 3 to 0, his third World's Series shutout suffered at the hands of the Giants and the second by that score to Mathewson.

Mack was in a quandary before the third game in New York, October 9. He had used his top pitchers, Bender and Plank, and now was reduced to using one of those kids Billy Weart wrote about against McGraw's third ace, Jeff Tesreau, before one of those partisan New York crowds. He had his pick from among Carroll Brown, Joe Bush, Bob Shawkey, and Byron Houck. All had plenty of stuff but were as wild as a flock of young hawks.

Eventually Connie decided on Bush. By this time Joe was twenty; he had a blazing fast ball and already had shown Mack great competitive spirit. "Joe had a lot of courage," said Connie, "and I wasn't afraid to start him before that hostile crowd. I felt that, if he had control and could get past the first few innings, he would be all right."

Though Eddie Collins and Frank Baker again made five hits between them the young battery of Bush and Schang stole the show. As the Athletics won, 8 to 2, Bush held the New Yorkers to five hits; while Schang, stealing Baker's thunder, smote a resounding home run.

The fourth game, seesawing back to Philly, gave Connie his share of thrills, the greatest defensive play of his eight World's Series and the sight of Bender almost frittering away a six-run lead, but eventually bringing the bacon into the Shibe Park clubhouse by a score of 6 to 5.

The A's spotted Bender a 6-to-0 lead at the expense of Al Demaree when the Indian perhaps took things too easy. New York first threatened in the sixth, when Mack called Oldring's catch on Moose McCormick, McGraw's crack pinch-hitter, "the greatest I ever saw in a World's Series and one of the best catches I have seen anywhere." With Murray and Cooper on base, Oldring, who had been playing fairly deep for McCormick, came in fast and took the Moose's stinging liner off a blade of grass after a diving, tumbling catch.

But Bender made Mack sweat in the seventh and eighth, when New York scored five runs and came within a run of a tie. Then, closing in a blaze of glory, the Chippewa blotted out the side in order in the ninth, getting two pinch-hitters, the dangerous Crandall of 1911 and Eddie Grant.

"Albert, you surely had me sitting on pins and needles for a while," said Connie when it was over.

Connie got his bump on the noggin winning the fifth and final game at the Polo Grounds on a Saturday afternoon, October 11, but it was worth it. He also had the satisfaction of seeing Eddie Plank, pitching a two-hit game, finally slay his old jinx, Christy Mathewson, 3 to 1.

With the A's breaking the scoreless drought for Plank by getting him three early runs, Eddie mowed down the Giants as fast as they came up. It wasn't until the fifth that they put a runner on base, when Shafer walked with one out. On the hit-and-run play, Murray hit a high fly over the pitcher's box. Shafer was on second base and apparently got bewildered at the frantic calls of coaches McGraw and Robinson for him to get back to first. It looked like a "duck soup" double play for the Macks.

Plank settled under the ball, but just as he was about to squeeze it, Baker pounced down on him and knocked the ball out of his hand. Everybody was safe. It was then that Connie stood up in the dugout, as though wishing to ward off Baker, and in doing so butted his head into the Polo Grounds concrete. For a few moments he saw plenty of stars. McLean then drove in Shafer with a single, but the Giants made only one more hit, Mathewson's single in the sixth.

7

The World's Series celebration was tempered by the serious illness and subsequent death of Harry Davis's young son, Harry, Jr., the boy breathing his last the Tuesday after the new title was clinched. Mack and the players all knew the boy, as he frequently had worked out with his dad and other Athletics. The members of the $100,000 infield, all men Harry helped to break in—Baker, Barry, Collins, and McInnis—were the pallbearers. Plank, who boarded with the Davises, was heartbroken and called off a celebration in Gettysburg planned in his honor. Connie felt as badly as he saw the bereavement of his former star and Mrs. Davis.

There was some talk of calling off the city's celebration; it was postponed, but after a conference between Connie, Ben Shibe, and the Mayor, it was decided to hold it a week after the funeral. Escorted by the Police Band, the club made the three-mile trip from Shibe Park to the Bellevue-Stratford, while the public lined the streets and acclaimed the greatest club in baseball. There was the usual dinner and speechmaking, but so shortly after the tragedy in the Davis family neither Mack nor his players had much stomach for it.

After the series, Connie, Mrs. Mack, and the children had gone down to Atlantic City to recuperate from a wearing season. There now was another son, Connie, Jr., born in 1912. Connie, Sr., came up from the shore for the parade and banquet. He had lost fourteen pounds juggling those young pitchers around, and he needed rest, relaxation, and plenty of sea air.

After returning from the shore, Connie got a lot of publicity, and much of it adverse, especially in Detroit, by picking Tris

Speaker, his own Rube Oldring, and his former recruit, Joe Jackson, as his All-Star outfield of the majors. When asked about Ty Cobb, Connie replied: "I wouldn't trade him even-up for Oldring. Rube is a much better center fielder."

A lot of argument resulted, but it finally was decided that Connie was having his joke, had his tongue in his cheek when he said it, and perhaps was being smart in getting Oldring to think he fitted into this stellar picture. And it wasn't so many years since the great Ty had spiked Barry and Baker!

8

Connie was 51 when he won his 1913 World's Championship; he was the first manager ever to win three blue ribbons, and critics were saying that his team, with its wealth of young material, could go on winning pennants indefinitely. It was the season before the Federal League war; he was at the very top of the baseball world, in command of a compact, harmonious, baseball-minded team.

"We were just one big happy family," recalled Eddie Collins. "We went to the Pacific Coast one time, and almost all of us had our wives along. But there wasn't an argument on the trip. I'd like to see any other club duplicate that record."

Before Eddie was married, he lived with the Harry Davises. One day Mrs. Davis had sliced pineapple for dessert, and Collins smacked out four hits. From then on his favorite dessert was sliced pineapple. There was a day when he didn't make any hits and fell down several times in the pinches, so Mack asked: "Didn't you have your sliced pineapple today, Eddie?"

Cy Morgan, the Crossroads Cutup, was one of the team's comedians and amused the players on long trips by putting on his one-man minstrel show on the train. Though most good-humored at night, Cy usually awoke in the morning with the world's worst grouch. In Chicago, coming down to breakfast in this mood, he tossed several pieces of silver into an electric fan. They clattered all over the room. Remembering Schreck and New Orleans, Connie said sternly: "Next time we go on a trip, Cy, I'll bring along some toys for you to play with."

And Ira Thomas, the catcher, already was winning fame with his recitation, comparing baseball with the greater game of life.

"You race to first, and you're young and full of spirit," said Ira. "You go along to second, and that's your prime. It gets tougher going to third; you're slowing up. Age is creeping on. And then you labor on to home; your race is run."

Sharing honors with Mack in bringing three world's titles to Philadelphia in four years was the little hunchbacked mascot, Louis Van Zelst. A kindly, good-natured boy, he had come to Mack in 1909 and said he was lucky, and indeed he was. Nothing but good luck followed in his wake. Louie had a regular uniform, made all the trips, and once in New York Connie sent him out on the coaching line. That offended the dignity of Tommy Connolly, who came over to the bench, saying: "You know, Connie, you can't get away with that."

A newspaper story which made Mack as mad as anything he ever read was printed while the club was in Cleveland. It was said Connie shouldn't exhibit little Louie around the country, his misshapen body was offensive to some eyes. "I was so mad I walked all the way out to the ball park so I could cool off and not say something I might regret," he related. "When I got there I was pleased to run into Ed Bang, the veteran Cleveland writer. He, too, had read the story, and felt about it exactly as I did."

CHAPTER XXII

A SEASON OF TRAVAIL

1

MACK WON another pennant in 1914, but he since has said that the season was the most unpleasant and unsatisfactory of his entire career. The Federal League, with the voluble Jim Gilmore president and some rich gullible businessmen backing his clubs, was in the field, and all season the independents made flattering offers to Mack's stars. The Athletic salaries weren't big as contrasted with those of the Babe Ruth period, but Philadelphia still was largely a 25-cent bleacher town, and Connie and the Shibes paid what they could afford.

With the bitterness of the Federal League raids of thirty years ago long since dissipated, Connie calmly and dispassionately sat down and told the story of some of his woes and vexations of that year, which subsequently resulted in his breaking up his greatest club.

"Thinking as I did at the time, I felt it was the most unhappy season I ever experienced," he said. "In view of conditions which existed on my ball team, the beating we took from the Braves in the 1914 World's Series was not surprising.

"The Federal League was after our players from the spring to the World's Series, and the season was one of trouble and unpleasantness. What made it even more bitter was that Danny Murphy, who had played on five of my championship clubs, was the scout for the Brooklyn Federals. That club was backed by the Ward brothers, rich baking concern, and they tried to put a strong winning club in Brooklyn. Murphy, who had been used largely as a pinch-hitter on our 1913 champions, went to the Feds early in 1914, as did one of my young pitchers, Byron Houck. And Danny was in a position to offer some of our players two and three times what we were paying them.

"We tore up some contracts in midseason, wrote new ones, entered into three-year agreements with Eddie Collins, Frank Baker, and other key players. Still the Feds kept raising their offers, and my players were dissatisfied. Some of them came to me and said they would finish out the 1914 season with me, but that in the next season they would be in the Federal League. I knew some of my players had signed with the Feds—or had agreed to their terms when we were in the 1914 World's Series.

"I was pretty sore at the time—awfully sore. I felt the players were letting down both me and the club, and that we had paid them as good salaries as baseball then could afford and made it possible for them to get into four rich World's Series. Today, over the perspective of the years, I feel a little differently. The players were taking advantage of a baseball war to get all they could, just as I took advantage of a baseball war to raid the National League when we first put a club in Philadelphia. I long have forgiven the players who gave me those 1914 headaches, and most of them have been back with me in some capacity."

2

As for the 1914 race itself, it was another runaway, though the second-place Red Sox threatened for a period in September and won their last eight games from the Athletics. After Detroit led most of the spring, the White Elephants never were dislodged from first place after May 29. The A's winning margin over Boston was 8½ games. But, after Connie closed the league campaign with 99 victories and 53 defeats, many long dreary years would pass before he was to see another Athletic club at the head of the American League standing on the last day of the season.

Despite the friction over contracts, Mack's men led easily in batting with .272, 14 points better than the Tigers. Eddie Collins batted second to Ty Cobb with .344, and Frank Baker and Stuffy McInnis were well up, with .319 and .314. Bender and Plank again carried the pitching staff. Jack Coombs still was incapacitated most of the season with his spine in a brace, but pitched a few games in the fall.

Of the young pitchers, Bush, Shawkey, and Pennock were coming along the fastest. Carroll Brown, the pitcher who had been permitted to hurl that 18-inning exhibition in the 1913 training season, was bothered with a lame arm and was released to the Yankees. Mack came up with another fine young left-hander, Rube Bressler, a youngster from Brookfield, Pennsylvania, who was acquired from the Harrisburg club. Though Bressler later was better known as a National League outfielder with Cincinnati and Brooklyn, as a nineteen-year-old kid pitcher, Rube had everything but control. He was one of the bright spots of Connie's unhappy year, as he won 12 games and lost 3 and ranked fourth in earned runs with 1.76.

3

The Athletics' 1914 World's Series opponents were the upstart Boston Braves, the club which was last in mid-July and then made its sensational dash through the entire National League. The club was led by George Stallings, called the Big Chief, who had led the Detroit Americans in 1901 and the Yankees in 1909 and 1910. Mack, of course, knew George well. Though Stallings was a cultured Georgia gentleman in a drawing room, a man who had taken several years of medicine, he was one of the most superstitious men ever connected with baseball, and when he cut loose he had a vocabulary that would sear a steel plate.

Before Connie was to suffer his worst and most humiliating World's Series defeat, he had an experience with Stallings that helped to make 1914 one of his most unpleasant years. The Braves closed their league season in Brooklyn with a double-header on a Tuesday, October 6. The Athletics went a day later, having an American League scheduled at home with the Yankees, October 7. The first game of the World's Series was on the Shibe Park card for Friday, October 9.

Stallings brought his club to Philadelphia immediately after the Brooklyn double-header and, getting in touch with Connie, asked whether his club could work out at Shibe Park on Wednesday and Thursday.

"I'll be glad to let you work out in the morning," said Mack.

"But that isn't what I want," continued Stallings. "I want the men to work out in the early afternoon, so they can get accustomed to the light and the shadow of your grandstand."

"We're playing the Yankees here Wednesday, George; and we'll be working out ourselves Thursday afternoon," contended Mack. "You can have the park until noon."

Stallings was miffed, and as there already were a lot of reporters in Philadelphia for the World's Series, he was quoted as saying that Mack was a cheap skate and a poor sport for not letting him work out at his park. "And just for that, we'll knock hell out of them," said Stallings.

Connie called up the Big Chief at his hotel and remonstrated with Stallings about the interview. "Those things you've been saying about me are unfair; I never denied you the use of the park." Stallings exploded over the phone, and relating the incident, Mack added: "I guess I was pretty hot myself."

"When I get out there Friday, the first thing I'll do is to punch you in the nose," said Stallings.

"Well, whenever you want to start punching, I'll be here," replied Connie.

There was no exchange of managerial fisticuffs before the first game, but the conduct of the players during the series was particularly distasteful to Connie. There were a bunch of tough hombres on that Boston club—Johnny Evers, Rabbit Maranville, George Whitted, and others, who were known for their sizzling adjectives. Inspired by their manager's feud with Mack, the Braves rode the A's unmercifully all through the series.

4

Before the first game there were reports that several of Mack's stars had been out to the wee hours of the morning. With the exception of Mack, the tendency of the entire Athletic club was to underrate the Boston champions. Hadn't they—the great A's—won 12 out of 16 games from National League pennant winners since 1910? So what had they to fear from Stallings' crew?

Mack had sent Bender to scout the Braves in New York when the Bostons played a September series with the Giants. Encountering the Chief near his own ball park, Mack said in surprise: "I thought you were supposed to be in New York."

"Oh, I didn't see any need for scouting that bush league outfit," said Bender.

If Mack feared the worst before the series, he realized fully how the wind was blowing after the first game. It was a 7-to-1 rout for the American League champions. The A's made only five hits off chunky Dick Rudolph, while the Braves batted out Mack's ace, Chief Bender, in the sixth inning. Whitted tripled with Evers and Connolly on base in the sixth, and Schmidt scored Whitted with a single to Barry. His face showing his displeasure over the Chief's showing, Connie got up from the bench and called to Bender, "That's enough," motioning to young Weldon Wyckoff to come in from the bull pen. And he couldn't help but mutter: "Pretty good hitting for a bush league outfit."

After six World's Series victories in nine games, Bender finally was driven to cover in his tenth start. His head hanging low, he was a disconsolate sight as he walked slowly off the field. Few knew it, but it was the last time Philadelphia fans would see the great Chippewa in an Athletic uniform. Hank Gowdy, who was to emerge the series hero, started in to annoy Mack with a triple, double, and single.

Where the A's made only five hits off Rudolph in the first game, Connie saw his players even more impotent at bat in the second; they got only two off Bill James, handsome young right-hander, as Eddie Plank suffered a tough 1-to-0 defeat. It was the same World's Series story with Eddie; the boys could get him no runs. Connie fretted up and down his bench as though sitting on a hot griddle; the only hits to bring him any comfort were a double by Schang and a single by Collins.

Even so, Plank held off James for eight innings, before Mack saw his men go down in a ninth inning when all the breaks went against them. With one down, Deal, Boston's substitute third baseman, got one of his two hits of the series, a double on a fly ball, which was misjudged by Strunk. Eddie fanned James for the second out, and then Mack gave a grunt of despair on the next play. Schang saw he had Deal trapped off second base; but, instead of coming well into the diamond before letting go his throw, Wally snapped it high to Barry from behind the plate. Instead of trying to get back to second, Deal broke for third and made the bag in safety. Connie then suffered a dozen deaths on Boston's winning hit. Les Mann arched a short fly to right. Cocky Collins back-pedaled for it; he got his fingertips on the ball but couldn't quite squeeze it, and it dribbled away for a hit, Deal scoring the only run of the game.

Mack and the fans had a brief hope the Athletics would get that run back, perhaps win, in their half. James walked Barry, fanned Schang, and then handed another pass to Jim Walsh, batting for Plank. Eddie Murphy sent a ball skimming over second for an apparent hit, when little Rabbit Maranville made a desperate running grab for the ball. It stuck; the Rabbit tagged second, forcing Walsh, and then shot the ball to Schmidt in time to double-up Murphy, ending the game. It also marked Plank's last appearance as one of Connie Mack's players.

5

Connie had a blue Sunday, October 11, to think over his two defeats before the series was to be resumed in Boston on Monday, October 12, Columbus Day. Apparently he had a feeling that both Bender and Plank would be in the Federal League in 1915, because he gave out an odd statement that, regardless of the future developments of the series, he would use only his young pitchers in the remaining games.

On the train to Boston he summoned Joe Bush to his drawing room. "You'll pitch the third game, Joe," he said. "If you pitch against these fellows the same way as you did against the Giants last fall, you can win. The Braves really haven't as many good hitters as McGraw had on the Giants."

The game proved another heartbreaker for Connie, one of his most painful World's Series setbacks. He knew he had to win this one to keep from suffering a humiliating series debacle at Stallings' hands. And the game was within his grasp, only to get away.

Stallings opposed Bush with George Tyler, a left-hander, and the third member of his "Big Pitching Trio." The clubs were all tied up at 2 to 2 at the end of the ninth; it looked as though the A's had finally crashed through when they scored twice in the overtime inning. Schang opened the tenth with a single; and, after Bush fanned, Eddie Murphy bunted and was safe on a fielder's choice. Oldring grounded out, but a walk to Collins filled the bases. Baker hit a hot shot to Evers in short right; Johnny knocked down the ball but couldn't field it. It was a hit for Baker, and Schang scored. Then the usually crafty Evers acted as though he had fallen in a trance; as he held the ball Murphy made a break for the plate and scored without even drawing a throw.

The score was 4 to 2 as the Braves came up for their half of the tenth, and for the only time in the series Connie felt a brief glow of pleasure. Bush had given up only five hits, and the two-run lead looked adequate. What's more, Evers had ridden his club hard, and he chuckled at Johnny's lapse. His joy was short-lived. Those Braves were hot, and Hank Gowdy was still hotter. First man up, Hank drove a terrific homer into the center-field bleachers. Bush fanned Devore, but Mack groaned out loud when Joe lost Herb Moran, a former Athletic player, walking him after a "two and three" count. Evers atoned for his day-dream with a long single on which Moran galloped to third, from where he scored the tying run on Connolly's long fly.

Neither team scored in the eleventh, but the end came suddenly and painfully in the twelfth. It was getting dark and unquestionably would have been the last inning even if Boston hadn't scored. Gowdy again was Mack's *bête noir.* He lashed Bush's second pitch to the left-field bleachers for a double. "What doesn't he hit?" moaned Connie. Pinch-hitter Larry Gilbert walked, and Les Mann ran for the slow-footed Gowdy. Moran tried a sacrifice bunt; Bush pounced on it and thought he saw a chance to force Mann at third. But his hurried throw to Baker was wild, sailed into foul territory, and the rollicking Mann raced home with the winning run while the bewildered, unhappy Athletics slowly made for their clubhouse.

No World's Series contender up to that time ever had been knocked off in the minimum number of four games. Even the Tigers got a twelve-inning tie out of it when routed, four games to none, by the 1907 Cubs. But Mack, who had a team which was favored to win, two to one, suffered that ignominy. It was a relief for Connie when it was over, though the short series meant the contending clubs made practically nothing out of it. And the Athletic treasury needed its World's Series receipts badly.

Stallings came back with Rudolph, his first-game pitcher, but Mack, true to his word that he would use only young pitchers, called on Bob Shawkey to save his waning fortunes. Bob pitched fairly well—gave up only four hits, but retired after five innings because of a bruised hand with the score 3 to 1 against him. Connie then called on his young left-hander, Herb Pennock, to take his baptism, and the kid from Kennett Square started his brilliant World's Series career by pitching three scoreless innings.

Many thoughts ran through Connie's mind on that train ride back from Boston. Visions of Hank Gowdy swinging his bat rose before him like an ugly ogre. In the four games Hank hit .545, his six hits including a homer, a triple, and three doubles; while Mack's pitchers walked him six times. The Athletics were almost as feeble at bat before Rudolph, James, and Tyler as they had been against Matty and McGinnity in 1905, hitting a sickly .172. Jack Barry made no hits, Oldring had only one, and McInnis and Schang only two. Frank Baker hit .250 and the great Collins only .214. The entire series was a hideous nightmare for the Athletic manager!

6

There were no parades or festivities for the Athletics when they returned from Boston. Some city officials and businessmen wanted to hold the annual pennant-winning banquet at the Bellevue, but Mack and Ben Shibe quickly nixed it. "No banquet this year," Connie told the committee with feeling. Deep down, he was sore and hurt.

Connie paid tribute to the gameness of the Braves and passed lightly over the shortcomings of his team, saying: "We never played our game," but some recriminations got into the newspapers.

A team of All-Americans and All-Nationals had gone to the coast and Honolulu after the World's Series. Mack was to have taken charge of the American League club, but at the last moment declined to go, saying he had other things to do. Ira

Thomas took over in his stead, and then came reports that some of the Athletic players couldn't get along with the good-natured Ira and changes would be made. It was a fall of rumors, and one week Connie had to make three denials—that Eddie Collins had been released to New York to manage the Yankees, that Chief Bender had announced his retirement from baseball, and that Connie had acquired majority holdings in the Athletics. "I'm getting darn tired of denying things," said Mr. Mack.

Then Hughie Jennings, the Detroit manager, who was doing a vaudeville turn, spilled an Athletic story while playing in Atlantic City and gave the Philadelphia public an inkling of some of the thoughts that were running through Connie's mind. Hughie told reporters that the Athletics had asked for waivers on their three great veteran pitchers, Eddie Plank, Chief Bender, and Jack Coombs.

Mack didn't deny it, but he was sore at Jennings for letting the cat out of the bag. There was little love between Mack and Hughie since the hot pennant fights of 1907 and 1909. He let go a few caustic shots at Jennings. "I'm an American Leaguer first, last, and all the time," he said. He left the inference that Jennings, though an American League manager, had rooted for his old fellow Oriole, John McGraw, against the Athletics in the World's Series of 1911 and 1913. Some even went so far as to say that Hughie tipped off McGraw on how to pitch to Mack's players.

Then Ban Johnson, powerful American League president, came to Philadelphia around Thanksgiving, and for several days Connie and old Ben Shibe were closeted with Ban at the Bellevue. "Something big is stirring," wrote Billy Weart.

The bomb exploded the week before Christmas. It wasn't much of a Christmas present for Athletic fans, but none of them suspected what dreary "A" happenings would follow the big news from Shibe Park. Mack announced the sale of Eddie Collins, crack second baseman and key to the infield, to the Chicago White Sox for $50,000, and that, waivers having been procured from other major-league clubs on Bender, Plank, and Coombs, the three members of the famous trio were given their unconditional releases.

Shortly afterward it came out that Bender had signed with

the Baltimore Federals and Plank with the St. Louis club of the same independent league. There were reports that Coombs would sign with the Brooklyn Feds; Jack's condition still made him a gamble, but eventually he tied up with Charley Ebbets of the Brooklyn Dodgers of the National League and helped pitch Brooklyn to the 1916 pennant.

Collins was one of the players signed to a new three-year Athletic contract in the summer of 1914, but the Federal League continued to put tempting bait before him. The Brooklyn Feds especially remained persistent. "I sold Eddie to Chicago to save him for the American League," says Mack today.

Whether Eddie would have hopped to the new league, only he knows; but Mack knew he couldn't match the latest offers of the rich Wards. Ban Johnson, who knew everything that went on in his league, was fully in touch with the Philadelphia situation. He knew that Connie was angry and vexed at most of his stars; eager to bolster his league in Chicago, he arranged for Collins's sale to the White Sox during his Thanksgiving visit. Ban then still was most friendly with Comiskey; and, as the White Sox had had no real contender since 1908, Johnson felt placing Eddie in Chicago was a master stroke.

Two men who did not think so were the wealthy New Yorkers, Colonel Jacob Ruppert and Lieutenant Colonel T. L. Huston, who had just purchased the New York Yankees from Frank Farrell and Chief Devery. They had been promised new players for the building up of their team. Mack let them have Pete Dailey, an outfielder, but for years they resented the fact that Johnson and Mack did not give them a chance to bid against Comiskey for the services of the great second baseman.

Connie Mack could have had Babe Ruth, baseball's great Bambino, in 1914, almost for the asking and at a price far below the $12,000 the Athletics paid for Clarence Russell, the Baltimore left-hander, in 1910. Mack was very close to Jack Dunn, the Baltimore owner-manager, in those days, and the pair had many player deals.

Dunn had a great team in Baltimore that season; he was running away with the International League race; but Baltimore fans, feeling the Baltimore Feds had returned the city to major-league baseball, snubbed their noses at Jack's club. He broke up his team in midseason. Conferring with Mack, Dunn said:

"I have two pitchers who can help you, Connie—my young left-hander, Babe Ruth, and that tall North Carolina college right-hander, Ernie Shore.

Speaking of it later, Connie said: "Jack had no money, and neither did we. Otherwise I might have been interested."

He replied to Dunn: "No, Jack, you keep those fellows and sell them to someone who can give you real money for them."

Dunn then sold Ruth, Shore, and their catcher, Ben Egan, formerly an Athletic recruit, to Joe Lannin, the former owner of the Red Sox, for less than $10,000 for the trio. Lannin, however, had been an angel to stricken International League clubs in their warfare with the Feds; he owned the Providence club, but also gave financial aid to Baltimore, Buffalo, and other clubs in distress.

"Of course, no one then thought of Ruth as a slugger," added Mack. "But I knew he had great promise as a left-handed pitcher."

CHAPTER XXIII

SEVEN BITTER YEARS

1

A MONTH after Collins' release, Connie Mack obtained the veteran second baseman, his 1901 batting king, Larry Lajoie, back from Cleveland. Lajoie by this time was thirty-nine; he had had a tempestuous career in Cleveland, including four seasons as playing manager—and once lost a pennant by four points—but he still was a graceful fielder and could hit.

"When I first sold Collins and released Bender, Plank, and Coombs, I did not think I was breaking up my club," said Mack. "I like to win as much as the next man. I knew I had good young pitchers in Bush, Shawkey, Pennock, Bressler, and Wyckoff; and I thought Lajoie might steady these kids at second base until I could develop a younger player for the position. I wasn't sure we would win again, but I thought we would have a strong first-division team."

For 1915 training Mack was back in Jacksonville, where Rube Waddell fought his alligator and dove into the soft ooze of the St. John's River twelve years before. Connie had a raft of young players there and even put on the catcher's mitt occasionally to see what his pitching rookies had in stock. Third base was Connie's big problem at his 1915 camp; for, though Baker had signed one of those new three-year contracts, he didn't show up. He, too, had had flattering Federal League offers. Mack experimented with two outfielders, Eddie Murphy and Jimmy Walsh, at the position, and even gave Rube Oldring a whirl at his earlier post.

"Eddie Collins was more forthright than Baker," said Mack years later. "Eddie told us frankly where he stood—and where we stood. Baker wasn't sure whether he wanted to play or not; he hemmed and hawed. We knew the Federal League had raised their offer to him, but we had him under a long-term contract and were in no mood to offer him more."

Shortly before the team returned home for its spring series with the Phillies, Louie Van Zelst, the little hunchback mascot and friend of Mack and his players, died in Philadelphia. It almost seemed as though little Louie was spared the sight of seeing "his" four-time champions fall on evil days. Writing of the little mascot, an unnamed Philadelphia sports writer could not have put Mack's feelings into words any better if he had read Connie's innermost thoughts. "In that misshapen little body, there was one of the greatest, gentlest souls that ever existed. Players and fans alike loved little Louie, and of all the mascots that have appealed to the baseball world from time to time in its history, he probably was the most famous and most appealing."

The club opened at Shibe Park, April 14; and, while the day was dedicated to Napoleon Lajoie, young Herb Pennock was the fair-haired boy as the fans filed out of the ball yard. The slender southpaw from Kennett Square pitched a one-hit shutout as he won a 2-to-0 pitching duel from Ernie Shore of the strong Red Sox. Mack's outfit that day wasn't a bad-looking team as it took the field: Eddie Murphy, third base; Walsh, right field; Oldring, left field; Lajoie, second base; McInnis, first base; Schang, catcher; Strunk, center field; Pennock, pitcher. Connie was pleased as he left the park and thought: "Maybe we'll surprise them."

A newspaper note said Frank Baker and his wife drove up from their Trappe, Maryland, home to attend the opening game. It went on to say that Frank exchanged pleasantries with coach-catcher Ira Thomas, but that Connie gave him only a cold stare when "Bake" looked in his general direction.

It is fortunate that men cannot look too far into the future. Suppose some Tibetan lama had told Mack that night: "That Boston club, which Pennock held to one hit, will be the new league champion in the fall with 101 victories. Your club will be last, with only 43 victories and 109 defeats for the hideous percentage of .283. And you will remain cellar-bound for seven years." Even the gentle-mannered McGillicuddy probably would have wanted to poke a bony finger right in the crystal-gazer's eye. Yet that is the fate that awaited baseball's wonder manager of the period from 1910 to 1914.

For a fortnight Mack remained with the elect; by May he had slid to seventh, and in July he settled for a long dismal stretch in last place. His pay roll still was high, as a result of the Federal League jacking up salaries all along the line. Connie thought his players didn't care. And there was no doubt about the disinterestness of the Philadelphia fans; they stayed away in droves.

More players were put on the mart. Jack Barry was sold, July 2, to the Red Sox for $8,000, a rather ridiculous figure; and a fortnight later Connie disposed of Eddie Murphy to the White Sox for an even smaller amount. Jack Lapp followed Murphy to Chicago. The one-hit pitcher of the opening game, Pennock, went to Boston on waivers; and Bob Shawkey was sold to the wealthy new owners of the Yankees. Barry, shifted to second base in Boston, was to continue sipping World's Series gravy, as his new club, the Red Sox, won World's Championships in 1915 and 1916; while Shawkey, and Pennock later, were destined to become high-salaried aces on famous clubs in New York.

Among the dreary things Connie sat through that season was the wild pitching debut of Bruno Haas, no relation to Mule Haas, Mack's later-day center fielder. Bruno, a Dean Academy youngster, walked sixteen batsmen in a dreary base-on-balls parade, as the Yankees, then no great shucks as a team, beat the A's, 15 to 7. Birdie Cree walked four times.

And a few days after the season started, April 22, Connie went through this believe-it-or-not afternoon: the great Lajoie, the most graceful of second basemen, was guilty of five errors, which still ties the modern record.

In the late summer Mack advanced a young shortstop, Samuel B. Crane, a Harrisburg, Pennsylvania, lad, from the Richmond club. He had drafted Crane from Greensboro, South Carolina, the year before and had him in mind as Jack Barry's successor at short. Perhaps Mack was attracted to the boy by his name; it was the same as that of Sam Crane, a National League player of Connie's day and for years thereafter a much-beloved baseball writer.

Crane didn't last long with the Athletics. He broke a wrist in the spring of 1916, was out most of the season, and then in 1917 he was traded to Washington. Later he played in the National League with Brooklyn and the Reds.

Then, in a sorry tragedy, Crane killed his sweetheart, Della Lyter, and a male companion, Jack D. Oren, in a Harrisburg café in 1929 and was sentenced April 14, 1930, to a term of 18 to 36 years at Pennsylvania's Gratersford Penitentiary.

Crane would have no place in this story but for the warm heart of Mack, who has befriended this player ever since, writing him letters of encouragement, sending Athletic players to visit him, and advising him "to keep a stiff upper lip." Year after year Crane applied for parole, and each time Connie sent his personal endorsement with the application. Finally, in the summer of 1944, the twelfth request for clemency was granted, after Mack told the parole board that Crane would be given employment at Shibe Park as soon as he was released.

2

If the season of 1915 was a bad one, that of 1916 was downright brutal. Connie hit absolute rock bottom that year, his club finishing with the horrible record of 36 victories and 117 defeats for a percentage of .235. It was the lowest in either major league in this century. Those 1916 A's came in 40 games behind the seventh-place Washington club.

"Yes, we were bad—very bad—that year," admitted Connie sadly. He had two pitchers that year, Jack Nabors and Tom Sheehan, who won 2 games between them and lost 37. Jack lost 19 straight for a major-league record before he won his first game of the year, and then lost his twentieth shortly thereafter. Sheehan, later a pretty fair pitcher and now coach of the Boston Braves, won 1 and lost 17.

By some miracle of grace, Joe Bush managed to win 15 games and lose 24; and Elmer Myers, another big right-hander, almost matched that record, 14 and 24. Connie did have one thrill that season, for on August 26 Bush pitched a 5-to-0 no-hitter against Cleveland. It was the third pitched by one of Mack's pitchers; the others were by Henley and Bender.

"Considering the team I had that season, it was the greatest no-hit game ever pitched," said Connie. "It was really a wonderful achievement." On that Cleveland club were such well-known hitters as Tris Speaker, who wrested the batting crown from Cobb that season, Jack Graney, Bobbie Roth, Chick Gandil, Ray Chapman, and Steve O'Neill. Bush beat Coveleskie, the pitcher who got away from Mack. Covey had a 23-to-10 record in 1916; how he could have helped Connie that year!

An odd sidelight of that game is that it was the last major-league game played by Lajoie, the player who meant so much to Mack when he first tried to sell American League ball to Philadelphia fans. King Larry went out with a bang, contributing a triple to Bush's victory; while Wally Schang, the catcher, playing left field, poked out three hits. For the remainder of that season, Connie played Otis Lowrey at second base.

Playing shortstop for Connie that season, alongside the veteran Lajoie and the novice Lowrey, was a kid extracted from Goddard Seminary in Vermont, Lawton (Whitey) Witt. The expression "as green as grass" was written for Witt. He never had seen a big-league town before going to New York to catch the Jacksonville boat for the club's training quarters. The boat ride down the coast was as much of an adventure for the kid as though he had sailed on Columbus' *Santa Maria*. He never knew when the liner would sail right off the ocean. Witt helped make life unhappier that season with 78 errors in 142 games. Charley Grimm, the present personable Cub manager but then a seventeen-year-old St. Louis scorecard boy, played 10 games for Connie at first base. And before the start of that disastrous 1916 season, Mack sold "Home-Run" Baker, hero of the 1911 World's Series, to the New York Yankees for $37,500.

3

Connie still was last in 1917, but he had a much more respectable tail-ender, winning 19 more games than the year before, while he finished only 1 game behind the seventh-place

Browns. And, surprisingly enough, he again was getting a punch in his line-up, as his club ranked second to the Tigers in team hitting, ahead of Clarence Rowland's White Sox, the 1917 World's Champions.

Mack took on Rube Schauer, a Russian-born pitcher who had been with McGraw in New York, and brought the picturesque Ping Bodie, former chubby White Sox outfielder, back to the American League. And he engaged a couple of young infielders who were to go far in American League baseball—Jumping Joe Dugan of Holy Cross and Mahanoy City, Pennsylvania, and Philadelphia's own homebred, the effervescent Jimmy Dykes. Dugan was one of Jack Barry's shortstop successors at Holy Cross, and a player with great promise. In his earlier association with Mack, Dugan frequently found tail-ending with the Athletics irksome and was AWOL; it led to his nickname of "Jumping Joe."

Jimmy's association with the club began the year before, when Mack was combing Philadelphia and the surrounding country for ball players. He was bringing them in by the hundreds. Dykes had been a caddy and a pretty fair sandlot ball player. One of Mack's Philadelphia operatives, Mike Drennan, saw Dykes and told him to report at Shibe Park with a group of other boys at 9 A.M. At 9:30 hitting practice started, but no rookie hit without permission. Then came two hours of infield practice when, with Connie personally supervising things, Ira Thomas batted grounders down to Dykes. That was followed by a five-inning game. "And by that time my legs were so tired I could hardly stand," related Jimmy.

Dykes came back to the clubhouse for his stuff the following Saturday. "Where have you been?" the clubhouse man asked. "I think you've made an impression. Mr. Mack has been looking for you."

"Well, he'll need to look for me no longer," said Dykes. "I'm not coming back. They kill you around here."

Jimmy didn't come back, either, but next winter Mack asked him to call at his home. "You've got possibilities, and I want you to play for me," he said. Jimmy signed a contract but spent most of the 1917 season with Gettysburg in the Blue Ridge League. After starting the 1918 season with Mack, Dykes went into the Army, and surely thrived on Uncle Sam's rations.

He went in weighing 160, and came out tipping the scales at 196.

"I've got just the place for you, Jimmy—Atlanta," said Connie, looking the chubby lad over. "That Georgia sun will melt some of that Army fat off you."

Among the many young players Connie turned over, he usually learned the character of a player after a few minutes of conversation. On some he immediately turned thumbs down. Occasionally he fooled with a so-called "bad actor" because he recognized unusual ability and thought he could tame the player. But few ever fooled him.

"He inherited that sense from his mother, my grandmother," his son Earle once said. "She never judged a person wrong in her life. When I was a kid I used to like to bring some of the gang home for dinner, maybe five or six of them. It always was all right with Grandmom. She used to sit and talk with us, but maybe two or three days later she would say: "Earle, I wouldn't waste too much time on that one"; or, "Earle, so-and-so is a mighty nice boy; he'll make a wonderful friend." And every time she had them exactly right.

"Well, Dad is the same way. He'll talk to a ball player a few minutes, and he'll know all he needs to know about that young fellow and his character. If the boy is sound, Dad will go a long way with him. If he isn't, Dad will try to change him; but if he doesn't make progress after a year or two that player will just disappear from our team."

4

After three straight tail-enders and the nation plunged deeply in World War I, Connie Mack ripped up what still remained of his great champions of 1913-14 in the winter of 1917-18. Harry Frazee, the New York theatrical man, had purchased the Red Sox the year before and finished second in 1917 after the Boston club had won World's Championships in 1915 and 1916. Harry, who subsequently became baseball's No. 1 wrecker, then still was in the chips; he was building up, rather than tearing down. He had lost his playing manager and Second Baseman Jack Barry, First Baseman Dick Hoblitzel, Outfielders Duffy Lewis, Chick Shorten, and Jimmy Walsh to the services and went shopping to Mack's Philadelphia bargain counter for war replacements.

The Athletic treasury was suffering from those lean eighth-place years, the disruption of the Federal League period, the uncertainties of the great conflagration. Frazee came to the December, 1917, baseball meetings with a big bankroll. He went into a huddle with Mack and Tom Shibe, and when it broke up Frazee had title to Wally Schang, the clouting catcher; Amos Strunk, the fleet-footed center-fielder, and Joe Bush, the no-hit pitcher. For the trio Mack took Vean Gregg, once a great left-handed pitcher but then suffering from a lame arm, Catcher Chet Thomas, and Merlin Kopp, an outfielder, who was called early into the Army. Frazee sweetened the deal with $60,000.

The deal was completed December 14, 1917, and on January 10, 1918, Mack had more bad news for Philadelphia. Stuffy McInnis, the first baseman and "the last of the Mohicans," also departed for Boston. Connie took a train for Jacksonville, Florida, and let Joe Ohl, the secretary, break the story that "McInnis had been traded to Boston for players to be selected later."

This was just about the last straw. Even Jimmy Isaminger, Mack's most loyal of loyal supporters in the press box, let out a blast in his weekly Philadelphia letter to the *Sporting News.* The headlines over the two-column story ran: "Connie Mack Hundred Percent Efficient as a Team Wrecker. He Has Himself and Home Plate. Remarks by Isaminger Brought Out as a Result of 'Trade' of Stuffy McInnis to the Boston Red Sox."

Jimmy's mad didn't last long, for in a subsequent edition he called for a fair deal for Connie Mack and hotly resented an implication that Connie would pay no player over $2,000 for the 1918 war season.

However, even Isaminger, along with other Philadelphia sports writers, speculated that, when the McInnis deal finally was completed, Mack would get a spavined outfielder, an old cigar box, and another Frazee bank roll. "What chance have we to get Larry Gardner, Everett Scott, Harry Hooper, or any of Frazee's better players?" wailed Jimmy in his column.

Well, Mack had a surprise for them. The completion of the deal didn't take place until just before the training season, and then Connie was happy to announce he had received Third Baseman Larry Gardner, Outfielder Clarence (Tillie) Walker, and Catcher Forrest Cady. It was fully a 100 per cent player return for Stuffy McInnis.

Mack had to ride up and down the bench with successive Tail-ender No. 4 in that abbreviated war season. But he had a respectable cellar champ, the club winding up with a percentage of .402. Those fellows obtained from Boston did pretty well, especially Gardner and Tillie Walker, who hit .294 and tied Babe Ruth for the league's home run honors with 11. George Burns, who succeeded Stuffy at first base, finished second to Ty Cobb in hitting with .354. Both of the Boston catchers, Cady and Thomas, flopped; but Mack came up with a new catching find, an aggressive youngster from Gloucester, Massachusetts, Ralph (Cy) Perkins.

Gregg's lame wing yielded 9 victories against 14 defeats, while Connie introduced the pitching marvel of the season, Scott Perry, and almost precipitated another war between the American and National Leagues. Despite the fact that the league season was shut down on Labor Day by the War Department's "Work or Fight" order, Mack worked Perry as he did "Pink" Hawley of his 1895 Pirates. Scott pitched 332 innings in 44 games, managed to win 21 games, while losing 19.

Prior to the war, Perry had been the property of the Browns and Cubs, and his title went to Atlanta. The Georgia club sold him to the Braves in early 1917, but Scott refused to report and joined an independent club in Joliet, Illinois. Mack procured Perry's reinstatement and engaged him in March, 1918, the Braves then showing no interest in the pitcher.

However, as Perry became Mack's one-man pitching staff, Connie's old nemesis and foe of the 1914 World's Series debacle, George Stallings, manager of the Braves, put in a claim for Perry and asked that he be returned to the Boston club. The case was brought before the old National Commission, with Ban Johnson voting for Mack, Governor Tener for Stallings, and Chairman Garry Herrmann throwing the deciding vote to the Braves. Garry ordered Perry to report to Boston. Then Mack and the Shibes went into the civil courts and procured a restraining order preventing the enforcement of the Commission's decree. Perry finished the season in Philadelphia.

Governor Tener, president of the National League, called upon his club owners to break relations with the American, even to the point of not meeting them in the 1918 World's Series. This was too drastic a suggestion for his league presidents in a war year; they refused to back Tener up, and he resigned.

"I do not pretend that Perry wasn't the property of the Boston club according to baseball law," said Mack. "But what irked us, and why we went into the courts, was that they knew we were dickering with him in the spring and filed no objection when I put Perry under contract. He was then just a mediocre pitcher. It was only after he began winning games for me, and enabled us to give a reasonably good account of ourselves, that they showed interest and demanded we surrender him. Had they approached us in the right way, we could have satisfied them over an inactive pitcher who had been doing them no good."

5

The end of the first World War brought no surcease to Mack's tail-end blues. In fact, with the other clubs getting their men back from the armed forces in 1919, Connie's fifth tail-ender again sank to the depths. From a .402 percentage in 1918, the A's receded back to a wretched .257. This time Mack trailed Clark Griffith of the seventh-place Washington club by twenty games.

"It was a most unhappy and disheartening season," said Connie, "and I started it with one of my worst deals. There was an outfielder in the league who was a known trouble-maker, Bobbie Roth, but he could hit. I had handled a few bad boys before and thought I could manage Roth. I figured if I could put more of a punch in my outfield, we might get somewhere. Well, I talked trade to Cleveland for Roth and offered them two real good players, Larry Gardner and Pitcher Myers, who had come back from the Army. They wanted a little bit more, and I agreed to throw in Charley Jamieson, who had been an extra pitcher and part-time outfielder on my club.

"It proved a bad mistake. I had little luck with Roth, and by midseason I traded him to Boston. As for Jamieson, the player

I tossed in, for the next fifteen years he was one of the best outfielders and lead-off men in our league."

When Mack traded Roth, along with Shannon, a young infielder, to Boston, he got back Jack Barry and Amos Strunk from the Red Sox; but Jack was near the fag end of his career, and Strunk soon moved on to the White Sox. As for Roth, called "Braggo," he made almost the entire American League circuit before he finished, skipping only the Browns and Detroit.

The American League split into a bitter feud that year over Ban Johnson's refusal to permit Frazee of the Red Sox to sell a disgruntled pitcher, Carl Mays, to the wealthy owners of the Yankees, Colonels Ruppert and Huston. The Yankees, White Sox, and Red Sox clung together in one faction against Ban's so-called "Loyal Five" clubs, with Mack and the Shibes of Philadelphia, Griffith of Washington, Phil Ball of St. Louis, Frank Navin of Detroit, and Jim Dunn of Cleveland supporting the veteran executive.

The feud became so bitter that it almost tore the American League wide open, and the three insurrectionist clubs combined with seven National League clubs to toss Garry Herrmann, the Cincinnati club owner, out of the chairmanship of the old National Commission. Though Herrmann decided against the Athletics in the Scott Perry case, he sided with Johnson in the more famous George Sisler controversy and was accused of being "Ban's man" on the Commission. The ousting of Herrmann paved the way for the election of Judge Landis to the post of one-man Commissioner a year later.

Talking of that fight, Mack said: "Ban was right. Both Tom Shibe and I felt a sense of loyalty to Johnson, but we also knew he was entirely correct in his stand. Frazee sold Mays after the player had walked out of a game he was pitching and left the club. While he was absent from the Red Sox without permission, he was sold to a better club. You just can't run baseball that way."

6

Mack still went bumpity-bump in the cellar in the seasons of 1920 and 1921, with the lowly percentages of .312 and .346, respectively. Getting out seemed a hard and almost hopeless task. But never did Connie quit on himself or his team. He wasn't having the same luck with players as when everything he touched turned to gold, but he was bringing up some good men and felt sooner or later he again would lead a team which would click. There was some grousing by the Philadelphia fans, an occasional pun in the newspapers as when Bugs Baer, the humorist, wrote, "The Athletics have reached a point where a base on balls constitutes a batting rally"; but on the whole the Quaker City public was patient. And Connie has been eternally grateful. "Mack must be a magician, or he has his own town hypnotized," Colonel Huston, the Yankee owner, said around that time. "Any other man who would have seven straight tail-enders in baseball would be run out of his town."

Gradually Mack was bringing up a crew of likely youngsters, most of them lads from Dixie, including Chick Galloway, a shortstop from Clinton, South Carolina, and Frank "Boog" Welch, an outfielder from Birmingham, and three six-foot pitchers—Bryan "Slim" Harriss, six-foot-six-inch right-hander from Howard Payne College and Brownwood, Texas; Rollie Naylor, a fellow from Denton, Texas, six feet, two and a half inches; and Bob Hasty, a six-foot-three-inch Cracker from Clayton, Georgia. Eddie Rommel, who was to bring Connie much joy with his knuckle ball, was a tall, talkative right-hander from Baltimore. He went south with McGraw in 1919, but there was some question as to his postwar title, and Mack acquired Eddie from Newark in 1920.

"For a while Cy Perkins, Eddie Rommel, and I were the old Guard on the team," reminisced Jimmy Dykes. "As we saw the players come and go we would look at one another and say: 'I guess we're next.' But somehow we weathered the storms."

Perkins soon developed into Mack's mainstay behind the bat and one of the ablest in the game; he was catching upward of a hundred games a season against some of the wildest, wooliest pitchers ever seen in the majors. Usually his fingers were bruised and battered. If ever there was a catcher who earned his "A" in those depression years, it was cheerful Cy.

Harriss, called the Texas Ranger, had a bad afternoon one day in Cleveland and was driven off the slab. Usually when a pitcher is knocked out he goes directly to the clubhouse, but tall Slim hung around the bench. "Get your clothes on, Slim," ordered his manager. "When I feel like it," answered the Texan. Mack grabbed a bat and chased the Lone Star beanpole all the way into the clubhouse.

On another occasion Slim had two strikes and no balls on Babe Ruth, then creating an entirely new game as he sent his home-run records into the stratosphere. Ruth knocked the next pitch over the roof of New York's Polo Grounds.

"What was the idea of giving him a fast one, with a two-and-nothing count?" demanded the enraged Mack.

"I tried to slip it past him," said Harriss.

"How marvelously you succeeded!" responded Connie.

Connie was heartsick when the Black Sox scandal broke late in the season of 1920, though the World's Series which the Chicago culprits had thrown was played the preceding fall. Baseball had been Mack's very life, something that he loved, revered, almost worshiped. And now the game's greatest annual show, the World's Series, had been corrupted, polluting the entire baseball stream. What hurt still more was that Joe Jackson, his early outfield find, was one of the accused players.

The Athletics had only a few September games left, and on a Saturday shortly after the scandal Mack left for the park in low spirits. He even thought: could baseball endure this shock? At best he expected a small turnout of mocking fans to look over his lowly tail-enders. It was difficult for him to face them. As Mack, with heavy heart, entered the runway leading to his bench, he encountered one of his players, who remarked: "A great crowd, Mr. Mack!" Connie thought the player was spoofing and in gentle irony meant to convey that there was only a handful in the stands.

As he came on the bench, the stands came to life. There was handclapping, whistling, and stamping of the feet. He peered out of the bench into the stands and saw a 15,000 crowd, a remarkable turnout with nothing at stake. As they saw him, the crowd cheered louder than before. Then he began to understand what it was all about. It was Philadelphia's way of saying: "There may have been a scandal, but we're still with you, Connie Mack." A lump arose in his throat; he was humble. but his heart no longer was sad.

Yet a year later skies again were dark for Connie Mack, for in his *Sporting News* letter of September 29, 1921, Jimmy Isaminger wrote: "It is telling no secret to say that Connie Mack has been very irritated over the apathy of some of his players in the final home stand, and there may be some sensational releases before the start of a new season."

CHAPTER XXIV

GOING UP!

1

THE LONG Athletic drought ended in 1922, when Connie finally shoved his nose one position out of the cellar. *Spalding's Guide* for 1923 tells the story of one of the oustanding happenings of the previous season: "The Philadelphia Athletics finished in seventh place in 1922. That was the big event in baseball in the Quaker City. After seven years of punishment at the bottom of the race, a combination of players was formed by Connie Mack which got him out of last place. He owes them an eternal debt of gratitude.

"Now that the Athletics are out of eighth place it is possible that they have determined to remain out, and that they will crawl up in the fight until they get back in the first division. Before their manager ceases his connection with baseball, they may even win another pennant. If they do, Mack may not disband that team until it falls apart from old age."

Yes, that paragraph was prophetic; Mack did win another pennant—three more in fact; but that team did not fall apart from old age. Again circumstances beyond Mack's control broke it up, but that belongs to a later chapter.

Prior to the season of 1922, Connie disposed of Joe Dugan in a big highly involved four-cornered deal, involving the A's, Yankees, Red Sox, and Senators. The rich New Yorkers sent their ace shortstop, Roger Peckinpaugh, and Pitchers Jack Quinn, Warren Collins, and Bill Piercy to Boston for Mack's old speedball artist, Joe Bush, Sam Jones (another first-string pitcher), and Shortstop Everett Scott. The Red Sox, in turn, sent Peckinpaugh to Washington for Dugan, procured from Mack for a pint-sized Cuban pitcher, José Acosta, who soon tumbled back to the minors. Connie also got some cash in the deal, supposedly furnished by New York, with which he was permitted to buy Edmund (Bing) Miller. Though Connie once let Bing go to the Browns, he quickly regained him in a subsequent deal, and Miller made his later pennants possible.

Later in that same season Jumping Joe Dugan gravitated to New York, where he joined his old pal on the Athletics, Whitey Witt, the old Goddard Seminary kid—by this time an outfielder—whom Mack sold to the Yankees early in 1922.

Old Ben Shibe died on January 14, 1922; and his oldest son, Thomas Stevenson Shibe, long vice-president of the A's, was moved up to the presidency. Tom's younger brother, John, became vice-president and secretary. However, while genial Tom was president in name, he let Connie shape the affairs of the club, especially as it applied to players. Whenever Tom was questioned about the club, he said: "See Connie; he's boss."

A few years before, Connie had purchased the quarter interest which originally was awarded to Frank Hough of the *Inquirer* and Sam Jones, the A. P. man, and now owned half of the club. Uncle Ben had been in failing health for some time, and even before his death Tom and Connie had talked of ways of building up the club to its former greatness, using the old saw, "You've got to spend money to make money." It was taking too long to try to come up with another Collins, Coombs, and Bender from the sandlots, and it was decided to spend money for players up to the limit of the club's credit. Despite the seven long years in the eighth slot, the "young fellows" who gambled on an Athletic football team in 1902 decided to remodel and enlarge their stand. The left-field bleachers were covered and a new bleacher built in front of the left-field fence.

That new bleacher and the remarkable pitching of Eddie Rommel helped make the emergence from the cellar possible. Helped by that new left-field home-run zone, the A's led even the Yankees, with their Ruth blunderbuss, in homers, showing the way with 111 circuit clouts. Tillie Walker, the chap obtained in the McInnis deal and a dead left-field hitter, smote 37 of them; and Bing Miller, the new man from Washington, 21. During the season Mack spent some of the money he and Tom talked about and purchased Joe Hauser, a first baseman with a home-run sock, from Milwaukee, and acquired Ralph (Pep) Young, another of those Philadelphia Central Manual boys, from the Detroit Tigers to play second base.

However, the wonder player of the year was Eddie Rommel, credited with being the father of the present-day knuckle ball. Though Mack used him frequently in relief, Eddie also pitched many complete games, worked in 294 innings, and closed with the amazing record of 27 victories, 13 defeats, and a percentage of .675, a believe-it-or-not mark with a seventh-place club.

That was the year Connie sprang Otto Rettig, a New Jersey semipro, on the St. Louis Browns, then a strong contender; and George Sisler, Baby Doll Jacobson, and other Brownies of that period still believe that Mack's cute little trick in pitching Otto in a midsummer series cost them the 1922 pennant. Rettig won his only major-league victory that day, and the Yanks nosed out St. Louis by one game for the 1922 championship. Frank Bruggy of Elizabeth, New Jersey, was second-string Athletic catcher by this time, and he brought in Rettig, another Elizabethan, shortly before game time.

Connie asked Otto: "When do you want to work?" Rettig replied: "Any time," so the lean manager said: "All right, warm up." Rettig warming up threw the Philadelphia press box into complete confusion. Bill Brandt says they not only never had seen Rettig, but the writers never even had heard of him. However, Otto had good control of his "nothing ball," fielded his position like a Fitzsimmons, achieved a well-deserved victory, and then never won another one.

In that same season the A's had the bases full, and Mack looked up and down the bench for someone who might bring in those runs. "I need a pinch-hitter," he said.

"Me! Me!" said Bruggy.

Frank took a powerful swipe and then raised a pop fly about ten feet in the air which nestled in the glove of the third baseman.

As Bruggy walked shamefacedly back to the bench, Connie

said: "Frank, whenever I call again for a pinch-hitter and you're the only one on the bench, don't you move."

In a Fourth of July game at the Polo Grounds, Babe Ruth hit perhaps the highest infield fly on record. The ball went so much higher than the roof of the grandstand that the spectators almost lost sight of it. Jimmy Dykes, playing second base that day, got tears in his eyes as he fiddled down below trying to station himself under the ball. When it finally came down, it fell in back of him, and Ruth got two bases. When Dykes returned to the bench at the end of the inning, Mack remarked: "My goodness, Jimmy, it took it a long time to come down, didn't it?"

Though he still helped out at training camps and occasionally during the season, Harry Davis gave up his captaincy. He had been elected a member of the Philadelphia city council, and also had a prosperous business. So Connie, always quick to forgive, gave the post of nonplaying captain and coach to his old second baseman, Danny Murphy, who was the Brooklyn Federal League scout during that vexing year of 1914.

2

Connie moved up another notch in 1923, when his club finished sixth with 69 victories and 83 defeats for the respectable percentage of .454. And for two and a half months he again knew what it meant to be in a race, as he had Philadelphia in the throes of pennant excitement. During the better part of May and June, his youngsters were running second and were the only club to make any trouble for the great Yankees, then on their way to their third straight pennant.

Wid Mathews, now a scout for Brooklyn, was as hot as a firecracker that spring. Never an outstanding player, Wid was a colorful little guy who captivated the fans with his peach-basket catches. For several weeks no one could get him out. While the home-run crop shrank from 1922's 111 to a more moderate 52, Bing Miller collected 21 while hitting .336. Connie bought Sammy Hale, a hard-hitting third baseman from Portland; he was getting a lot of good baseball out of Boog Welch; Joe Hauser was coming along fast as a first baseman and home-run hitter, and Connie worked the knickers off Ralph

Perkins, catching him in 148 games. He also added a pair of burly left-handers to his pitching staff, Freddy Heimach, from near-by Camden, and Rube Walberg, from the distant Northwest. The latter came from the Giants on waivers, after McGraw had passed him up. Freddy now is a copper in Miami; Rube an innkeeper in the Philadelphia suburbs.

After Connie's kids chased the Yankees all through the spring, the bubble burst in a four-game series at Yankee Stadium in the last few days of June. Just before the big New York series, the A's knocked out Walter Johnson with a 20-hit barrage and crushed Washington, 16 to 7; but it was the high tide of Mack's 1923 campaign. After that came Gettysburg. It didn't make it any sweeter for Connie that his former pitching finds put him on the skids. In the first game of the series, June 28, Bob Shawkey nosed out Rommel, 4 to 3; on the twenty-ninth New York finished ahead in a slugging match, 10 to 9; and on the thirtieth, Herb Pennock set back the A's, 6 to 1. Connie tried to come back with the hard-worked Rommel in the fourth game, but Sam Jones closed with a 4-to-0 shutout. From then on the club never stopped skidding until it rested in sixth place, but Mack considered it an improvement when he finished ahead of Chicago and Boston.

Connie attended the all-New York World's Series that fall and got quite a kick out of the Yankees' first blue-ribbon victory. "Yes, we did very nicely," he said, smiling, after the Yanks turned back McGraw's team, four games to two. He could say "we" quite appropriately. All four Yankee victories were chalked up by pitchers he developed; Herb Pennock won two games, and Joe Bush and Bob Shawkey one each. Wally Schang did all of the Yankee catching; Dugan played third base as it rarely had been played before and hit an important home run, while Whitey Witt did a swell job in center field.

3

The season of 1924 came near being one of Mack's most disappointing, yet it finished in a blaze of glory, with great promise for the future. From May 5 to August 8, in the very heart of the season, the A's were back in eighth place. After two years out of the cellar damp and of breathing a little fresher air, Connie seemed back where he was in 1915 to 1921. At times there was a blue funk over Shibe Park so thick you could cut it with a knife. And then, in the last two months of the race, Connie found the combination; his team played the best ball in the league and finished in fifth place, the top spot of the second division.

The great disappointment of the early season was Outfielder Paul Strand, the rookie most in the limelight in the 1924 training camps. Strand wasn't exactly a youngster, as he was a young southpaw pitcher with Stallings in 1914 when the Braves tomahawked Mack. Out in the Coast League, they converted Paul into an outfielder; and, playing with Salt Lake City in 1923, he had marks which were scarcely human. Playing 194 games, he cracked out 325 hits, including 66 doubles, 13 triples, and 43 home runs, as he topped the league in batting with .394. He scored 180 runs and drove in 187. It didn't seem possible a ball player could be that good, even in Salt Lake's rarified atmosphere. Connie scouted Strand personally in the summer of 1923, decided it was all true, and blew the roll on Paul. The purchase price at the time was given as $70,000; Mack now says it was $40,000. Strand flopped so badly with Mack in 1924, hitting a lowly .228 in 47 games, that he was tossed with Pitcher Rollie Naylor into a midseason deal with Toledo, whereby Mack acquired Outfielder Bill Lamar, a former Yankee.

Eyes were focused on Strand to such a degree at Mack's 1924 Montgomery, Alabama, training camp that the boys almost overlooked a sturdy Polish youngster from Milwaukee, Al Simmons, né Aloysius Szymanski. A third-string Milwaukee sports writer had trouble jockeying the z's and y's in Al's name while taking down his amateur box scores over the telephone and changed it to Simmons. About this same time Al became an Athletic fan and wrote Mack asking for a trial. "Al says he wrote to me, but I don't remember it," said Connie. "We get hundreds of such letters each year from boys who want to join us." Anyway Simmons was signed by his home-town team, Milwaukee, which farmed him to Shreveport in 1923. It was while Al was in Louisiana that Mack bought him. He finished that season with Milwaukee and gave some indication of his hitting greatness by poking out a .398 average for 24 games.

Had Milwaukee held on a while longer, they could have sold Simmons at a much stiffer price. Compared to the price tag on Strand, Al was a basement bargain.

Neither baseball men nor sports writers were sold immediately on Simmons. He had an odd batting stance—kept one foot "in the water bucket." They said he never could hit big league pitching from such a stance, but he got tremendous power into his swipes and hit .308 in his freshman year. Even that was to be a puny figure for the big Pole, for in the next ten years he fell under .340 only once. He became one of the great right-handed hitters of baseball history; twice led his league at bat; has a twenty-year lifetime major average of .334; and in his prime got a three-year contract from Mack calling for $100,000.

The second costliest rookie at Connie's Montgomery camp was Max Bishop, Jack Dunn's great second baseman at Baltimore, whose price was given as $50,000, though that, too, was perhaps a little exaggerated. Though never a Simmons, Bishop was destined to become a valuable regular on Mack's later-day champions.

A pitching pickup of 1924 who helped Mack for several years was an addition to his Texan brigade, Sam Gray of Van Alstine, drafted from Beaumont, where he supposedly was a Detroit "cover-up." Mack also took on a former Phillie right-hander, Stan Baumgartner, a University of Chicago man and now Jimmy Isaminger's successor as first-string baseball writer on the *Philadelphia Inquirer*. Stan had a splendid year, winning 13 games and losing only 6.

One of Stan's games that season still brings chuckles from Mack. Baumgartner was knocked out early by the Indians, and in the seventh inning, Cleveland led, 13 to 2. Connie thought Rommel, his relief pitcher, was taking things too easy and remonstrated with Eddie between innings: "I want you to bear down out there, no matter what the score is. There is no telling what may happen in a ball game." The words were scarcely out of his mouth when his team went on an eighth-inning rampage, scored 14 runs and pulled out the game, 16 to 14. Baumgartner, who left the park early, was squirting water on his lawn when he heard the final scores come in on his radio. When he heard: "Athletics, 16; Cleveland, 14," he thought someone was playing a prank or that he had better check up on his hearing.

Heimach, the big Camden boy, also started to come along in 1924, as he won 14 games while losing 12. Freddy also hit .322 that season, and Mack found him useful as a pinch-hitter and substitute first baseman. However, in his early years with the club, training rules meant little more to Heimach than they did to Connie's earlier playful southpaw, Rube Waddell. Frequently at Montgomery he violated Mack's midnight curfew. When the club broke camp, the players had to leave at an unearthly hour to catch a New Orleans express. "We leave at 2:30 A.M.," Connie informed his players, and then, turning to Heimach, asked: "Do you think it will be possible for you to make it, Freddy?"

In Chicago that little bundle of energy and ginger, Jimmy Dykes, came back to the hotel at three o'clock in the morning. "I really took a girl home for another player," explained the present White Sox manager.

Reaching the hotel, Dykes used the freight elevator to get to his floor, actually running it himself. Apparently no one saw him. Next day at luncheon Mack passed him in the dining room and remarked: "Jimmy, you're not in the habit of doing that, are you?"

"No, Mr. Mack, I'm not," said the perplexed Dykes, "but I don't know what you are referring to."

"That little matter of coming in at three o'clock," said the manager quietly. "Well, we'll say no more about it, but don't let it happen again."

To this day it still is a mystery to Dykes how Mack found out about his early-morning outing. He has asked him a number of times, especially after becoming Chicago manager, but each time Connie dismisses the matter with a broad grin.

In 1924 Earle Mack, with eleven years of managerial experience with Raleigh, Charlotte, Hanover, Pennsylvania, Moline, and Martinsburg, West Virginia, returned to Dad's team as coach, and has been one of his father's valuable lieutenants ever since. In the meantime the Athletics had acquired a controlling interest in the Portland club of the Pacific Coast League; and Connie and Tom Shibe sent Tom Turner, the Athletic scout, and Roy Mack, Connie's oldest son, out to

Oregon to run the club. "We really bought the Portland club so that we could buy Mickey Cochrane, the Portland club's great catcher," admitted Mack. The Athletics turned over $50,000 to their new affiliate Portland club for "Black Mike," a former Boston University all-around athlete, soon to become Mack's No. 1 all-time catcher.

And in the fall of 1924 Mack and Tom Shibe made the Athletic's highest player investment, $100,600 for Robert Moses (Lefty) Grove, the tall sinewy pitcher of Dunn's then-perennial Oriole International champions. Grove, a Cumberland mountaineer with a fiery temper—it mellowed with the years—was to give Connie a few additional headaches but many a compensating thrill. Some even called him faster than Rube Waddell, and when tall Mose eventually hung up his shoes he had the best won-and-lost record of any top-ranking pitching star in baseball. He came cheap at his price, and this figure wasn't exaggerated, or stage money. The A's bought him for ten yearly payments of $10,000; the extra $600 was interest charges during the decade.

4

It almost happened in 1925, when Connie Mack came closer to a pennant than any year since 1914. His White Elephants led the pack a good part of the season, from May 9 to June 29, July 15 to 20, July 22 to August 20; and at one point Connie enjoyed a comfortable five-game margin over his old rival, Clark Griffith, whose Senators had won the 1924 World's Championship. But this time the bottom fell out of the club's pennant bid on their last Western trip, as Mack suffered the agony of a 12-game losing streak and 17 defeats in 19 games. At one time the slump approached a rout, but Mack was able to rally his shattered forces in September and managed to beat out strong St. Louis and Detroit teams for the runner-up position. While he trailed Washington by 8½ games at the finish, second place after 10 years in the second division was a godsend, especially in a year when the proud Yankees tumbled to seventh place.

Connie says today he could have won in 1925 but for an early-season accident which incapacitated his first baseman,

© *Sporting News*

AL SIMMONS

Mack's great left fielder and American League's Batting Champion, 1930-1931.

© *Sporting News*

JIMMY FOXX

Possesses more home runs than any hitter other than Babe Ruth.

Hey, move over to the right.

Just a little bit more.

I guess that's just about right.

© *Sporting News*

Now, let me mark that "out" down.

CONNIE WIGWAGGING WITH HIS FAVORITE SCORE CARD

Joe Hauser, in one of baseball's oddest injuries. Joe suffered it in one of the preseason exhibitions between the A's and Phillies. An ordinary grounder was hit to Shortstop Galloway, but when he looked over to first base there was no one there. Hauser was squirming painfully on the ground. Apparently as he was springing to cover his bag, he suffered a lateral fracture of the left kneecap; it fairly tore the bone apart. It kept Hauser out for practically the entire season. They wired the knee together, and Joe tried to come back in 1926. His fielding was all right, but his power at bat was gone, though later it came back in the American Association, where he set a home-run record with 65.

With Hauser out, Connie scoured the land for the best first baseman available. The A's Portland club had a holdout first baseman, Jim Poole; Mack quickly satisfied Poole, ordered him to Philadelphia, and without any spring training stuck Jim into his line-up. He proved a fair stopgap for one season. Despite the injury to slugger Hauser, Mack showed his fans plenty of hitting. The A's lost the pennant, but they were well ahead of the league in hitting with .307. Connie had seven hitters from .318 up. Young Simmons really put the wood to the ball in his second year, clouting out an average of .386, with Walter French, the former West Point football-baseball star, now a major in the Army Air Corps following Aloysius with .370. Bill Lamar hit .356; Sammy Hale .345; while Cochrane, the young catcher, broke in with .331 and caught 134 games. Jimmy Dykes was up there with .325, and Bing Miller followed with a lusty .318.

Despite the August crash, Connie also got some fine pitching behind his hitting. Sammy Gray was the new pitching hero of Shibe Park, much more so that year than Grove. Though out a month with a broken finger, Sam won 16 games and lost 8. Rommel had another fine year with a 21-to-10 record, while Harriss had his best season with Connie, 19 and 12. The forty-year-old spitballer, Jack Quinn, was purchased in midseason from Boston. The youthful Grove whiffed 116 batters in 197 innings, but he won only 10 games against 12 defeats. Moreover, he lost the club's 1925 heartbreaker—a 1-to-0 15-inning Fourth of July defeat to Herb Pennock at Yankee Stadium. Steve

O'Neill, Mack's rookie catcher of 1911, drove in New York's lone run, the tally which sent Grove fuming to the clubhouse.

Stan Baumgartner was Mack's chief relief pitcher. Once, when Stan wasn't overly happy with his lot he muttered on the bench: "If I could get a job for $40 a month, I'd quit this lousy game."

Overhearing the remark, Connie said: "I have just such a job in the office; do you want it?"

However, on another occasion when Baumgartner did a particularly meritorious relief job, Mack said: "Go down to Wanamaker's and buy yourself a suit of clothes. You earned it."

"What kind of a suit shall I buy?" the pitcher asked.

"A real good one."

So Stan bought himself an expensive English tweed, with two pairs of pants. It cost $125, but when he gave Connie the bill the manager never batted an eye.

During that season Frank Baker visited Connie Mack in his Shibe Park tower. The coolness between Mack and his old third baseman over Frank's failure to play in 1915 long since had been dissipated. "There's a kid down at Easton, Maryland, in the Eastern Shore League, who looks like a real hitter," said Baker. "His name is Jimmy Foxx; he's only seventeen, but he's as strong as a young bull." On Baker's tip Connie acquired Foxx, then a kid catcher, for a song. He farmed him to Providence most of that season, but Mack employed him in ten games in the fall. Baker said the boy could hit, and the hefty East Shore lad made him look like a good prophet by hitting a fancy .667. Those arms and shoulders were to grow with the years, and Jimmy was to hit 527 home runs, more than any right-handed hitter in the history of baseball and second only to the magic 714 total of the fabulous Ruth.

5

That 1925 season started at Fort Myers, Florida, Mack's first of a long series of training camps in that pleasant west coast town. It was a winter gathering place for those famous three geniuses of the nation, Thomas Edison, Henry Ford, and Firestone. What an atmosphere for that wizard of baseball, Connie Mack! Jimmy Isaminger was there, as usual, with such other well-wishers of the Athletic press box as Bill Brandt, Stoney McLinn, Bill Dooly, Eddie Pollock, and Don Donaghy.

They were "all aboard" when Mack started his last western trip in middle August three games ahead. They were calling it "the Pennant Special." They were there to tell the Quaker City of Connie's seventh pennant. The first stop was St. Louis. The story is that French, the West Pointer and a pretty good jockey, got so under George Sisler's skin with barbs that passed Mack's censorship that George played like a veritable demon. The Browns bowled over Connie's sluggers, 7 to 6, 9 to 8, and 7 to 6. The tall tactician had little stomach for his dinner after the second and third games; in the 9-to-8 affair the A's scored 6 runs in the first half of the ninth, only to have the Browns come back with 3, and St. Louis also pulled out the third game with 2 runs in the ninth.

Moving on to Chicago, Connie saw his club lose its fifth straight. The venerable gentleman had a two-day surcease. as Slim Harriss and Sammy Gray turned back the White Sox, 6 to 1 and 3 to 0, and Simmons and Bing Miller hit crushing homers in Gray's victory.

Then came one of the most agonizing two weeks in Mack's sixty years in baseball; the Pennant Special went into reverse as his boys blew the next twelve games. The Elephants were taken to the cleaners in straight games in Cleveland and Detroit. In the former city, Connie saw a game slip away, 4 to 3, when Chick Galloway ruined what looked like a promising rally by lining into a triple play. In Detroit he thought he had a game in hand when the Tigers teed off on Quinn and Grove for seven runs in one fruitful inning.

Back in the East, the A's blew two games to their closest rival, Washington, and another pair to the then seventh-place Yankees, one to that old jinx, Pennock. But, returning to Shibe Park for Labor Day, two loyal crowds totaling nearly 70,000 came out for the holiday games with the Senators, anxious to show the Grand Old Man of Baseball they still were with him and hadn't given up the ship. The turnstiles hummed merrily, but the music brought no joy to Mack. Grove's Labor Day luck was no better than it had been on the Fourth of July; he lost the morning game to Walter Johnson, 2 to 1; and the Senators outslugged the A's in the afternoon, 7 to 6, for Philadelphia's twelfth straight defeat. It left the erstwhile leaders nine games behind.

One of Connie's most fearful slumps ended next day, September 8, when Gray and Harriss collaborated on a 6-to-4 victory over the Senators, but he knew 1925 pennant hopes were dead and already was thinking of the next season.

CHAPTER XXV

TY COBB JOINS CONNIE'S COLORS

1

REACHING SECOND place after a steady four-year climb, Connie felt he again had the Athletics clicking and could look any man in the eye. By this time he had taken up golf, and went down to Fort Myers early in 1926 to get in a few late-winter licks. For years he got a lot of fun out of smacking the little hard rubber pill down the fairway. Later his golfing partners frequently were his own players, Dykes, Cy Perkins, and Mickey Cochrane. In the North he played usually at Philadelphia's Cedarbrook Club, where his favorite golfing partner was Charles Rehfuss. Connie didn't hit such a long ball, but he could keep it straight. "Down-the-middle Connie," Jimmy Dykes used to call him.

A new coaching acquisition at that 1926 Fort Myers camp was Kid Gleason, the old White Sox manager, ex-Oriole, and a former Phillie second baseman. The Kid came from Camden, and the general impression was that kindly Connie made a job for him.

Among the rookies at Fort Myers were a pair of mountaineer pitching brothers Ira Thomas had lassoed in Weyers Cave, Virginia, deep in the Blue Ridge Mountains. Their names were Orie and Kit May. Connie always was partial to big ball players—especially pitchers; and when the hillbilly moundmen reported, well under six feet, Mack stroked his chin and remarked wistfully: "My goodness, I thought you were big fellows; but go in the clubhouse and get your uniforms."

If the A's blew the 1925 pennant in that deadly late summer slump, 1926 was a tantalizing season. Connie had a good club, but just not quite good enough. It ran second to the Yankees most of the season, but Speaker's Cleveland team finished fast, passed the Mackmen in September, and almost caught New York. Though the Indians nosed him out for second place, Connie really was closer to the top than in 1925—he finished only six games out of first place.

He did a lot of midseason horse trading. In June he swapped Bing Miller to the Browns for another outfielder, Baby Doll Jacobson. "Jake" didn't stay long enough in the Shibe Park clubhouse to get acquainted, as Mack dispatched him to Boston, along with Pitchers Slim Harriss and Freddy Heimach, in exchange for Howard Ehmke, the tall veteran right-hander, setting the stage for a World's Series drama later on. However, Connie hated to give up Miller and regained Bing from the Browns the following winter in a deal for Sammy Gray.

Mack's pitching find that season was Joe Pate, an old-timer resurrected from the Texas League. Though employed largely in relief, Joe just couldn't lose. He was credited with nine wins and no defeats. Walberg the big Seattle left-hander, was showing almost as much smoke as Grove, and Maryland Mose finished his sophomore years with thirteen victories and as many losses. The tall mountaineer often went into a blue funk after losing tough decisions. "Just leave him alone and don't say anything to him," Connie advised his players. Dykes was Grove's roommate and one of the few players on the club who could tell Mose where he got off.

As for Dykes, Mack still was shifting him around the infield; in 1926 he divided his time between second base and third. A fan in the upper stand didn't like Jimmy's third basing, and said so in raucous abusive tones. And Jimmy didn't like the fan. After the seventh inning of a game the A's were losing, Dykes asked Connie: "Can I be excused, Mr. Mack?"

"And why, Jimmy?" responded his manager.

"Well, there's somebody upstairs that I think I have a little business with."

Mack looked him quietly in the eye before answering and

then said: "Jimmy, there's only one up there now; by the time you get up in the stand, there will be five more; and shortly after that there might be twenty-five. So, as I think you're a pretty valuable man on this team, I feel you might just as well spend the rest of the afternoon at third base. Have a good sleep on it, and by tomorrow you'll forget it ever happened."

2

Shortly after the close of the 1926 season, the Detroit club announced that Ty Cobb, playing manager of the Tigers for the past six years, would not direct the club in 1927. Subsequently Ty was given his unconditional release, November 2. On top of that, word came from Cleveland that Tris Speaker, highly successful playing manager of the Indians, would leave baseball to go into business.

Shortly afterward Judge Landis admitted having a letter from Dutch Leonard, a former Red Sox and Detroit left-hander, mentioning the two stars in connection with a questionable game late in 1919—after the American League race had been decided. It was a winter for washing dirty linen. Swede Risberg, one of the expelled Black Sox, supported by Chick Gandil, a fellow culprit, made other charges against players on the Detroit and Chicago American League clubs. After public hearings, Judge Landis absolved Cobb and Speaker of any wrongdoing and also acquitted the Tigers on the Risberg charges; and it always has been a keen regret among admirers of Ty and Tris that even a shadow should have been thrown over their great careers.

Anyway, after Cobb's twenty-two seasons in Detroit, he was a free agent and there was quite a scramble for his services. Ty was approaching forty, but had hit .339 in 1926. "I think I'll go after Cobb," Mack told Tom Shibe. "Ty still has a lot of good ball in him and can help us in the outfield. And we'll get everything we pay him back at the gate." "Sure, go after him," Tom replied.

Connie had to fight off several other high bidders, including Brooklyn and other National League clubs. Eventually he got Ty's name on an Athletic contract. Cobb drew around $70,000 for his 1927 season's work with Mack, $40,000 in salary and the rest in a bonus for signing and another when the season's gate exceeded a specified figure. The spikings of Baker and Barry in 1909 long since had been forgotten and forgiven. Philadelphia was thrilled at having the great Cobb in its outfield, and Mack was thrilled at playing him. And in Cobb's opening game at Shibe Park in Athletic regalia Mack wig-wagged him around his outfield with his scorecard just as though Ty had been Kit May.

Mack went all-hog for star old-timers that winter. He also brought back Eddie Collins after twelve seasons in Chicago, the last two as playing manager, and signed Brooklyn's old slugging left fielder, Zack Wheat, released by the Dodgers after playing eighteen seasons in Flatbush. He had in a bid for Tris Speaker, but the Texan signed with Griffith in Washington. And Connie laid it on the line in purchasing Bishop's former double-play partner in Baltimore, Shortstop Joe Boley. Like the mighty Szysmanski, Joe shortened his name from the Polish Bolinsky; he came from Joe Dugan's old home town, Mahanoy City, and gave Mack the cream of the minor-league shortstops.

The Athletic chief says his 1927 club was strong enough to win the average major-league race, but he battled that season against one of the superteams of baseball, Huggins's great Yankees, winners of 110 games, the American League high. If Connie finished with the credible record of 91 victories and 63 defeats, he trailed the mighty New Yorkers in second place by 19 games. Mack, in turn, was 6 games ahead of Clark Griffith, whose Washington club ran third.

Though Simmons was out of some 40 games with an injury, clouting Al hit .392, second only to Harry Heilmann. Cobb still had the old batting knack and clicked off an average of .357 in 134 games. Collins, at forty, demonstrated to Connie that he was another spry "old man" by hitting .338 in 95 games. He divided second base with Bishop. Wheat also had some power left, with .324 for 88 games. Grove had his first real winning year, 20 victories and 13 defeats; while Quinn, Walberg, Ehmke, and Rommel gave Mack many pleasant afternoons with fine pitching performances.

3

Early in May, when the 1927 race still was tight, Connie got more incensed at an umpire than at any arbiter since the 1907 blow-off with Silk O'Loughlin. This time the object of his wrath was Emmett (Red) Ormsby. The Red Sox were playing at Shibe Park, May 5, and Grove had a 2-to-1 lead over Wiltse, when Ira Flagstead, a Boston pinch-hitter, hit Mose for a two-run homer in the first half of the eighth, putting the Red Sox ahead, 3 to 2. Cobb, first up for the A's, gave Connie a pleasant moment when he drove the first pitch over the right-field fence just inside the foul line. The ball obviously was fair when it left the park; and Mack, his players, and the crowd thought it was the game-tying home run.

However, Red Ormsby, the plate umpire, called Cobb back, insisting it was a foul ball. He admitted the ball was fair when it sailed over the fence, but said it had curved foul by the time he lost sight of it. It precipitated a violent argument, but Cobb wasn't chased then.

Batting over again, Ty drew back his bat, and as he did so he hit Ormsby on the chest. Red claimed Cobb did it on purpose; Ty said it was accidental. He ordered Cobb out of the park. Simmons, who was the next batter up, got into the argument, in which Ormsby was pushed and jostled. Al also was chased, as Connie got sorer by the minute, and the crowd grew more belligerent, throwing a shower of bottles.

Ban Johnson immediately wired indefinite suspensions for Cobb and Simmons, which didn't sit too well with Connie, who felt Ormsby's poor decision precipitated the entire incident.

The Athletics were scheduled to play their first 1927 game in Detroit, May 10, and it was to be a big home-coming for Ty, something similar to Waddell's game with the Browns at Columbia Park in 1908. Detroit fans sent Johnson a petition asking him to reinstate Cobb by the tenth. Ban did so, saying the report of Brick Owens, the base umpire, on the Shibe Park near-riot held Simmons more blameworthy than Cobb.

Connie smoldered inwardly over the incident and Ormsby's decision for some time. After the season Bill Dooly of the *Record* asked him: "Are you going to file a protest with the league against Ormsby's work."

"Oh, no, Bill, I wouldn't do that," Mack replied. "It might cost Red his job. I'd never take away any man's bread and butter."

Ormsby, by the way, needed plenty of butter; he had thirteen children.

Only two months after the Cobb-Ormsby incident, Ban Johnson, American League president since its inception, was forced out of office at a meeting in New York, July 10. It was a difficult confab for Connie and Tom Shibe, so intimate with Ban since the early days of the league. Johnson had gotten into one dispute after another with Commissioner Landis; Ban's health was none too good; and it was a case of Ban or the Judge. Johnson's term still had eight years to run at $40,000 a year, but his club owners voted to ask for his resignation. Ban locked himself into his room, and when a committee of Colonel Ruppert, Clark Griffith, and Bob Quinn went to see him, he wouldn't open the door and said he would speak only to Phil Ball of St. Louis, the old Federal Leaguer, who alone stuck by him. Eventually Ban stuck his hand through the door and handed his resignation, scribbled on notepaper in lead pencil, to Ruppert. It was to take effect at the end of the 1927 season.

Voting against Ban was one of the saddest votes ever cast by Mack in a League meeting room. It brought back recollections of the 1900 meeting in Chicago when Johnson, young, vigorous executive of the new league, asked Mack to take the Philadelphia franchise. There were some reports that Connie too, had turned on Johnson because of the Ormsby ruling and the Cobb and Simmons suspensions. Such a thought was unworthy; Mack is the last man to hold a grudge.

"The Philadelphia club and I stuck to Ban as long as we could," said Mack. "He had been a great man and a great executive. But he had lost his grip and wouldn't play ball in the new order which came in with Landis. The American League club owners had to act as they did in 1927 to protect their interests and investments."

4

By 1928 Connie Mack had his pennant winner built; it put up an amazing—even heroic—fight against the Yankees, but couldn't quite make it. But the venerable baseball general still was trying to beat out a club good enough to sweep two successive World's Series in eight straight games.

Connie acquired the last two cogs necessary to complete his great machine. In the previous winter he had purchased the loquacious Jerseyman from Montclair, George (Mule) Haas, from the Atlanta club, and in June he took the last remaining prize from Dunn's Orioles—the big pitching moose, George Earnshaw. Haas, now a White Sox coach, along with Bing Miller, was to develop into one of Mack's great center fielders. Earnshaw, a Swarthmore graduate and social registerite—now a commander in the Navy—started in slowly, breaking even in 14 games; but he was destined to become Connie's right bower, balancing Grove, the left bower. With his flair for showmanship, Connie also signed Tris Speaker, released by Washington. Tris hit .267 in 64 games, but Mack's new machine didn't really go into high until Haas succeeded the veteran in center field.

For two and a half months it looked like another runaway for the Yankees. By July 4 they led the second-place A's by 13½ games. The brash New Yorkers had been poison to the White Elephants. The American League had a freak schedule that year, and Mack had to play 18 of his 22 games with Huggins before July 4. The Yanks took 13 of them.

They were saying the Yankees could win by 25 games if they wished, and then Connie pulled out the throttle. His club became a veritable baseball hurricane, sweeping everything in front of it. Day after day, and week by week, the A's whittled down the New York lead. Finally, in Boston, September 7, they tied the Bronx Bombers by winning a double-header, one of the games being a 1-to-0 pitching duel in which Grove won the decision from Red Ruffing. And then Mack's heart sang the following day, a Saturday, when his men smacked down the Red Sox in another double-header as Huggins was taking only a single game from Washington. Day of days, the A's led the great Bronx Bombers by a half-game!

Immediately afterward, Connie took his team and his precious three-point lead to New York, where the A's were scheduled for a four-game series, the only games left between the leading contenders after the crazy spring schedule.

"If you can win three out of four, you'll play in the World's Series; if we break even our position will be good," Mack told his players, but the Yankees still had their early-season Indian sign on the Elephants; it was they who took three out of four.

A crowd officially given out as 82,000 paid, the greatest to see a ball game up to that time, attended the Sunday double-header at Yankee Stadium, September 9. In view of the growing Athletic pay roll, the check Joe Ohl took from Ed Barrow made pleasant reading for Connie; but what happened on the Stadium diamond was gall and wormwood. Another pennant was being knocked from under him!

George Pipgras, the present-day umpire, was enjoying his greatest season and gave the White Elephants an extra coat of whitewash in the opener by a score of 5 to 0. The second game was even more painful for Connie. He started Walberg and felt fairly content as Rube carried a 3-to-1 lead into the seventh inning. Then the Yankees bats got busy and reached Rube for two runs, tying the score. Mack yanked Walberg and waved to the bull pen for Eddie Rommel to take over. But shifting from Rube to Eddie was like leaping out of the frying pan into the fire. With the bases full in the eighth, Rommel served one of his famous knucklers to Bob Meusel, and Connie's heart sank to his knees when the lanky Californian knocked it into the stands for a grand-slam homer. It gave the Yanks the game, 7 to 3.

There was no game on Monday, but on the eleventh, Mack's taut nerves took the same beating as in the second game of the Sunday double-header. Grove pitched this one against Henry Johnson, who, though no shucks as a pitcher, tossed five harpoons into Connie's Elephants in six tries in 1928. Grove blanked New York for six innings as the A's amassed three runs off Henry. The Yanks scored one run in the seventh, and in the eighth the Bronx Powerhouse really went to work on Grove. Ruth hit a homer with Gehrig on base, and two additional runs scored before Mose could put out the fire.

With little Bishop hitting Hoyt for a crucial homer, the Athletics grabbed something out of the wreckage by winning the fourth game, 4 to 3; but where Mack came to the big town a half game in front, he was leaving a game and a half in arrears.

Each team still had to make its last western trip, and it was a nerve-tingling one for Connie. His A's still had a chance, but every time they won, the Yankees won also, and on the few occasions the Mackmen lost, New York also lost. Only one who has traveled with a ball team in such a situation knows the emotional strain on every one from the manager down to the bat boy. In Detroit, Grove apparently had a game won when Harry Rice knocked it from under him with a ninth inning homer. That was almost the last straw.

Hearts were heavy as the team took the train for Chicago. Connie sat in the smoking compartment of his pullman with Bill Brandt, then of the Philadelphia *Ledger* and Don Donaghey of the *Bulletin*. And can you guess what Mack was peeved about? He was talking about the 1910 World's Series with the Cubs. "I still think we should have taken four straight from the Cubs in that series," he was saying. "I should have followed my hunch and let Topsy bat for Thomas against King Cole. Some of my players argued me out of it. And I'll never let any one talk me out of it again when I've made up my mind on what's the right thing to do."

Mack stayed in the 1928 race until September 28, two days before the end of the season. New York's eventual winning margin was two and a half games, almost the same as when the big Stadium series was over. New York won 101 games and lost 53 for .656; Connie won 98 and lost 55 for .641. "Anyway, we let them know they were in a fight," said Connie, when his team was mathematically eliminated.

CHAPTER XXVI

HAPPY DAYS ARE HERE AGAIN

1

WHEN Connie Mack hit the pennant jackpot again in 1929, winning his first flag in fifteen years, it came easy—almost ridiculously easy. The momentum of that furious finish in the second half of the 1928 season still was pushing the Athletics forward when the new season got under way. For the second time in his career, little Huggins was trying to bunch four straight Yankee pennants. This time, the little mite didn't even see the finish, as he died four days before the end of the 1929 season. Long before that, Connie had clinched his seventh flag. The Athletic margin over the second-place Yankees was 18 games, practically reversing the procedure of two years before, when New York excelled Mack's runner-up A's by 19 games. Connie's team won 104 games and lost only 46 for a percentage of .693, a higher peak than achieved by any of the Collins-Baker-Bender-Coombs teams.

Simmons again was terrific in left field, hitting .365, four points under Lew Fonseca, the league leader; while "Bucketfoot Al" connected for 34 homers. After experimenting with Jimmy Foxx behind the plate, at third base, and at first base, Connie eventually decided that the latter position was Jim's best spot. The broad-shouldered Marylander, by this time twenty-one, hit .354, and his home-run output was only one under that of Simmons. Cochrane, full of pep, fire, and conversation, stood out as the game's foremost catcher and hit .331.

Bing Miller was up there again with .335. Cobb's contract was not renewed, and Ty, at forty-three, bowed gracefully out of the picture with a lifetime average of .367 for 24 major-league seasons. Haas, the new center fielder, hit .313 and covered his patch like a carpet. With Boley and Bishop working beautifully around second base, Dykes, the former infield Jack-of-all-trades, was stationed permanently at third base.

Grove's contribution to Mack's new pennant was 20 victories and 6 defeats, and Earnshaw blossomed into a full-fledged star with a 24-to-8 record. Walberg, the third member of the Big Three, won 18 and lost 11. Rommel was the game's best relief pitcher, with 12 victories and 2 defeats, while Connie found spots for the veterans, Quinn and Ehmke.

Of course, on the ball field everything didn't go quite as smoothly as that final 18-game margin might indicate. It was a season of hard, driving play, bench explosions, and clubhouse blowups. And Lefty Grove was in the middle of a number of them.

In Cleveland, late in the game, Bishop kicked one behind Grove, and on the next play Dykes booted another easy chance. The two putouts would have retired the side. Mose was red-headed, and in pitching to the succeeding Cleveland batsmen he served the ball right over the middle of the plate. Indian hits rattled off the fences.

When the regulars came in after the inning, they gave Grove some dirty looks, and there were angry murmurs under their breaths.

"Stop muttering," said Connie sharply. "Do you want him out of there?"

The question was answered by a chorus of "yes" from almost the entire bench.

"All right, get Quinn ready," said Mack. "He'll go in the next inning."

Lefty was burned up. He wouldn't speak to Dykes, his roomie, that night. The pair usually took the same taxicab to the ball park. Next day Jimmy asked him in the Hotel Hollendon lobby: "Are you going out to the park, Mose?"

"No, I ain't goin' out yet," said Grove in his iciest tone.

However, when Mack again called on Lefty to pitch, he

poured in his No. 1 pitch faster than ever and won his next six games.

Dykes had a great western trip that season, the best in his twenty years as an active player. He hit .500 and was feeling pretty good and proud when the club returned home, and Philadelphia also was Dykes's home town. The A's opened against Detroit, and in Dykes's first time at bat George Dauss made the third baseman look bad as he struck him out. Dauss was the hardest pitcher in the league for Dykes to solve. When Jimmy came up again, Connie called for a pinch-hitter. Dykes was so mad that he angrily threw his bat, and Connie had to jump to avoid being hit.

In relating the incident Dykes said: "Then I made my big mistake. Instead of getting dressed and leaving the park, I stayed around the clubhouse until the game was over. Mr. Mack rarely came into the clubhouse, but this day he did.

"Come over here, young man, I want to talk to you," said Connie.

"What is it, Mr. Mack?" Jimmy asked meekly.

"I never want you to do that again," Mack said sternly.

2

Winning the 1929 World's Series from the Chicago Cubs, 4 games to 1, provided two of the great kicks of Mack's baseball life; and, while the Athletics overcame an 8-run deficit by scoring 10 runs in the seventh inning of the fourth game, he terms his first victory of that series, won by Howard Ehmke, 3 to 1, the greatest thrill of his long career.

The Cubs were managed that season by Joe McCarthy, the famous present-day Yankee skipper and the Philadelphia boy who had stood with the crowd at the Broad Street Station to help welcome Mack and his 1910 Athletic World's Champions back from Chicago. Joe had a terrific .302-batting club, with a line-up of almost all right-handed hitters—Rogers Hornsby, Kiki Cuyler, Hack Wilson, Riggs Stephenson, Woody English, Zack Taylor. Gabby Hartnett had a lame arm but did most of the pinch-hitting. Among the Cub regulars, Charley Grimm, the present-day Chicago manager and a Mack rookie in 1916, was the only left-handed batter.

Connie dazed the sports world, also his own players, by pitching long, angular Howard Ehmke, now a Philadelphia manufacturer of tarpaulin infield covers, in the first game of the series in Chicago, October 8, 1929. Ehmke, formerly a great picher, then was thirty-five and near the end of his career. During the 1929 season he had appeared in only 11 games, pitched a total of 55 innings, equivalent to 6 nine-inning games, had a record of 7 games won and 2 lost, but worked only 2 complete games.

Only in recent years has Mack told the real story of how he came to pitch Ehmke in the first game, and that for over two weeks before the series it was a secret between Ehmke and himself that the tall right-hander would draw the opening assignment in Chicago.

Shortly before the Athletics left on their last Western trip, Mack called Ehmke to his little office in Shibe Park. "Howard, there comes a time in everyone's life when there has to be a change, and I think we've reached the point where we soon must part company."

"All right, Mr. Mack. If that is the way it is, it has to be," said the pitcher. "I haven't helped you much this year, and it's lucky you didn't need me. But I've always wanted to pitch in a World's Series, and I'd like to work in the series, if only for a few innings."

Then Ehmke flexed his arm like a prize fighter and remarked: "I think I've got one more good game left in there."

"So do I," agreed Connie. "Now, you needn't make our last western trip, but stay in the East and catch the Cubs in Philadelphia and New York. See what they like to hit, make notes on them; for I am going to pitch you in the first game."

The night before the first game, it was whispered in the Chicago press room that Mack would pitch Ehmke, the 55-inning pitcher, against Charley Root, McCarthy's top man. The sports writers grinned—it was just Connie trying to confuse Marse Joe. Both of Mack's aces, Grove and Earnshaw, expected to get the call and were surprised that Connie hadn't spoken to either of them.

As the players reached Wrigley Field, and Ehmke left the bench, he must have had doubts that Mack would carry out his September plan. "Is it still me?" he asked.

"Yes, Howard, it still is you."

When it came nearly time for the pitchers to warm up, Earnshaw, of his own accord, started to toss a few pitches to Cy Perkins. Then Ehmke took off his windbreaker to warm up, and there was a little grumbling on the Athletic bench.

"Are you going to let that guy pitch?" Simmons asked Mack, half belligerently.

"Yes, I am, Al," Connie replied quietly.

The great outfielder started to say something, but quickly thought better of it. "Well, if he's your selection, it's all right with me," he said.

Ehmke, warming up for the Athletics, threw the stands, especially the press box, into utter confusion; and Connie—with that twinkle in his eye—thoroughly enjoyed it. "Why, they tell me that Bob Quinn, who then was president of the Red Sox, almost fainted in his box," Mack laughed, relating the incident. In the press stand they were asking: "Has the old man gone screwy, soft in the head or something?"

Probably even Mack could not have suspected the game Ehmke still had tucked away in his arm, for Howard pitched one of the World's Series classics. Before that autumn afternoon was over, Ehmke had established a new World's Series strike-out record of 13. It was an unusually warm day for Chicago in October, and the fans in the center field bleachers were in their shirt sleeves. Pitching side arm from his right hip, Howard kept the ball concealed from the Chicago batsmen and then let the Cubs lose it in that bleacher background. The Cubs got 8 hits to 6 for the A's, but Chicago didn't score until the ninth, when they were helped by Dykes's two-base wild throw.

For six innings Charley Root fought off Ehmke on even terms, but in the seventh inning that broth of a boy from the Eastern Shore, Jimmy Foxx, brought joy to Connie and grief to the Chicago stands by driving a homer into the center-field bleachers. Root retired in the second half, so pinch-hitter Gabby Hartnett might strike out for him, and the A's closed with two runs on Guy Bush in the ninth. A pair of errors by Woodie English, McCarthy's shortstop, set the stage for the Philadelphia tallies and brought a successful outcome to Mack's great pitching gamble.

"I've thought since what people might have said if I had lost that game—with Earnshaw, Grove, and Walberg sitting on my bench," said Connie.

"It's your turn tomorrow, George," Connie said smilingly to Earnshaw, after Ehmke had completed his brilliant first-game victory.

3

The second game, also played in Chicago, was another "lovely day" for Mr. McGillicuddy, even though he had to remove Earnshaw during a Cub rally in the fifth inning. However, between the "Big Moose" and Grove, his successor, the famous pair matched Ehmke's 13 strike-outs of the first game. The A's hit Pat Malone and a company of relief men, Sheriff Blake, Hal Carlson and Art Nehf, with everything—including the kitchen stove. Foxx and Simmons, both of whom hit homers, were especially devastating, driving in seven runs between them. Jimmy started the Athletic scoring parade in the third, when his second round-tripper in two days followed a single by Cochrane and a walk to Simmons.

The final score was Athletics, 9; Cubs, 3. Mack was letting his mind revert back to the series with Chance's Cubs nineteen years before. The two series were running a strange parallel. The score of the first 1929 victory was almost the same as Bender's opening victory of 1910, which was 4 to 1. The second games of both series produced the same score—9 to 3. It boded well for a new Athletic World's Championship.

Immediately after the second game, the clubs caught their special trains for Philadelphia, where the series was resumed, with only one day's intermission, on Friday, October 11. Using his big right-hander, Earnshaw, much as he employed Jack Coombs nineteen years before, Connie came right back with Earnshaw in the third game. "Just take your time, George," he advised. "You had everything in Chicago, but were pitching too fast."

One who had attended an Athletic-Cub World's Series game at Shibe Park in 1910 would have found difficulty recognizing the plant when these clubs tangled in the first Philadelphia game of 1929. Gone were the old left- and right-field spacious bleachers; the covered grandstand now ran around the entire park. Mack and his associates had put in additional improvements costing around a quarter of a million. There were no standees this time in the outfield, and Connie and the Shibe boys also voted against any standing room in the grandstand. When the park was sold, that was that; each of the Philadelphia games of the 1929 series drew exactly the same crowd—29,991. They asked Connie why the club didn't let in nine more and make it an even 30,000.

"Well, we just didn't have nine more seats," he laughed.

The Cubs finally bagged a game, winning the third contest by a score of 3 to 1. Earnshaw again was good, struck out ten men, and gave up only six hits against nine off Guy Bush, his opponent. But the Cubs ganged up on Connie's Moose in the sixth, scoring their three runs on singles by Hornsby and Cuyler, a walk for Bush and a fumble by Dykes.

4

If Connie can chuckle over winning the first game with his mystery pitcher, Ehmke, his face expands into a broad grin when he recalls his Columbus Day victory in the fourth encounter. "Yes, we surely put over a beautiful rally that afternoon," he admits, "and if we hadn't scored those ten runs in the seventh inning, I was prepared to put in the biggest bunch of rookies anyone ever saw at a World's Series game. I had planned to put every substitute on my bench in the game the last two innings."

With the possible exception of the 1908 play-off game, which Frank Chance's club lost to the Giants, the loss of that Columbus Day game—after piling up an 8 to 0 lead for Charley Root, McCarthy's ace—was the most painful defeat in the sixty-eight-year history of the Chicago National League club.

Mack opened the game with old Jack Quinn, the veteran spitballer, who held off Root for three innings. The Cubs reached old Jack for two runs in the fourth, and then shelled him out in the sixth, rolling over five runs as Connie rushed in Walberg and then Rommel. Eddie gave up Chicago's eighth run in the first half of the seventh, and the Philadelphia fans yawned. It looked like the worst Athletic World's Series defeat since Matty beat Andy Coakley, 9 to 0, in 1905.

The Athletics had made only three hits off Root, and there was only a ripple of enthusiasm in the Philadelphia dugout when Simmons opened the A's half of the seventh with a lusty home-run clout to the roof of the left-field stand. "Well, we won't be shut out, anyway," Jimmy Dykes said to Connie, hoping to contribute a little optimism to the general gloom.

However, the homer seemingly touched off a rally, as Foxx, Bing Miller, and Dykes each paddled out singles, bringing in a second run. As Boley started for the plate, Connie began to take a real interest in the rally. "I think that fellow has lost his stuff," he said. "Swing at the first good one you see, Joe, and hit it."

Boley followed instructions to the letter, and his single fetched in Miller. There was a lull in the rally as George Burns, batting for Rommel, popped to Shortstop English; but, when little Bishop also cracked out a single, scoring Dykes, the entire Athletic bench jumped into action. The Elephants had cut the Chicago lead in half, and still had two runners on base.

McCarthy didn't like the way things were going; he dismissed Root and called in Art Nehf, the former Giant left-hander, to pitch to Mule Haas, a left-handed batter. Mule hit a screeching line drive to center, but a ball which was playable. But Hack Wilson, the Cub center fielder, misjudged it badly. He first started to come in for the ball, then apparently was blinded by the sun and lost the sphere completely. It cleared his head and rolled out to deep center field, as Stephenson ran over from left to retrieve it.

Boley and Bishop scored, and then "the Donk," too, was waved in from third by Coach Eddie Collins. "He's goin' to make it! He's goin' to make it!" yelled the excited Dykes. Then, giving the next player to him on the bench a resounding slap on the back, Jimmy cried: "We're back in the game, gang!"

However, Jimmy didn't smack a fellow player, but the tall lean tactician himself. In the excitement Connie had gotten up and sat next to Dykes. He was leaning forward, watching Mule's slide, and Jimmy's vigorous thump knocked him off the bench and out among the bats. Again it was 1910 all over again.

"I'm sorry, terribly sorry," said Jimmy, reaching out to give his boss a hand.

"It's all right, Jimmy. Everything's all right," said Connie.

"In fact, anything you do is all right. And isn't this a wonderful rally?"

Haas's three-run gift homer reduced the Cub lead to 8 to 7. McCarthy didn't blame Nehf and let him stay in long enough to walk Cochrane. Joe then switched to Sheriff Blake, a right-hander, but in a jiffy Simmons and Foxx—up for the second time—both bumped out singles, and the score was tied at 8 to 8. McCarthy was getting desperate and now called in Pat Malone, who promptly plunked Bing Miller in the ribs, filling the bases.

Here was another laugh! Runs had scored so fast that Jimmy Dykes had lost track of them; he thought the A's still were a run behind and went up to swing from his hip, hoping to bring in what he thought to be the tying run from third with a long fly. He hit a fast ball and pulled it to left. But it went beyond Jim's expectations. Stephenson jumped for the ball, got his fingertips on it, but couldn't hold it; it went for a double, as the joyful Simmons and Foxx streamed over the plate. Malone then struck out Boley and Burns, the pinch-hitter providing two of the putouts of the inning; but the A's now were ahead, 10 to 8.

During the big rally, Connie had called to Grove, "Get yourself ready, Bob." Mose tried to watch the game from the bull pen and warm up at the same time. But when he came in he surely was ready. In the eighth and ninth innings he retired the six Cubs who faced him as fast as they came up, striking out four of them.

5

The amazing fourth-game victory put Connie Mack in the driver's seat, three victories to one, and he needed only one more game to regain the coveted World's Championship. The Athletics gave it to Connie, October 14, with another dramatic victory, again snatching the game right from under the noses of the snarling Cubs; but there was an incident before the game which annoyed and provoked Mack.

President Herbert Hoover came up from Washington to attend the game. As he marched to his box, accompanied by Secret Service men, boos were mixed with the cheers, and there were loud cries of: "Beer! Beer! We want beer!" from the stands. It was the year after the Hoover-Al Smith election, when prohibition was one of the nation's moot questions.

"It was a most regrettable occurrence," said Mack. "And I was sorry any of our Philadelphia fans were guilty of it. I never have been a party man. I vote for the man, not the party; and in my day I have voted for good men of both parties. But every good citizen should show proper respect for the President and his office."

In his fifth game Mack again started Ehmke, but without the element of surprise and the help of that Chicago bleacher Howard wasn't the pitcher he had been in the opener at Wrigley Field. Connie took him out during a Cub rally which netted McCarthy two runs in the fourth. From there on, big Rube Walberg pitched shutout ball; but, as the Athletics had been helpless before Pat Malone for eight innings, it again looked like a Cub victory and a trip back to Chicago for a sixth, and possible seventh, game. Up to the ninth, big Pat had a two-hit shutout in his grasp.

But Connie's 1929 boys just didn't know how to lose. The inning started inauspiciously enough when Walter French, the West Pointer, struck out for Walberg. But Bishop set a new rally into motion with a single to left; and Mule Haas, one of the heroes of the previous game's explosion, set off a new bomb under McCarthy's bench. He sent a beautiful line-drive home run sailing over the right-field wall for a clout which tied the score.

When the cheering on the Athletic bench abated, Connie grinned and remarked to the Donk: "Well, George, they can't say Wilson misjudged that one."

More fireworks were to come for Connie and his fans. Hornsby threw out Cochrane for the second out, but Simmons hit the top of the right-field scoreboard with a dynamic double, the ball bouncing back into the playing field. Had the ball gone to the right or left of the scoreboard, which extended beyond the fence, it would have ended the game then and there. The honor of driving in the winning run was left to Bing Miller. With the count two balls and two strikes, he, too, rifled the ball against the scoreboard, as Simmons, with big loping steps, tore in with the run which made Mack the World's Champion manager again after a period of sixteen years. He also became the first to win four blue ribbons; previously he had been tied with McGraw and Huggins with three.

After the game, Joe McCarthy, the Philadelphia boy, came into the Athletic clubhouse and offered his congratulations.

"You've a great fighting team, Connie," said Joe.

"And I'm glad I don't have to play against your right-handed hitters all season," said Mack.

Despite Connie's dislike for vulgarity and rough stuff in baseball "riding," the two clubs had been pretty crude in their conversation in the early games of the series. The Cubs had some pretty good jockeys in Pat Malone, Guy Bush, Charley Root, Wilson, Hartnett, and Grimm; and the A's—with their Cochrane, Haas, Dykes, and Rommel—weren't exactly baseball sissies. They gave back what they received and tried to add a little interest.

It reached such a point that Judge Landis called the two managers, Mack and McCarthy, to his quarters and said: "If this indecent language doesn't stop, I will fine the players guilty of it a full share. Often it is difficult to tell who is yelling. In that case, I will fine the manager."

Mack called a meeting in his clubhouse and brusquely announced; "From now on, all jockeying is off. I'll not hear another word of it."

Prior to the last game, Cochrane yelled at the silenced Cubs: "After this game, we'll serve tea in the clubhouse."

Mack was afraid this had reached the Commissioner's ears. "Do you want it to cost you money, Mickey?" he asked.

However, when Landis came into the Athletic clubhouse to congratulate the victors, he threw his arms around the happy Cochrane and said: "Now let's have that tea."

Connie escaped from the clubhouse as soon as he could. Rud Rennie, the observing *New York Herald Tribune* baseball writer, followed the grand old leader. Office girls kissed and hugged him as he made his way to his own private office in the tower. He stood for a few minutes like a man in a daze, his fingertips shaking against his hips.

"You must excuse me a minute," he said. "I am afraid I overdid it a bit."

Then he lay down on a low leather couch and pressed his hands against his throbbing temples. Nearing sixty-seven, the excitement of those last two games was beyond anything he had experienced.

6

Topping that new World's Championship came an honor for Connie Mack such as had never heretofore been given to a baseball man. He had gone to Mount Plymouth, Florida, for his winter vacation, prior to the 1930 training at Fort Myers, when in February he made a surprise return to Philadelphia. Sports writers weren't left long in doubt as to the reason for his visit. At a private dinner at the Bellevue-Stratford, he was presented with the Bok award for having rendered greatest service to Philadelphia in 1929. With it went $10,000, a gold medal, a scroll and chest.

The award was endowed by Edward Bok, Philadelphia editor and son-in-law to the late Cyrus Curtis. Prior to giving the award to Mack, the baseball manager-owner, it had gone to learned men who had won distinction in professions and the arts—science, medicine, music, literature. It touched Connie, the former East Brookfield shoe hand, deeply. Editors throughout the country termed it not only a wonderful tribute to Mack, the man, but to all baseball. And Connie was proud that his game was thus honored.

In gaining the award, Mack's sportsmanship and the example he had set for the youth of the land during his fruitful career were big considerations. And the committee also considered the object lesson he gave to elderly men who were buffeted by misfortune. In those fifteen long years he had never quit, and his dauntless courage had carried him back to the top seat in the national game when many men of his age were ready to retire to their carpet slippers and a seat on the front-porch swing.

CHAPTER XXVII

PENNANTS BUT NOT PLENTY

1

FOLLOWING his overwhelming victory in 1929, Connie confidently expected to repeat in 1930. "I knew I had another good club and would have been disappointed if we hadn't won again," is the way he put it. However, even though Connie had a comfortable eight-game margin over the second-place Washington club, led by Walter Johnson, the Senators gave him a few restless afternoons during the season.

Al Simmons proved an awfully tough man to sign that spring, and Connie didn't get the big Pole's signature on a contract until the morning of the opening game, when a crowd of 34,000 overflowed Shibe Park to see the A's, with Grove in the box, defeat the Yankees, 6 to 2. Simmons, playing in his first opening game since 1927, helped seal the compact by blistering George Pipgras for a lusty home run.

But Washington proved a tough nut to crack in the early part of the season. After George Walberg blanked the Senators, 9 to 0, in the first spring game between the two contenders, Washington won the next seven games. It annoyed Mack. "What's the matter with you fellows whenever you play Washington?" he asked. "You look like a bunch of old women."

After a mediocre May, the A's had a good June, winning 21 games out of 30; but they were trailing the Senators by 4½ games when Washington came to town for the Decoration Day series. Griffith's club was hot, and the Old Fox had Manager Johnson send Pitchers Ad Liska and Bump Hadley 48 hours ahead to rest up for the holiday games. It was an unforgettable Memorial Day holiday for Mack—also for Simmons. Clubs then still played morning and afternoon holiday games, and with Grove shellacked pretty hard, the Athletics trailed, 6 to 3, when Simmons came up in the ninth with two A's on, and two out. In three times up, Al hadn't hit anything that looked like a dangerous foul. Dykes rode him from the bench as Al went to bat; the crowd also climbed on the big slugger. "Put in a pinch-hitter, Connie; Al ain't awake yet," some taunted. Simmons was mad all the way through; he knocked the ball out of the park, tying the score.

In the thirteenth, Simmons led off with a double and reached third as Dykes beat a slow hopper down the base line. Simmons rounded the base and then had to scamper hastily back to third. As he did so, he felt something pop in his knee, and, standing on the bag, he could feel the knee swelling under his uniform. As Boob McNair singled, Simmons limped painfully home with the run which won for the Athletics, 7 to 6.

Mack followed Simmons into the clubhouse. "What is it, Al?" he asked.

"I don't know, but the knee don't feel right," the slugger replied.

Simmons pulled off his long knickers and stockings, and Connie saw that the knee already had swollen to twice its normal size. He called up Dr. Carnett, the club physician, asking whether he could come right over. "Simmons has an awfully bad-looking leg," Connie told the doctor.

"Simmons has a broken blood vessel and will need a little rest," said Carnett, after giving the knee an examination.

"Do you want to take him to the hospital?" asked Mack.

"Maybe later, but not now," Dr. Carnett said. "I've come to see your second game. You can let him get in uniform and sit on the bench. He is not to play, as he can't run, but I guess he can pinch-hit if you need him. Come to think of it, when the spot comes up, I order it. I'll tend to the knee later."

With Earnshaw opposing Hadley, it was a free-swinging, free-scoring game. By the time the A's came up for their fourth inning, Washington was ahead by a score of 7 to 4. Three Athletics were on base, when it came the turn of young Harris, Al's fill-in in left field, to bat. Mack looked at Al, and Al at him.

"I guess this is the spot the doctor ordered," said Connie. "See whether you can walk around the bases."

Simmons saw to it that he walked around; he belted a homer into the left-field stands, and the A's went ahead, 8 to 7. At the finish they led, 14 to 11, with Simmons' four-run pinch homer the margin of victory.

That double win broke Washington's spell, and, though Mack suffered through a five-game losing spell in June, his boys followed it with a ten-game winning streak. On July 13 they pushed Washington out of first place, and never let go after that date.

If a 14-to-11 game over the Senators helped the A's slay their Washington jinx, a 14-to-10 victory over the White Sox in Chicago, September 18, was the last spike nailed into Connie's eighth pennant. It was a freak ball game, with the Sox tearing into Earnshaw for five runs in the first inning. But the A's had a twenty-hit day, and enjoyed five-run innings in each of the fourth and seventh. Simmons hit a homer and three singles; and Grove, last man in a parade of pitchers, was credited with the pennant-clinching game.

The season closed less than a fortnight later, with Al Simmons nosing out the Yankees' Lou Gehrig for the batting crown, .381 to .379, on the last day of the season. Despite Connie's many great players through the years, Simmons was his first batting champion since Nap Lajoie hit that .401 for him at old Columbia Park in 1901, Mack's first year in Philly.

Speaking of those days, Simmons said: "I was a fighting, snarling player on the field. I am proud, not ashamed, of that reputation. I played to win; so did Dykes, Cochrane, Grove, Earnshaw, Mule, Foxx, and the rest of that crowd. We were champions, and we battled just as the Yankees did for so many years, and as the Cardinals have done in the National League. Connie held a bridle on us if anybody got too tough, but he wanted us to fight. There was a spirit in those later-day Mack champions that I've never seen on any other club of which I was a member."

© *American League Service Bureau*

JIMMY DYKES

Home town boy who made good.

© *American League Service Bureau*

GEORGE EARNSHAW

"What a pitcher he was against the Cardinals!"—Connie Mack.

© Charles M. Conlon

YOUTHFUL ATHLETICS BATTERY WHO STOLE SHOW IN 1913 WORLD'S SERIES

Catcher Wally Schang (*left*)—Pitcher Joe Bush (*right*).

2

Connie anticipated trouble from the Cardinals in the 1930 World's Series, and got it. "We're a good club, even a great club," he told his players in a clubhouse talk, shortly before the series. "But those hot clubs can be awfully tough. Eddie [Collins] can tell you what the Braves did to us in 1914."

And Gabby Street's St. Louis Redbirds were really red hot, having won 39 out of their last 49 league games for a percentage of .796, finishing ahead of strong Cub, Giant, and Brooklyn clubs.

For a good part of the 1930 season, Robinson's Brooklyn club led the National League, but the unhappy Dodgers toppled from first place to fourth in the last ten days of the race.

"For weeks it looked as though we would play Brooklyn in the World's Series," said Connie, "and I was looking forward to it. I always had an affection for Wilbert Robinson, and I believe he had a good opinion of me. It would have been nice to have played him in the series." And then, with a sly smile, he added: "I think Brooklyn would have been less troublesome than Gabby Street's team."

Gabby Street was the same fellow who caught for the American League All-Stars in 1910 and 1911, who helped tune up Mack's team for the successful World's Series of those years.

Mack won the series from Gabby, four games to two. It was his fifth and last world's pennant, but put him out in a class by himself, though the mark since has been passed by his old hero-worshiper, Joe McCarthy. The hitting in the 1930 series was very light; the winning A's hit only .197, against .200 for the Cardinals. "But we had a lot of long hits and wasted mighty few, and I had Grove and Earnshaw," said Connie. Each of the illustrious pitching pair won two games. Grove also was charged with a defeat; the other "A" reverse went to Walberg.

Despite those shouts of "Beer" in the last game of the 1929 World's Series, President Hoover came up from Washington for the first game at Shibe Park, October 1. He sat in a box near the Athletic dugout and threw out the first ball. "It is a pleasure, Mr. President, having you with us again," said Mack, shaking the Chief Executive's hand. "You know you brought us luck when we beat Pat Malone in the fifth game last year."

Connie's remark that his team made its hits count was amply borne out in the first game. The Athletics got only five off the veteran spitballer, Burleigh Grimes, while the Cardinals made nine off Grove; but the Philadelphians won, 5 to 2. Each of the five Athletic blows was an extra-base hit and converted into a run. Cochrane and Simmons hit home runs, Foxx and Haas triples, and Dykes a double.

The next day it was Earnshaw's turn to weave his magic over the St. Louis batsmen. Connie had an enjoyable afternoon as the A's scored runs in pairs—in each of the first, third, and fourth innings. With the kind of ball the Big Moose was heaving, Mack could sit back, rest, and relax. His team again scored almost a run per hit, winning 6 to 1 with the aid of only seven hits.

After a one-day break in the schedule, the series was resumed in St. Louis, October 4. Back on their own Sportsman's Park, the Cardinals braced and tied up the series by winning the third and fourth games, 5 to 0 and 3 to 1. Wild Bill Hallahan, Street's game left-hander, pitched the shutout against Walberg, Shores, and Quinn; and old Jesse Haines defeated Grove. The latter contest again was a game of few hits; the Athletics making only four and the Cardinals five. An error by Dykes cost his roommate, Grove, the game in the fourth inning. With two out, Hafey doubled, and Blades grounded to the third baseman. Hafey was near Jimmy when he fielded the ball; he might have tagged Chick, but elected to make the sure play at first, but his peg was low and eluded Foxx. It paved the way for two St. Louis runs. Grove was so burned up that only one other Cardinal reached base the rest of the game.

Connie was disturbed. In the two games in which his club won, his team had made only twelve hits, and now they had scored only one run in two defeats. That wasn't the kind of hitting he had been looking at all season. What's more, he was to see many more goose eggs stacked on the scoreboard as Earnshaw dueled with Grimes in another grim battle. It was one of the historic ball games of St. Louis, and both Connie and Street realized the fifth-game winner in all probability would win the series.

For seven innings neither side even threatened to score as Earnshaw and Grimes bore down on every pitch, and the crowd held breathlessly to their seats. In the eighth inning, with one man out, Connie suddenly changed his tactics. "Let's try bunting on this fellow," he said, "See whether you can lay one down, George," he added to Haas.

The Donk followed instructions, laid one down, and beat it out. Mack flashed the signal to Collins for Haas to go down to second on the first pitch. Jimmy Wilson's good peg would have shot Haas down, but Frisch spilled the throw, and the Mule was safe. Boley also left the bench with orders to bunt. The ball squirted by Burleigh, but he picked it up belatedly and threw to third in a vain effort to get Haas. Runners now were on third and first with only one out.

It was Earnshaw's turn at bat; he had given up only two hits, but perhaps the fall afternoon in 1913 when he failed to lift Plank for a pinch-hitter popped into Connie's mind. This time he didn't hesitate. "Grab a bat and hit for George," he said to Jim Moore, a young outfielder who had hit .303 that season. Grimes declined to give Moore anything good to hit; he walked the young pinch-hitter, filling the bases.

It brought up the top of the line-up, and the failure to let Moore hit upset Mack's strategy. He thought Jim would have been good at least for a long fly. "Shall I try to wait him out?" asked Bishop, the lead-off man. Burleigh had given only two walks up to this time. "No, he's got too good control; hit anything good you see," instructed Connie.

Bishop then hit straight down to Bottomley, and Sunny Jim's throw to the plate forced Haas. The St. Louis crowd yelled as their anxiety was partly relieved. Then Dykes rolled to Gelbert for the third out. Connie felt a sore sense of disappointment; his hatband was wet with nervous sweat, as he felt his club had blown its great scoring chance.

As soon as he sent Moore to bat for Earnshaw, Grove had gone to the bull pen, even though he had pitched the day before. Frisch hit him for a single with two out, when Mose quickly fanned Jim Bottomley.

Then came the dramatic ninth inning, one of the most thrilling frames of Mack's career. Cochrane, first up, worked Grimes for a pass; but the crowd whooped when big Simmons raised a gentle fly to Shortstop Gelbert. And then curtains for St. Louis fans and pandemonium on the Athletic bench! Jimmy Foxx got his sturdy East Shore shoulders behind a swing, and there was no doubt where the ball was headed from the moment it left Jim's bat. It landed far up in the left-field bleachers. The collective stomachs of that 38,844 crowd sagged with the hit; it was so quiet Mack could hear the footfalls of Cochrane and Foxx as they jogged around the bases.

"A very nice hit, Jimmy; a very nice hit," beamed Connie. This time no one shoved him off his own bench.

Grove quickly blotted out the side in the Cardinal half, and the excited, jubilant A's dashed off to their Special, which whisked them back to Philadelphia. The players were in such gay spirits that Connie had to warn some of them the series wasn't over. But the players replied: "That was it! Jimmy's clout was it! There won't be much fight left in those Cardinals when we get them back in Shibe Park."

The players had it figured out correctly. The sixth game was anticlimax, with Earnshaw pitching his third game and winning easily, 7 to 1. Mack, of course, had the same hunch—that the sixth game would prove easy; but he couldn't pass it to his players. He always has warned his teams of the danger of overconfidence. Oddly enough, the Athletics closed as they started the series. Connie saw his men make only seven hits, but again each was for extra bases and good for a run. Dykes and Simmons slammed homers; Miller hit two doubles; and Dykes, Foxx, and Cochrane each one.

"Earnshaw really was wonderful in that series," said Connie. "No one ever gave me greater pitching; the Cardinals made only thirteen hits and scored two runs off George in twenty-five innings."

3

Connie Mack won his third straight pennant and the ninth of his career in 1931. It put him only one under John McGraw, his great National League rival. And he won his greatest victory total, 107, and his highest percentage, .704. It proved another easy flag to win. The A's stumbled through April but went into high in May, when they won 23 out of 27 games for an .852 gait and soon outdistanced New York and Washington.

At the finish Connie topped McCarthy, the new Yankee manager in second place, by 13½ games.

One-sided races were proving a problem for Mack and Tom Shibe, just as the earlier runaways were financial headaches for Ben Shibe and Mack in the Collins-Barry days. Baseball thrives on keen competition, and the profits are made when two or more teams are all snarled up in a hot August and September finish. With his three-time champions winning by margins of 18, 8, and 13½ games, there wasn't much left of the race by Labor Day, and it was just a case of Mack playing out the schedule. The pay roll had zoomed higher and higher. Simmons had a new three-year contract calling for $100,000, or $33,333 a season; Grove and Cochrane were up to $20,000, with other stars not far behind them. The great depression which started with the stock market crash of 1929 was eating deeper and deeper into the national income. Many of Mack's most faithful fans, employed in Philadelphia's numerous factories, already were out of work or on part time. Connie and Tom Shibe wrinkled their brows when they compared their high payroll with the lean gate receipts. Some 3,000 more seats had been added to Shibe Park in another expensive remodeling project.

It was Grove's phenomenal year, 31 victories and only 4 defeats for the fabulous percentage of .886. Earnshaw and Walberg remained up with the league leaders with 21 to 7 and 20 to 12, respectively; while a pitching newcomer, Leroy Mahaffey, hung up a 15-to-4 record. Waite Hoyt, the former Yankee ace, was acquired from Detroit in midseason.

At the start of the season, Connie had said to Simmons: "A man never is a real champion unless he repeats." Al took Connie at his word; and, though he missed a number of games with swollen ankles, he presented his manager with his second successive batting championship, hitting .390. Cochrane hit .349, and Haas .323; Foxx slumped to .291 but lashed out 30 homers. Boley suffered a good part of the season from injuries; and two able Dixie kids, Eric McNair and Dibrell Williams, vied with each other for the shortstop vacancy.

Connie also came up with another fine young outfield prospect in Roger Cramer; he was a fielding fool like Haas and showed signs of becoming a star hitter. Cramer was a Beach

Haven, New Jersey, carpenter and semipro pitcher; Cy Perkins found him on a Sunday outing to the Jersey coast when he was invited to umpire a game.

Grove's great pitching record produced its share of excitement—and explosions—for Mack and Grove's fellow inmates of the Athletic clubhouse. In the spring, following a ten-game winning streak, the great southpaw lost a tough game as a relief pitcher at Shibe Park. Fonseca's two-run homer in the twelfth beat him. Mose tore up things in the clubhouse, raised hell in general, and then got in his big car and drove to his home at Lonaconing, Maryland.

Three days later, he was back and sat rather demurely on the Athletic bench. Connie had taken no notice of his absence, and when Grove started to get up to warm up, Mack remarked: "Oh, you want to pitch for us again."

Grove pitched the game, won it handily from the Tigers, and then went on to his sensational winning streak of 16 straight, tying the American League record of Walter Johnson and Joe Wood in 1912. Grove went for a new record in the first game of a Sunday double-header in St. Louis, August 23; and Connie, of course, rooted hard for his great competitor. The game was tragedy for Mose; he lost it, 1 to 0, to Dick Coffman, with a mediocre record; and the only St. Louis run came when Jim Moore, substituting for Simmons, horribly misjudged a line drive by Oscar Melillo, and the ball cleared Jim's head for a double.

Grove had another brainstorm in the clubhouse as he ripped up his uniform, threw around his glove, his shoes, and the furniture, while the hapless Moore tried to keep away from his wrath. Then, to add to Mose's cup of woe, in the second game the A's bashed out 17 hits, scored as they pleased, and won for Waite Hoyt, 10 to 0.

Simmons and Dykes also irked Connie by bickering one day. Jimmy thought Aloysius was slow in retrieving a ball. He didn't say anything to Simmons, but gave him a pained look when the pair came in to the bench. Neither spoke, but both sat glaring at each other. As Simmons's batting turn came around, Al was slow in leaving the bench. "All right, Pollock, don't take all day; get up there and hit," growled Dykes. Al replied in kind.

Connie had heard enough and said: "Shut your mouths."

Dykes added a few more words, when Mack turned on him sharply and repeated: "Dykes, I said shut your damn mouth."

As Dykes and Simmons walked out to their positions as the Athletics again took the field, the flare-up was forgotten; they were grinning and saying to each other: "Wasn't the old gentleman mad? Didn't we get him hot?" And, on the bench, Connie read their thoughts. "I know exactly what they are saying," he said to the players sitting next to him. "They are saying: "Didn't we get the old man sore, and wasn't he hot?"

In his disciplinary measures, Connie often was quite subtle. Max Bishop, his second baseman, was a little guy with a big appetite. In a game at Yankee Stadium Max smashed out a hit to deep right center—it looked like a sure triple—but Bishop was nailed at third, breaking up a rally.

At breakfast the next morning Connie paused a moment at the table where Bishop was seated. In front of the second-sacker was a plate of wheatcakes almost as high as Max's head. "Max, if you hit a triple today, I think you had better stop at second," said his manager.

And once, when Cochrane was thrown out at first base, he remarked: "What's the matter, Mickey; a little tired today?" The catcher was so sore that in his next time at bat he hit the longest home run of his career.

4

The Cardinals again were Mack's World's Series opponents in 1931. This time there was no uncertainty as to who the Athletics would play, as Gabby Street won his pennant as easily in the National League as did Connie in the American. The Athletic chieftain had a chance to be the first manager to win three straight World's Championships. He had twice bunched two—in 1910 and 1911 and 1929 and 1930. Chance had won two with the Cubs in 1907-8, Carrigan with the Red Sox in 1915-16; McGraw with the Giants in 1921-22; and Huggins with the Yankees in 1927-28. But three straight had eluded all of these great leaders. It was a mark within Connie's grasp and, approaching his sixty-ninth milestone, he was keen for this new distinction.

However, the honor eluded him also. A wild-running Pepper Martin, who won national fame as "the Wild Horse of the Osage," galloped madly through the series and proved as much of a nuisance for Mack as did the redheaded Brave catcher, Hank Gowdy, in 1914. For five games the A's just couldn't get Pepper out. Though he went hitless in the last two games, Pepper closed with an average of .500 and stole five bases on the annoyed Cochrane. Largely through Martin's efforts, and aided by some great pitching by Bill Hallahan and Burleigh Grimes, the Cardinals pulled out the series in seven games. It was the only one of Mack's eight series to go to a deciding game.

The series opened in St. Louis, October 1, and Connie was pleased when Grove, his 31-game winner, defeated Street's sensational freshman, Paul Derringer, by a 6-to-2 score. Grove didn't really pitch his game. The Redbirds jumped on Lefty for two runs in the first inning and straightened out his left-handed fire ball for twelve hits. And Pepper Martin served notice on Connie that he was going to play rough by lacing Mose for a double and two singles and stealing a base. However, the A's ganged up on young Paul for four runs in the third inning, and Simmons hit the big Kentuckian for a mighty homer with Cochrane on base in the seventh.

Mack knew it was going to be a tough series when the Cardinals tied it up in the second game by downing Earnshaw, their 1930 jinx, as Bill Hallahan, the left-hander, pitched a three-hit shutout. Martin had another great day and had become a pain which extended the full length of Connie's long neck. "Can't anyone stop that fellow?" he asked impatiently. "What's he hitting?" "Everything I am throwing him," replied Earnshaw.

In the second inning Martin hit to left; big Al didn't pick the ball up cleanly, and the Wild Horse slid safely into second ahead of Simmons' throw. Then Martin stole third, as Wilson bluffed a sacrifice bunt, and Pepper came in on Wilson's fly. In the seventh Pepper stole his way around again. He singled, stole second, took third on an out, and scored on a squeeze play as Gelbert bunted safely to Earnshaw's left. The Moose tried for a play at the plate, but his throw was a little high, and Pepper slid in under the angry, frustrated Cochrane.

There was a wild scene in the ninth inning, when quick-witted action by Eddie Collins almost snatched victory from the jaws of defeat. Wild Bill had a flurry of wildness and walked Foxx and Dykes, Miller flying out between the two passes. Young Dib Williams struck out, and Connie called on Jim Moore to hit for Earnshaw. Moore also fanned, for what should have been the last out; but Wilson, picking the third strike out of the dirt, foolishly threw the ball down to Third Baseman Jake Flowers. And Jake, thinking the game was over, started to walk off the field, as did some of the other Redbirds. In the meantime, Moore still was standing at the plate.

"Run! Run! What are you standing there for? Run!" Connie yelled from the bench, but in the noise of the crowd he could not be heard. But Collins was going through all kinds of gyrations in the third-base coacher's box and finally prevailed on Moore to run to first, with the Cardinals making no play on him. There was wild commotion, with the fans not knowing exactly what had happened. Finally Nallin, the plate umpire, called Moore safe at first and ordered the game resumed. Connie thought it might be a break, but Hallahan refused to fluster; he returned to the mound and retired Bishop on a foul to Bottomley.

5

With the scene shifting to Philadelphia, the Cardinals also won the third game, 5 to 2. They continued their hammering of Grove, while Simmons spoiled Grimes's one-hit shutout by homering with two out in the ninth and McNair, running for Cochrane, on base. Again the Wild Horse had a busy afternoon, hitting a double and single and scoring two runs.

"You've got to put us back in this, George," Connie said earnestly to Earnshaw before the fourth game. George did, pitching another beautiful game, winning 3 to 0 as he held the Cardinals to two hits, both going to the irrepressible Martin.

With the series tied at two victories apiece, Mack tried Waite Hoyt, with a background of six Yankee World's Series victories; but again it was too much Martin. The Cardinals won

5 to 1, as ol' Pepper drove in four of St. Louis' runs with a homer and two singles. By this time the colorful Oklahoman was hitting .667.

There were recriminations and bickerings in Mack's usually harmonious club. Cochrane was having a bad series; not only was Martin running wild on him, but Mickey was having a difficult time at bat. Some of the pitchers felt he wasn't supporting them properly, and Cochrane felt Grove and Earnshaw weren't holding the runners—especially Martin—to their bases. Cochrane, a born fighter—who loved to win, fretted over his showing, and his eyes were bloodshot from loss of sleep. And George Earnshaw poured salt in Mickey's wounds with a suggestion that young Joe Palmisano, rookie second-string catcher, catch him in his next game. Connie paid no attention to it, but it burned Cochrane up. Some of the Athletics also were deep in a falling stock market which hit new bottoms while the series was being played, and margin calls delivered by telegram to the Athletic clubroom and bench did not help the morale of Mack's players.

Following Hoyt's defeat, there was another one-day break in the schedule, as the clubs made the jaunt to St. Louis to end the series. President John Shibe didn't make the trip, as he was slightly ill, and his physician forbade the trip. However, Mrs. Shibe accompanied the expedition. Of the other Athletic wives, only Mrs. Mack and Mrs. Eddie Collins were in at the finish. Connie chatted freely with the players on the Special as it lapped up the miles roaring through Indiana and Illinois. "We've got nothing to alarm us," he said in his most encouraging tones. "We have Lefty and George to throw against them in St. Louis, and they won't need much hitting to win. Somebody is sure to break out again in their park, as Jimmy [Foxx] did when we beat Grimes last year."

The boys broke out all right in the sixth game and easily tied the series at 3 to 3 when Grove pitched his best game of the set, a five-hitter, as he won 8 to 1. And for the first time in the series Pepper was held hitless. Things definitely were looking up! Street again pitched young Derringer, and for the second time in the series the A's sailed into him for a fat four-run inning. And, for good measure, the Mackmen

© *Sporting News*

CONNIE WITH TWO OF HIS GREAT BATTERY CHAMPIONS

Mickey Cochrane (*left*). Lefty Grove (*right*).

© *Charles M. Conlon*

EDDIE COLLINS

Second base wizard and coach of later Athletics champions.

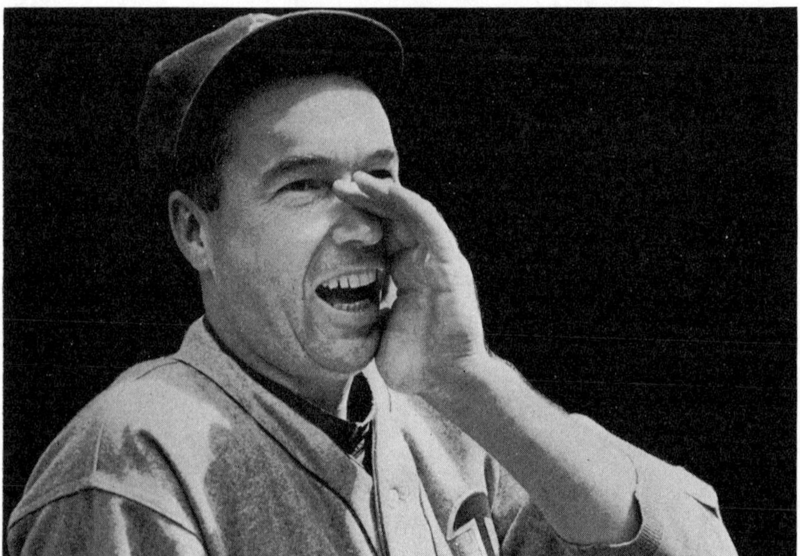

© *Sporting News*

GEORGE "MULE" HAAS

Connie: "George, you said all there is to say. You now hold the championship."

hung a second "4" on the scoreboard at Sylvester Johnson's expense in the seventh.

Connie felt pretty good on the morning of the seventh game as he talked over plans for the contest with his coaches, his son Earle, and Eddie Collins. "Today is the first time I've ever been in the seventh game of a World's Series," he remarked, "but I think George will make everything all right."

All St. Louis feared the worst. Cardinal fans had a wholesome respect for George Earnshaw, who had been poison to the Redbirds for two autumns. The crowd dropped from 39,041 for the sixth game to a mere 20,805 for the seventh. And those who filed into the park looked as though they were preparing to attend a wake. The Athletics were 8-to-5 favorites to win, so impressed was everyone with Earnshaw's magic.

Yet, despite the fact that Earnshaw pitched a magnificent game, he went down to defeat, 4 to 2; and after it was over Connie had to shoulder his way through the crowd to the Cardinal clubhouse, where he returned Gabby Street's congratulations of the previous October. But that seventh game defeat wasn't an easy pill to swallow; it was one of the most bitter of Connie's long career. "It was mighty hard sitting on the bench and looking at George lose that game," he said. "The Cardinals made only one real hit off him in the seven innings he pitched. He never had more stuff than he did that day."

Connie's Irish grandmother would have said that leprechauns, or the "bad little people," were after him or Earnshaw that day. Maybe no one left any milk outside the Chase Hotel for the little gnomes. For three innings every conceivable piece of luck befell Cornelius and George, and all of it was bad. After Grimes retired the Athletics in the first, High opened for St. Louis with a pop fly in back of third. It was out of Williams', reach, but too far in for Simmons. Watkins followed with an almost identical hit. Two little punk flies which should have been easy outs, and the Cardinals had two men on with none out. "Goodness gracious, can't anyone catch those things?" Mack exclaimed. Frisch advanced the Redbird pair with a sacrifice, and High scored when a wild pitch squirted out of Cochrane's glove, Watkins going to third. Martin walked and stole second. Then Orsatti fanned, but Cochrane dropped the third strike, and Mickey had to throw him out at first. Watkins dashed in from third when Foxx returned the ball poorly to the plate. Then George struck out Bottomley.

There was more trouble for the Moose in the third, when High skipped a single just barely out of Bishop's reach. Max tried for it but couldn't quite subdue it. Then Watkins hit to the right-field pavilion roof for a home run, the only real hit off Earnshaw, the happy High jogging in ahead of him. From then on, the unlucky Earnshaw retired fifteen Cardinals in order until Mack sent Phil Todt to bat for him in the eighth inning.

Connie did get a parting thrill out of the game in the ninth, but it flickered out entirely too soon. In a last desperate rally, the A's threw quite a scare into Street and St. Louis' faithful 20,000. Grimes's spitter had mowed down the A's for eight innings, but, for the second time in the series, Burleigh blew a low-hit shutout with two out in the ninth.

Simmons opened the Athletics' ninth with a walk. Foxx fouled out, and Miller forced Al. The jig seemed up, but Dykes walked, and Williams arched a single over High's head, something akin to Andy's own hit in the first. That filled the bases; and Roger Cramer, batting for Walberg, Earnshaw's successor, whistled a single to center; and Miller and Dykes scored. Two runs in, and the tying runs on base! Bats flew into the air, and there were other high jinks on the Athletic bench—even Connie was yelling. Street realized thirty-nine-year-old Grimes had tired and called in Hallahan. As in the second game, Old Man Opportunity again knocked at Bishop's door, but found the Bishop out. Max hit a loping liner, and for a few moments it looked as though it might fall safe; but quite appropriately Martin, the hero of the series, snared it on a dead run and dashed happily into his clubhouse.

Immediately after the last game, Al Simmons, Grove, and Cochrane, along with Captain Frank Frisch of the victorious Cardinals, flew with Herb Hunter and the author to San Francisco, the first hop of an All-Star baseball jaunt to Japan and the Far East.

As Connie shook hands and bade good-by to his stars, he said to Cochrane: "The series is over, Mickey; now forget about it. We all worked hard and did our best." He knew Mickey's nerves were badly wrought, but figured the ocean trip would put his great catcher back on his feet. And, the spirit of adventure coming over him, he decided the next time there was an oriental baseball junket, he would go along.

CHAPTER XXVIII

GOING DOWN!

1

IF IT took Connie Mack eight years to make the trip from the bottom to the top from 1921 to 1929, it required only half that long after the 1931 season for him to toboggan down to the basement again. There is an erroneous belief that Mack started to break up his second great team immediately after Pepper Martin derailed his Athletic Express in the 1931 World's Series. Mack tried, to the very best of his ability, to make it four straight in 1932. No stars were sold, and he even paid a pretty price for Tony Freitas, crack Coast League southpaw, to bolster his pitching staff; and the pony left-hander paid a little dividend, winning a dozen games while losing five.

However, Joe McCarthy was putting his genius to work in New York, and Marse Joseph matched the 107 victories Connie had won in 1931. Mack again had a club which could have won 7 races out of ten; but with 94 victories he couldn't even make it close for the new Yankee champions. After three rich World's Series pots, his players had to be satisfied with runner-up money.

The kick of Connie's 1932 campaign was the great battle waged by Jimmy Foxx, his larruping first baseman, to match or excell Babe Ruth's home-run mark of 60. The strong-shouldered Marylander was as hot as a firecracker from April on; he hit .364, losing the batting championship to Dale Alexander by three points; drove in 169 runs for Connie, while his extra-base harvest included 33 doubles, 9 triples, and 58 homers. After the pennant race was lost, Mack and all the team rooted hard for Jim to bat Ruth's record out of the book. Foxx probably would have succeeded if they hadn't selected just that year to put a screen in front of the right-field pavilion in St. Louis. Foxx hit that screen five times in 1932. The Babe had had an open St. Louis stand to shoot for when he bagged his 60 home runs five years before.

If Foxx was Mack's wonder boy that year, his former king slugger, Simmons, slipped from .390 to .322; and Cochrane, still feeling the reaction from his poor 1931 World's Series, slumped from .349 to .293. Connie felt both those declines in the standing of his clubs. Grove, however, continued to explode his fire ball for baseball's grand old man, winning 25 games out of 35, while he led the league's pitchers in low earned runs and high percentage of victories. Earnshaw and Walberg gave Mack 19 and 17 wins respectively, but young Mahaffey fell back to a 13-to-13 record. Cramer, the new deer in the outfield, hit .336 in 92 games, and young Eric McNair took over at shortstop.

By this time the depression had the nation in the subcellar; it was the season before the bank holiday, and Mack says he had the highest payroll in the game—even higher than that of the Yankees. He talked it over with the Shibes, Tom and John, and they reached the decision that they simply had to cut down the overhead. The elder Comiskey had died in 1931, but his son, Louis, sent out feelers to Mack that he would like to have Simmons. From the time the Black Sox scandal wrecked a great Chicago club in 1920, the Comiskeys hadn't had a first-divison team.

After considerable negotiations, Connie agreed to sell Simmons, Mule Haas, and Jimmy Dykes to the White Sox for $150,000. For one thing, it would lighten the payroll by Simmons' $33,333. The deal was closed September 28, the morning of the opening game of the Yankee-Cub World's Series in New York. Simmons and Haas then both were twenty-nine, Dykes thirty-six. Connie announced the deal with a heavy heart, but again he had no more intention of breaking up his club than he did in 1914 when he sold Eddie Collins to the White Sox. He had immediate and younger replacements for

Haas and Dykes in Cramer and Pinky Higgins. The latter was a sturdy lad Connie plucked off the University of Texas campus in 1929; later Higgins was developed in Dallas and Portland. Lou Finney, Simmons' expected replacement, was with the A's for a spell in 1931; in 1932 with Portland he was voted the most valuable player in the Pacific Coast League. Lou didn't do so well, but later became a valuable player with the Red Sox.

Connie was fond of all the players he let go, especially of Dykes and Simmons. Maybe he recognized Jimmy's managerial possibilities and felt he might develop them in Chicago. If so, the hunch was right, as Dykes became White Sox manager in 1934 and has been in charge ever since. And even though Connie had to caution the Donk, Haas, about his bench-jockeying, he often had enjoyed Mule. In Haas's last season under Mack, the Mule got into quite an argument with Pipgras of the Yankees and called him everything in the book. "George, I don't think there is anything else you can say," said Connie. "I don't think you overlooked a thing. You have the championship. So that will be all for today."

2

Connie slipped back another position in 1933, finishing a poor third with a percentage of .523, while Washington and the Yankees fought it out for the pennant. He had a new batting champ that season in Jimmy Foxx, who hit .356 and clouted 48 homers. Bob Johnson, a half-Indian outfield recruit, showed great promise; Higgins and Cramer, the new regulars, performed credibly; Cochrane was back at .322; and Grove had another fine 24-to-8 season. A former soldier from Georgia, Sugar Cain, flashed a lot of latent stuff on the mound, winning 13 games and losing 12; but two former aces of the Big Three—Earnshaw and Walberg—gave Connie an unhappy summer. They toppled from the heights with a mighty crash. The Moose's fast ball seemed to go out of the window overnight, as he won only 5 games and lost 10; while Walberg just couldn't find the home plate and won 9 while losing 13. It was the collapse of these pitching standbys which hurt Mack far more in 1933 than the loss of Simmons.

A signal honor was conferred on Connie Mack during the season. As part of the Century of Progress Exposition, and inspired by Arch Ward, *Chicago Tribune* sports editor, the American and National League played the first of their midsummer All-Star games in Chicago on July 6, 1933. In a nice display of sentiment the two league presidents, Will Harridge and John Heydler, appointed their outstanding generals, Connie Mack and John McGraw, to manage their respective teams. McGraw had retired to the front office of the Giants the year before and died the following winter. It marked the fourth meeting of McGillicuddy and McGraw in important interleague competition, and Connie prevailed, as he did in 1911 and 1913. Connie enjoyed the game immensely; it was fun to manage for a day when he had that heavy Yankee artillery, Ruth and Gehrig, on his side. Again he had Al Simmons in his outfield and Jimmy Dykes on third. And with Babe cracking out a two-run homer, Dykes getting a pair of hits, and Gomez, Crowder, and his own Grove rolling back the National League sluggers, Connie's team emerged the victor, 4 to 2.

Mack had some more distressing news for Philadelphia fans around the time of the December, 1933, league meetings. Shortly after the season ended, Frank Navin, owner of the Tigers, got permission from Colonel Ruppert to talk to Babe Ruth with the idea of making him his manager. Ruth had a trip planned to Honolulu and told Navin he would see him on his return. Navin got miffed, showed no further interest in Ruth, but called up Connie Mack and asked him whether he would consider a deal for Cochrane if it meant Mickey's promotion to the Tiger management. Connie was interested. With the Athletic treasury still empty, he agreed to accept $100,000 for Cochrane, with Navin throwing in John Pasek, a young catcher, who soon was included in another deal. Mickey, now a lieutenant commander in the Navy, proved a managerial sensation in Detroit, winning league pennants in 1934 and '35 and the World's Championship in the latter year.

Tom Yawkey, young millionaire and a nephew and foster son of William Yawkey, early owner of the Tigers, had purchased the Boston Red Sox the same year. As a prep-school boy the younger Yawkey attended Irving School in Tarrytown, New York, where Eddie Collins' deeds on the diamond and gridiron are part of the school's hallowed traditions. Yawkey once won one of these Eddie Collins annual sports awards, and Collins became his No. 1 sports hero. So it was not surprising that he should want Collins associated with him in his baseball venture, and promptly offered Eddie the job of vice-president and general manager of the Red Sox. In Philadelphia there was a feeling that Mack was grooming Eddie to be his eventual successor, but Connie readily gave his coach and assistant permission to accept the better post in Boston. Lena Blackburne, former White Sox shortstop, who had tipped Mack off to New Jersey players, became Eddie's coaching successor.

Yawkey took over a badly run-down club in Boston. With Eddie doing most of his negotiating, he tried in vain to buy a pennant and did much of his shopping at Mack's Philadelphia store. Connie swung his first big deal with Tom and Cocky shortly after the Cochrane sale, when he gave the Red Sox millionaire Pitchers Bob Grove and Rube Walberg and Second Baseman Max Bishop for $125,000, Boston tossing in Infielder Hal Warstler and Pitcher Bob Kline.

Lefty came up with a lame arm in 1934, the first of his long career. He pitched only 109 innings and won 8 games and lost as many. Connie fretted over Mose's showing. Good sportsman that he is, he told Yawkey he would take the pitcher back and refund his money. Tom, of course, wouldn't hear of it; and Grove's arm happily came back in 1935. He gave Tom seven good years of service and pitched his 300th major-league victory in a Red Sox uniform in 1941. In his last game of that season, he pitched against the Athletics. Later Grove said at a Philadelphia sports writers dinner: "I started in with Connie Mack, and I finished at least in the same ball park with him."

Despite Earnshaw's poor record, the White Sox were willing to gamble on him and paid Connie $20,000 and Catcher Charlie Berry for the Big Moose and Pasek, the catcher who was acquired in the Cochrane deal. Berry, now an American League umpire, came to Mack as a green kid from Lafayette in 1925; he was an All-American football star and was regained by way of Boston and Chicago.

3

The next resting place for Connie on the way down was fifth place in 1934; he slid into the second division as Cochrane lifted the Tigers from fifth to a sensational pennant. This time the A's won only 68 games and lost 82 as they receded to a percentage of .453. Foxx continued to bring Connie some joy as he hit .334 and increased his growing home-run collection by 44. The youngsters Higgins and Cramer blossomed into real stars; Cherokee Bob Johnson hit 34 homers; but from there down, the line-up had little power.

Connie was recruiting almost an entirely new pitching staff. A towering Kentucky mountaineer with the biggest feet in baseball, "Footsie" Johnny Marcum, came from Louisville, and did the best work on the staff, bringing Mack 14 victories while he lost 11 games. Always eager to give an opportunity to former Philadelphia scholastic stars, he engaged two home town right-handers, Bill Dietrich and Joe Cascarella, also a six-foot-four-inch Oklahoman, Al Benton, who later was to win All-Star distinction with the Detroit Tigers.

Following the 1934 season, Connie and Mrs. Mack accompanied a team of American League stars, directed by Babe Ruth, to the Orient. While Connie was Judge Landis' representative and the official head of the party, Babe Ruth did the actual managing. Athletic players predominated on the team—Foxx, Bing Miller, Infielders Warstler and McNair, Pitcher Cascarella, and young rookie Catcher Frankie Hayes. Other stars were Babe Ruth, Lou Gehrig, and Lefty Gomez of the Yankees; Charley Gehringer of Detroit; and Earl Averill of Cleveland. The team played 18 games in Japan, and other contests in Honolulu, Shanghai, and Manila.

"It was a grand trip," said Mack, "and I was glad of the opportunity to make it before the war. They gave us a wonderful reception in Japan; we played to immense crowds, and they surely made a fuss about Ruth and our other players. But you never could tell what was going on behind their smiling faces. The seeds of war already were being sowed at that time. We knew our rooms constantly were being searched and that they shadowed us wherever we went."

Back in 1931, when Grove, Cochrane, and Simmons were on their mission to Japan, Grove highlighted the trip by going in as a relief pitcher and striking out the side in each the eighth and ninth innings on 19 pitched balls, one above the minimum number. They sent Connie a card: "Old Mose still is mowing 'em down."

Connie had a chance to enjoy a similar exhibition when the Yankee Gomez, with his own Foxx catching, struck out 19 of the Nips. "Gomez really had to strike out four in one inning," chuckled Connie. "Jimmy missed a third strike on one of the hitters."

4

It was back to the cellar for the Grand Old Man of the game in 1935. And Connie finished deep in the coalhole with a percentage of .389—61½ games below the Browns. Weak pitching again weighed his club down. Marcum won 17 and lost 13, a surprising record with a tail-ender; but Dietrich, Cain, Benton, and Blaeholder, who came from the Browns, all had mediocre seasons. Foxx continued to slug away, finished third in batting and lashed out 36 home runs. Cramer, Higgins, Johnson played well, and Mack came up with two more promising rookies, Outfielder Wally Moses and Shortstop Skeeter Newsome; but somehow the club never clicked. Dib Williams, who played shortstop in the 1931 season, and Joe Cascarella joined the Athletic colony on the Red Sox in midseason.

In breaking up his first great club, the last to go was First Baseman Stuffy McInnis. Jimmy Foxx also was the last of the great 1929-30-31 champions to leave Shibe Park, and Mack didn't part with the mauling Marylander until he again struck bottom. Tom Yawkey had tried to buy Foxx for several years, and at the 1935 League meetings Mack finally yielded. This time Foxx and Pitcher Marcum went to the Red Sox for $150,000 and a mediocre battery, Pitcher Gordon Rhodes and Catcher George Savino.

Connie had gone down so rapidly since the 1931 World's Series that he was dizzy from the speed of his descent from the top to the bottom. It was an agonizing period. As with most people at that time, his personal investments shrank in value. He even had tried to help out some of his boys when they got their margin calls. And the club, having remodeled its plant just before the crash, was deep in the red.

"Having gone through the heartache of breaking up our earlier championship club, I disliked doing it again, but we had to do it to live. We had incurred obligations of between $700,000 and $800,000 in renovating our park. Our payroll at one time was terrific. We didn't have a man under $10,000 on the club. We operate in an industrial city, where the depression hit especially hard. I do not enjoy managing a tail-end club, but in those troublesome years we were confronted with situations which were beyond our control."

CHAPTER XXIX

RIDING THE BUMPS AGAIN

1

IN INTRODUCING Connie Mack at a dinner, the toastmaster spoke eloquently of the man who had won nine American League championships and five World's Series. When Connie got on his feet, he said quite humbly: "The gentleman who introduced me spoke of my pennants, but didn't say anything about my tail-enders. I had a lot of them, too."

Of course, a man who has managed in forty-four American League races, and is preparing to take his team into a forty-fifth, had to take a lot of sour with his sweets. It was mostly sour in the standing of the clubs after 1935, but there were sweets to compensate it as the nation showed greater and greater love, affection, and admiration for Philadelphia's Grand Old Man of Baseball. And the Quaker City fans were wonderfully loyal, coming out whenever Connie gave them anything at all to root about. Philadelphia and Pittsburgh by this time were the last big-league cities to get Sunday ball. From the start, Sunday games at Shibe Park were popular and well attended; it helped the club get back on its financial feet. Lights were put in at Shibe Park in 1939, and night games drew well—even with Connie in the basement. The Phillies became tenants at Shibe Park in 1938, which cut down the plant's overhead. And at no time did Connie become discouraged, as he dreamed and talked of building up "just one more winner."

He spent a lot of money and came up with good players, too;

but he couldn't whip them into winning combinations. Prior to the war, the American League was full of pitchers who got away from Mack—Potter and Caster of the Browns, Eddie Smith, Dietrich and Ross of the White Sox, Al Benton of the Tigers, and Chubby Dean of Cleveland—a pretty formidable staff. Some didn't fit into Connie's scheme of things—Dietrich had a few explosions of temperament; with others there was a little difficulty in the matter of discipline. As Mack grew older, he had less patience in humoring players as he did when he had his great battery of Waddell and Schreck. As Earle put it, Dad talked to a young player a few times like a Dutch uncle. If he paid no heed, he soon was wearing the uniform of another club.

However, it again was a period of bumping the bumps. From 1935 to 1943, inclusive, Connie again had seven tail-enders. Only twice in that period, 1937 and 1939, did he rise as high as seventh. In those two years Mack managed to beat out two Brown misfits. On September 13, 1936, Connie, who saw Waddell strike out 16 of his 1908 Athletics, was treated to another whiffing spectacle with his A's the goats. Young Bobbie Feller, then not quite eighteen, tied Dizzy Dean's strike-out record of 17 at the expense of Mack's tail-ender, a mark which Bobbie subsequently raised another notch.

Around the time the nation entered World War II, Mack thought he was really making progress and had a club which might suddenly find itself overnight. Ty Cobb had strongly recommended Sam Chapman, an all-around athlete at the University of California. Connie had to outbid a number of wealthy clubs to get Sam, but the collegian was worth it. He was Mack's outstanding player in 1941, hitting .322, smacking 25 home runs and driving in 106 runs, when he went into naval aviation.

Mack also went high to get Second Baseman Benny McCoy, a former Detroit substitute infielder and farmhand, and a player Mack expected to develop into his greatest second baseman since Eddie Collins. In December, 1939, he traded Outfielder Wally Moses to the Tigers for McCoy and Pitcher George Coffman, a younger brother of the fellow who stopped Bob Grove's 16-game streak in 1931. Later in the winter Judge Landis called off the deal and made free agents of a number of young Detroit players, including McCoy, for alleged "cover-up" shenanigans while they were in the minors.

It threw young McCoy on the open market, and he could "sell" himself to the highest bidder. Mack's leading competitor was Larry MacPhail, then of Brooklyn, but Connie raised the ante to a $45,000 bonus for the young second baseman and a two-year contract at $10,000 a season. McCoy suffered from being too much in the spotlight in 1940, but started to show in 1941, when he joined the Navy after Pearl Harbor.

A Philadelphia-born shortstop of Italian ancestry, Al Brancato, promised to develop into another Jack Barry. He was a spectacular fielder, and, though he didn't appear high in the batting averages, like Black Jack of Holy Cross, he could raise a lot of havoc with a .234 percentage. He, too, put on Navy blue after 1941.

Mack also signed Eddie Collins' son, Eddie, Jr., who was a fair outfield prospect before he went into service. Unlike his dad, Eddie, Jr., went to Yale instead of Columbia and could play the outfield without endangering his head. In a pretty baseball romance, Junior married Herb Pennock's daughter, Janet, and there now is an Eddie Collins III. With that baseball heritage, some of these days Eddie III no doubt also will be wearing the big "A" of Connie Mack.

Phil Marchildon, a French-Canadian who won 17 games while losing 14 for Mack's tail-ender of 1942, joined the Royal Canadian Air Force after that season and was a prisoner in Germany when last heard of. All told, Connie has 35 players on his service list. They aren't all Chapmans, McCoys, and Marchildons; but they put quite a crimp in his plans.

As the team wallowed in the cellar, Mack disposed of some of the men who had been replacements for the 1931 champions. In 1936 he sold Roger Cramer and Eric McNair to the Red Sox for $60,000, Pitcher Henry Johnson, and Infielder Al Niemiec. Johnson was the same fellow who knocked Connie out of the '28 pennant by defeating the Athletics five times that season. A year after the Cramer-McNair deal, he traded Third Baseman Pinky Higgins to the Red Sox for Billy Werber. Connie called that "a pretty bad deal." Werber, a Duke University honor student who won a Rhodes scholarship, never lasted long on any club. He played for Mack only one season.

"I tried to make a deal in our league for Werber, but nobody wanted him, so we sold him to the Reds on waivers."

Connie had a number of other Duke boys on his later-day teams. Jack Coombs, a member of Mack's "Big Pitching Three" of the World's Champions of 1910-11, had become baseball coach at Duke and sent his old mentor several of his outstanding pupils. Some had greater reputations in football than in baseball. In some cases Mack paid their tuition at Duke. The list included Ace Parker, Chubby Dean, Eric Tipton, Wayne Ambler, Raymond Coombs (Jack's nephew), Hal Wagner, and a few others. Few of them stayed long at Shibe Park. Wagner, a catcher from Riverton, New Jersey, was the best of the lot. Needing an outfielder badly early in the 1944 season, Connie traded Hal to the Red Sox for Floyd Garrison. Soon thereafter Wagner went into the Navy.

Connie's third son, Connie, Jr., was another of Jack Coombs's boys at Duke. Unlike the two older sons, Roy and Earle, Junior grew tall like his dad, and is even an inch taller than Connie, Sr.—six feet, five inches. "He would have made a fine pitcher if he hadn't hurt his arm," said his father proudly. "Connie could get a lot of stuff on the ball." Junior served under his dad as coach and was assistant secretary of the Athletics when he put on khaki early in 1944. He married a daughter of the late Senator Shepherd of Texas and has four young McGillicuddys.

Mack guessed wrong on another collegian, Bill Nicholson, now of the Cubs and the National League's No. 1 man in home runs and runs batted in the last few seasons. Ira Thomas found Bill in Washington College, Maryland, and signed Nicholson to an Athletic contract on his graduation day in 1936. Perhaps Bill's failure to get a single hit in 11 games with the A's in 1937 weakened Connie on the young slugger. The next year he had a chance to buy a fleet-footed outfielder, Dee Miles, a former Washington player, from Chattanooga. As part of the purchase price, Connie gave Joe Engel, colorful Chattanooga impresario, the pick of the Williamsport club, in which Mack then was interested. Joe picked Nicholson, the Athletic farmhand. Engel turned a smart deal, for less than a year later he sold "Big Nick" to the Cubs for $35,000. Big Bill's Maryland wagon tongue, like the bats of Baker and Foxx, could have brought a lot of sunshine into Mack's life the last few seasons.

If Coombs fed Connie players from Duke, his great Indian pitcher, Albert Bender, has been beating the brush for Athletic talent the last five years. The Chief re-entered Mack's service as scout in 1939. The incidents of 1914 and the Federal League long since had been forgotten. Since leaving Mack, Bender had pitched for the Baltimore Feds and the Phillies; managed clubs in New Haven, Johnstown, Richmond; coached for the Giants, White Sox, and the Naval Academy; and worked in Wanamaker's sporting goods department. He was as happy to get back with Connie Mack as when he first signed that $300-a-month Athletic contract in 1903.

2

Connie was down in the standing of the clubs, but his wits remained as keen as ever. A play in Cleveland in 1943 bears that out. With the Indians at bat, Oris Hockett on third base, and Manager-Shortstop Lou Boudreau on second, Ken Keltner grounded to Orie Arntzen, Mack's pitcher, whose throw to Catcher Bob Swift trapped Hockett between third base and the home plate. Swift chased Hockett back to third, where Boudreau by this time was occupying the bag. Hockett then continued on into short left field, apparently intending to relinquish the bag to his manager. Swift tagged both men, as a catcher will do in such a case, and Umpire Rue called Hockett out. As far as a crowd of 5,000, the umpires, and players were concerned, that's all there was to it: Hockett was out and Boudreau was safe on third.

However, Connie motioned to Rue to come over to the bench. "It seems to me, Mr. Grieve (Umpire Willie Grieve wasn't even in the ball park), that Boudreau is out for passing Hockett on the base line," he said. "The moment Hockett took one step beyond third base, Boudreau was closer to the plate than him. That's just the same as if Boudreau ran past him, so Boudreau's out. Now Hockett, of course, was tagged while he was off the base. So he's out, too; don't you think?"

Rue thanked Connie for setting him right, and, much to the consternation of the Indians and their fans, he called both players out. Mack had the wrong umpire, but the right decision. Of all the persons in that park, the 80-year-old Mack was the only one who saw that play correctly. Connie subsequently lost the game, which made him think that he would have done better had he kept his mouth shut. "If I had known we were going to lose the game, I could have kept quiet and let the umpires call it wrong," he told Red Smith that night. "Then I could have protested the game. The league would have had to uphold me, as I was absolutely right. The game would have been thrown out, and we would have had another chance to win it."

Lou Boudreau, the then twenty-four-year-old Illinois Bachelor of Arts, was named manager of the Indians in 1941. At the Chicago American League meeting in December, John Hoffman of the *Chicago Times* thought it would be a fine idea to get a picture of Connie Mack and Boudreau, the oldest and youngest major-league managers. Connie readily consented. He always has been most obliging to writers and cameramen. The photographer wasn't too well up in his baseball and asked Mack for Boudreau's first name. "Excuse me, Mr. Bou-deer, but what is your first name?" Connie asked.

Connie's pronunciation of names always has been a source of great joy to Philadelphia baseball writers. The great Cleveland pitcher, Addie Joss, used to be Addie Josh; and Hank Bonura, the White Sox slugger, was Boneer. His center fielder, Doc Cramer, was Crame; and the two famous Yankees, Lou Gehrig and Tony Lazzeri, were Gehridge and Lazurhie. When he talked of Charley (Gabby) Hartnett, the former Cub manager, on the loud-speaker before an Athletic-Cub game at Wrigley Field, Los Angeles, he referred to Gabby as Pat. And Long Beach, California, was Long Branch. So, when he called Joe Rue "Mr. Grieve," he was staying in character. Such little slips have made him even more delightful to those who come into intimate contact with him.

And he continued to use his scoreboard to give his signs. For three or four days he would give the signs. Then someone else from the bench gave them, while Connie went through the same motions with his card. Only they didn't mean a thing; it was only a ruse to throw off the opposition.

In his early years as White Sox manager, while he still was playing third base, Jimmy Dykes tried to steal Mack's signs.

Connie's hands were down low. That used to be the steal sign. Dykes called for a pitchout and got Doc Cramer trying to steal third.

Meeting Dykes after the game, Connie said: "I see there is nothing wrong with your memory, young man. But I could have told you the sign isn't the same today. You were just lucky to make that play."

Another time Dykes thought he caught a bunt sign. As he charged in, the batsman drove a terrific drive down the third-base line, a ball that singed the White Sox manager's hair without any extra charge.

"You know, we change 'em sometimes, Jimmy," volunteered Mack.

"Change 'em; I'll say you do," said Jimmy. "You nearly got me killed."

Some big men are small in little things, but not Connie; he is big in all directions. One of his players had a wife ill in Texas. The pitcher said nothing to Mack or any of his fellow Athletics, but he looked worried, and it was easy to see his mind wasn't on his work. Connie quietly found out what was wrong with the boy. He called him into his little office. "Here's a ticket for Texas," he said. "Take a week off. See how your wife is getting along and come back when she feels better."

In an exhibition game at Yuma, Arizona, the crowd early filled the little stands. Two elderly ladies came late and had no place to go; they looked frightened and bewildered. Connie had his trainer dig up a bench for them and let them sit in front of his players, where they had a real ringside seat.

As manager of one of the two tail-enders, Connie got first or second crack at the minor-league stars at draft meetings. At one of these sessions, Leslie O'Connor, Landis' secretary, sitting next to the old Commissioner, whispered to Landis that Mack was one over his player limit. He had drafted two players.

"I am sorry, Mr. Mack, but you can have only one of these men," said the Judge.

"All right," replied Connie. "Which one can I have?"

"Either one," said the Judge.

"Well, you can throw out whichever you want to," continued Connie. That got a laugh from everyone in the room. "I'll leave it entirely up to you, Judge; maybe you can pick one better than I can."

3

The death of old Uncle Ben's two sons, Thomas Stevenson Shibe and John D. Shibe, within a year and a half of each other, thrust additional burdens on Connie Mack at an age when most men want to take things easier. Tom, president of the Athletics since Ben's death in 1922, died on February 16, 1936. There was some talk of Mack's taking over the presidency then, but Connie threw his influence to John Shibe, who had been vice-president-treasurer-secretary under Tom. While John was an ardent Athletic fan, his big hobby was speedboat racing, and he spent a fortune trying to win the American Cup. Connie and his associates often called him Thomas Lipton.

However, even then John also was in poor health, and Connie succeeded him to the presidency on January 11, 1937, in his seventy-fifth year. John died on July 11 of the same year. After John Shibe's death, Connie acquired his stock, giving him control in the Athletics. Mack became president-treasurer-manager; and Roy, back from the Portland venture, was named vice-president-secretary. While the sons, including Connie, Jr., tried to take as much detail as possible from Dad's shoulders, the presidency brought additional duties and responsibilities.

After training in Fort Myers for eleven years, President Mack, always full of the spirit of adventure, took his club to Mexico City for late winter conditioning in 1937. The Mexican "hayride" wasn't an overly happy venture. There were hotel difficulties; the boys didn't like their meals and complained to Connie in real baseball vocabulary of the stenches which came out of the kitchen. The players suffered from nosebleeds, and Trainer Ebling learned early that cuts and bruises healed slowly in that 7,349-foot altitude.

Connie, himself, was one of the casualties. A grounder hit him on the right shin, knocked off a little skin. He thought nothing of it at the time, but the bruise failed to heal, and the leg became infected. Mack spent several days in the American Hospital in Mexico, but said the extent of the hurt was exaggerated.

One of his pleasant recollections of that trip is that Earl Brucker, one of his present-day lieutenants, came to him that spring as an energetic, talkative young catcher.

After the Mexican experience, Connie decided to stick to the good old U. S. A. for his baseball training. He was in Lake Charles, Louisiana, in 1938 and 1939. At the '38 camp, Wally Moses, the fleet-footed Georgia outfielder, drove right into camp with Mrs. Moses and drove right out again when he failed to come to terms with Mack. Moses had had a great season with the A's in 1937, hitting .320 and getting 48 doubles, 13 triples, and 25 home runs. Wally wanted a lot more money than Mack was willing to pay; it gave Connie a chance to pull another one of his famous lines. "Moses thinks he is a heck of a player, but he has too strong a weakness."

If the 1937 experience in Mexico City was only a mild infection, Connie became really ill in 1939, an illness which alarmed the entire country. He was stricken on the train, June 28, as the Athletics were on their way to Boston. Dr. Edward O'Brien, Red Sox club physician and a great friend and admirer of Mack, early recognized he had a mighty sick patient in his care. He told the Athletic president-manager he would have to go to a hospital at once. "You'll have to call up Mrs. Mack and see what she thinks about it," said Connie.

Mrs. Mack came to Boston and helped get him back to Philadelphia. He is so tall that when the train reached the North Philadelphia station, it was necessary to remove some panels to get his stretcher out of the Pullman. Ill though he was, he made a quip about it.

However, he was critically ill, and from President Roosevelt down the entire nation was deeply concerned about its most beloved baseball figure. In the July 13 issue of the *Sporting News,* his old friend, Jimmy Isaminger, wrote: "Connie Mack is very ill. No doubt his friends are a bit puzzled over reports of his condition from Philadelphia. It is untrue that he hears details of the A's games over the radio. He knows how sick he is and has no visitors or distraction in his sickroom."

Earle managed the club for practically the remainder of the season. There were reports that Connie never would try to run the club again, and that if he recovered he would become nominal president and let the younger Macks run the club.

They didn't know the old McGillicuddy spirit. He was a skeleton when he started to get around again some six months later, but a mighty alert, active one. He hadn't the slightest thought of quitting. At Atlantic City he put some pounds back on his sparse frame, and the color returned to his cheeks. By the early winter Isaminger was able to send out the encouraging word: "Connie Mack's comeback is real. He now is as alert, mentally and physically, as he was before his first serious illness late in the season of 1936."

As for Connie—always willing to learn by experience, he found an object lesson in the weeks he lay on his back. "I have learned enough from my illness to go on," he said. "I find that at my age I must watch my diet. Men of my age get alarmed when they lose a little flesh. To get it back, they overeat. That was my trouble. I will never again pay attention to a few pounds."

In 1940 Connie switched his training camp again, this time to Anaheim, California. This was another innovation—a Philadelphia team training in the Far West. And he learned of the great love and esteem the people of the hospitable state of California felt for him. Bringing a tail-ender to the Pacific Coast, he was touched with the homage which was paid to him and his team. It was the same wherever he went—San Diego, Los Angeles, Hollywood, San Francisco, or the smaller cities. At Hollywood, Joe E. Brown and Harry Ruby, the song writer and gagster, vied in showing him the sights.

On March 29, 1941, the San Francisco Junior Chamber of Commerce, along with the baseball old-timers of northern California, threw a big party for him at the Burma Grove of the Empire Hotel. Bill Lange and George Van Haltern, who played against Mack in the National League, were there; so was Jimmy Byrnes, his old scout; and Sam Sandow Mertes, early White Sox infielder, who was in left field for McGraw when the Giants threw all that whitewash in Mack's eyes in the 1905 World's Series. Judge Hugh L. Smith of San Francisco, a former Los Angeles catcher, was general chairman; and the funny man, Joe E. Brown, brought tears to their eyes as he told of what Mack meant to him, the nation, and its greatest game.

Abe Kemp, veteran San Francisco sports writer, told of running into Connie Mack at a minor-league meeting in Montreal a few years before. Back in 1909, when Abe was little more than a kid, he asked Connie for some old baseballs. Connie gave him a boxful. He walked up to Connie and said: "I guess you don't know me."

"Just wait a minute," said Mack—and then, after a pause: "You're the boy I once gave a box of baseballs."

4

As Connie got along into his seventies, each of his birthdays was an occasion at Shibe Park. The Philadelphia baseball writers made celebrating it an annual custom. In 1932, when he reached his seventieth birthday, he advised moderation in everything and said his good health was due to nine hours of sleep, an ability to relax, and a good digestion.

Five years later, 1937, when he celebrated his first three-quarters of a century, it really was an occasion. He had been a little under the weather, and there was some doubt as to whether he would show up. But he couldn't let down his boys. "You can rest assured that if he can walk, he'll be there," said son Roy. Shortly before the luncheon he appeared with his youngest son, Connie, Jr., and two physicians. Among those who greeted him were many of his old players—Bender, Davis, Oldring, Pennock, Dykes, Witt, Strunk, Keefe, Walberg, Ehmke, Berry and Blackburne—also players from other teams and a delegation of umpires. Dykes voiced the sentiment of them all when he said: "Whatever we are in baseball, we owe to Connie Mack."

Messages were read from President Roosevelt, Vice-President Jack Garner, former Postmaster-General Farley, Judge Landis, the major-league presidents, and many of the nation's leaders. The President's message read: "You have been a great inspiration to the national pastime and to the youth of the nation."

And before the party broke up, Connie said: "You know, my brother, Michael, always contended my birth was December 22, but I thought it was the twenty-third. I see now where it's finally been decided as the twenty-second."

However, the birthday still is being celebrated on the twenty-third, and when he was eighty, he stood for more than an hour, holding his listeners spellbound with his stories and reminiscences.

He showed his hands and exhibited only one "baseball finger," the first joint of his right index finger shaped like a marble. Some old catchers have hands which look like gnarled oaks. "Look at that," he said proudly. "Maybe I was lucky, but this is the only mark I have to show for my catching days. I can't even bend it now, but when I suffered that injury in Pittsburgh, I kept right on catching. We didn't have twenty-five-men rosters."

And he admitted there was a skeleton in his closet. He once had been put out of a game. And by none other than his old Washington battery mate, Hank O'Day. It happened while he was managing Pittsburgh in 1895, and nearly half a century later he wasn't contrite.

"There was a play at second base, involving Patsy Donovan, my outfielder, who was as safe as any runner can be safe; but O'Day said he was out. I was pretty sore, and protested strongly; but Hank not only insisted that Patsy was out, but fined me $100 and ordered me off the field.

"I refused to go, and O'Day called a policeman to assist me out of the park. I told the officer he had no right to put me off the field; he hadn't seen me do anything wrong. That sort of stumped him. He didn't know what to do, so he called the sergeant. Well, by that time I had cooled a little and decided to go.

"But it's foolish to argue with umpires, and ninety-nine times out of a hundred they are right. Not so long ago, while McNair was playing second base for me, I thought he tagged out a runner, but the umpire called him safe. I did a lot of hollering that afternoon, especially at the man who had made the decision. But before the game was over, McNair admitted to me he hadn't actually tagged the runner. So I waited for that umpire after the game and in front of his two associates I apologized for what I had said."

5

With the rolling by of the Mack milestones, the nation showed greater and greater appreciation of this wonderful Old Man of Baseball, and new honors tumbled into his lap. In 1938 he was given the Buffalo Award from the National Council of Boy Scouts, for distinguished service and the great inspiration he was for the boys of America.

In 1937 he was voted a plaque at the Cooperstown, New York, Hall of Fame. The designation was "for service to baseball apart from playing of the game," and for being one of the shining lights of the nation's great summer sport. In 1939, the year of baseball's centennial, one of the events at Cooperstown was a special Connie Mack Day, July 24. It was at the time of Mack's illness, and he couldn't attend; but Earle Mack took the Athletics to baseball's birthplace and shrine and pinch hit for his famous father. With Governor James of Pennsylvania pitching the first ball, and son Earle catching, the A's won the day's ball game from the Penn A. C., 12 to 6.

Inspired by Connie's lifelong devoted friend, Judge Harry S. McDevitt, and assisted by Philadelphia's sports-loving Jack Kelly and Speaker Elmer Kilroy of the Pennsylvania House of Representatives, May 17, 1941, was officially made a holiday, Connie Mack Day, by action of the state legislature. In setting May 17 aside as a special day, Governor James said in his proclamation to the people of his great state: "The name of Connie Mack has long since been carved in the halls of fame reserved for baseball's immortals. The name of Connie Mack has long since become a vital part of America and the American way of life.

"This tribute which we now pay by the designation of Connie Mack Day is but another honor to be paid this great American who already knows the highest distinction which can be given to a man—a place in the hearts of his fellow men."

Unfortunately, the elements didn't co-operate in the holiday, as heavy rains fell until 1 o'clock, restricting the attendance to 15,000. However, it was a great occasion in Mack's life, with Speaker Kilroy master of ceremonies, and Judge Landis, president Will Harridge, many bigwigs of baseball, Philadelphia neighbors, and former Athletic players helping to pay homage to the great septuagenarian.

George Cohan, Brookfield's other famous son, was in attendance; he had written a song for the occasion: "Connie Mack Is the Grand Old Name!" and George helped the Police and Firemen's Band to sing it. It started:

At old East Brookfield in Massachusetts,
A kid with a bat and a ball.
At old East Brookfield in Massachusetts,
A kid heard the big city call.

Over the loud-speaker the famous actor and showman said: "This is the thrill of my life. Mr. Mack, my song is a labor of love, and I wouldn't miss being here."

Among the many gifts presented to Mack, two which touched him especially deeply were a $150 wrist watch from the umpires of the American League and a silver plate on which was etched his favorite photograph of himself, with the inscription: "To Connie Mack, American patriot of clean sports, May 17, 1941, from the citizens of Philadelphia." The presentation was made by Gerry Nugent, president of the rival Philadelphia National team.

Connie's voice choked as he thanked his well-wishers. "Thank you! Thank you all! I sincerely hope in the near future I can in some way return this great kindness."

A parade of old Athletic stars, Harry Davis, Eddie Collins (accompanied by young Eddie), Grove, Dykes, Oldring, Bing Miller, Rommel, one of the umpires, Walberg, Simmons, etc., were introduced, after which two Athletic players, Chubby Dean and Sam Chapman took their famous manager on their shoulders and carried him to his dugout as the crowd roared its pleasure. If the elements were unkind, so were the Detroit Tigers. Even with Chapman and McCoy hitting homers for him, Mack saw his A's lose on his big day to the Detroit Tigers, 8 to 5.

A month later, June 10, at the commencement exercises of the Pennsylvania Military College at Chester, Pennsylvania, the former shoe-factory assistant foreman put on a cap and gown as he was made an honorary doctor of physical education.

In the fall of the same year, during the 1941 Yankee-Brooklyn World's Series in New York, the Sportsmanship Brotherhood presented Mack with the Sportsmanship Certificate of Award as the nation's No. 1 sportsman for 1941. In accepting the new honor, Mack paid tribute to the two great New York managers, McGraw, his early World's Series rival, and Joe McCarthy of the Yankees, who had just won his seventh pennant and was then in the process of winning his sixth World's Championship, placing him one ahead of Connie. "I used to think—and say—that John McGraw was the greatest manager of all time," he said. "But I think I have to change that now and put Joe McCarthy at the head of my list. He has earned first place."

The author is an officer in the Sportsmanship Brotherhood and had occasion to repeat Mack's words to McCarthy. "Connie was very kind to say that," said Joe. "But let's not kid each other. There is one man who is baseball's greatest all-time manager, and no one else can be spoken of in the same breath with him. The name is Connie Mack."

CHAPTER XXX

STILL GOING STRONG AT EIGHTY-TWO

1

THE SEASON OF 1943 was an especially unhappy one for Connie, inasmuch as it started out quite promisingly. The A's did unexpectedly well in the spring and early summer, and for two and a half months gave the Philadelphia fans much to shout and enthuse about. On June 15, with two months of the season over, the Mackmen were in fourth place, only 5 games out of the lead. By July 1 they had slipped to sixth, but they had a percentage of .474, and the clubs were so closely bunched that Mack was only 6½ games behind the front-running Yankees. Persons were saying that any club—even the A's—could win. And Connie saw plenty on the ball field to give him satisfaction.

He was host to the annual All-Star game at Shibe Park, July 13, which the American League team, with his own Dick Siebert on first base, won in a night contest from the National All-Stars, 5 to 3.

The A's went into a nose dive after this game, never came out of it, and soon were deep in the pit. On their last swing through the West, Connie had to sit through his second Athletic losing streak of 20 straight, the other being in that terrible season of 1916. "I can't understand it," he said. "I know we are a light-hitting club, but we have fair pitching, and are a good fielding team. It would seem, under the very law of averages, that we would get in a winning game somewhere." The club which trailed the leading Yankees by only 6 games in early July was 49 games behind New York at the finish.

However, again Connie didn't whine or twiddle his thumbs. War replacements are difficult to obtain, but he did more shifting of playing personnel. He added the wayfarer of the baseball trails, Buck (Bobo) Newsom to his 1944 caravan, getting the burly South Carolinian in a deal with Washington for another pitcher, Roger Wolff. They asked: "What is Connie thinking of, trying to take on a tough hombre like Newsom at his stage of the game?"; but it worked out all right. "Bo's language sometimes was pretty strong, but he pitched good ball for me," said Mack. So did Russ Christopher, a 4-F bean pole from the Far West; Jesse Flores, the little Mexican; and Don Black; while Jittery Joe Berry was one of the best relief pitchers in the two majors.

Connie came up with a pretty good batch of young infielders in Shortstop Eddie Busch and Third Baseman George Kell. He shifted Irv Hall, his 1943 shortstop, to second base, and after an injury to Dick Siebert he bought a veteran minor-league first baseman with a big sock, Bill McGhee, from Little Rock. When Siebert recovered, Dick went to the outfield. After having traded Catcher Frank Hayes to the Browns in 1942, Connie regained the stalwart Jersey boy in a later transaction and permitted Frank to catch all of his 155 games of 1944 for an American League record.

And, lo and behold, Connie tied Lou Boudreau, the young Cleveland manager, for fifth place, as Mack's 1944 club won 23 more games than did the feeble tail-ender of a year before. Maybe fifth place wasn't much for a man who had won nine championships, but after nine years no higher than seventh, it was a lower baseball heaven. It wasn't a club like the great Athletics of the past, but nobody was shoving it around. It proved quite a determining factor in the Browns' winning the first pennant of their American League existence, also in preventing New York from winning its fourth straight flag and its eighth in nine years.

The A's were scheduled to play a night game with the Yankees at Shibe Park, September 14. It was the last scheduled game between these two clubs in Philadelphia. It rained, and it was necessary to shift the game to New York, where the

© Sporting News

YOUNGEST AND OLDEST MANAGERS IN MAJORS
Lou Boudreau, Indians *(left)*, Connie, and Herb Pennock, General Manager of Phillies *(right)*.

TWELVE IMMORTALS WHO HELPED PUT OVER WAR BOND GAME AT POLO GROUNDS, NEW YORK, 1943
(*Back row, left to right*): Duffy Lewis, Eddie Collins, Roger Bresnahan, Connie Mack, Bill Klem, Jack Murray, George Sisler. (*Front row*): Hans Wagner, Frank Frisch, Babe Ruth, Walter Johnson, Tris Speaker.

Mackmen were scheduled for brief week-end series on September 16 and 17.

Ed Barrow, the veteran Yankee president, was sore about the transfer of the game to New York, forcing an extra double-header on the faded Yankees, and blistered Mack and the Athletics in a New York interview. He said the Philadelphia grounds were in no condition for the September 14 game because of a football game having cut up the field the night before. He sharply criticized baseball clubs who rent out their grounds for football before their league schedule is completed.

It annoyed Connie Mack, as he thought Barrow's barbs were unfair and uncalled for, and insisted that rain prevented the September 14 game at Shibe Park. So before the final series in New York he told his players: "I want you to go out and take all three of those games. We're going to fight for everything."

And did those boys fight? Ed Barrow had already sold his 1944 World's Series tickets, but by the time the A's finished with the Yanks there wasn't much need for them. With Bobo pitching, Mack won the Saturday game, 6 to 3. And then, before a 51,235 Sunday crowd, Connie's joyous A's knocked the Yankees out of the lead by setting them back on their heels in both games of a double-header, 5 to 4 and 2 to 1. Larry Rosenthal, an early-season Yankee castoff, won the first game with a pinch home run. New York never recovered from that triple defeat. It just doesn't pay to get the old gentleman riled.

2

The 1944 season saw Philadelphia pay another grand tribute to its eighty-one-year-old president-manager. It started in the brain of Eddie Pollock, the *Bulletin* sports writer; but all Philadelphia and baseball pitched in to make it a glittering success. It was the celebration of Mack's Golden Jubilee as a manager. As the Athletics were scheduled to be on the road on the exact date that Mack took over the Pittsburgh club fifty years before, the great day was held on August 4 instead of September 3. Lieutenant Governor John C. Bell was chairman of the Golden Jubilee committee, and Judge McDevitt again helped put the affair over.

If Connie Mack Day was almost washed out by rain in 1941, the Golden Jubilee ran into a streetcar strike, which completely tied up the transportation of the nation's third largest city. Despite the fact that the fans had to walk or get to the park with whatever gas rations were available, the crowd was 29,166, only some 4,000 short of Shibe Park's capacity.

It was a day of festivities for Connie, his fans, and old players, from morning to night. The high spot was Connie personally introducing the members of what he termed baseball's greatest living team: Babe Ruth, Hans Wagner, Walter Johnson, Lefty Grove, Frank Baker, Eddie Collins, Tris Speaker, George Sisler, and Bill Dickey. The latter attended in his naval lieutenant's uniform. Ty Cobb and Lieutenant Commander Mickey Cochrane, others named on Connie's team, were unavoidibly prevented from attending.

After calling out the names of the great stars, Connie beckoned to Al Simmons, who had returned to his team as a coach. "I want to introduce my substitute for Cobb," he said, "our own Al Simmons, one of baseball's greatest players, especially in the clutch."

Lieutenant Governor Bell presented Mack with a box containing a $5,000 check, in behalf of the committee. There were other gifts, and quietly Joe McCarthy, New York manager, slipped Connie a $150 gold pen and pencil set, a gift from his old baseball enemies, the Yankees. "Something with which to scribble on your scorecard," said Joe. Ted Husing was master of ceremonies; funmakers Bud Abbott and Lou Costello put on Athletic uniforms; Miss Elizabeth Hill, wife of Abner Doubleday's grandson, sang "The Star Spangled Banner," and President Roosevelt sent Connie a message: "Long may your scorecard wave." But just as the Tigers delivered a little sour note to the big day of June 17, 1941, so the Yankees wouldn't let the day be a complete success for Connie. Hank Borowy nosed out Bobo Newsom, 1 to 0, with Stirnweiss, the Yankee speed-boy, scoring the lone run of the game in the ninth inning.

Three days after the Golden Jubilee, Connie Mack went over to New York to direct the Eastern team against the Westerners, led by Mel Ott of the Giants, in *Esquire's* All-

American Boys' game at the Polo Grounds. Connie's Eastern lads won, 6 to 0.

For the next few days he was absent from Shibe Park, and the family admitted he had overdone things a bit. He also said that in future double-headers he would manage his club only in the second game. Frequently the Athletics played so-called twi-night double-headers, the first game starting at 6 o'clock, the second well after 8. He was asked why he didn't take the first game instead of the second.

"Why should I?" was his response. "I never go to bed early, so I prefer to do my managing in the second game."

3

That fifth-place finish of 1944, Connie's best since 1934, brought about a busy fall at Shibe Park. "We should see another fine race in the American League in 1945," Mack said. "And anything may happen." It could even be a tenth pennant for baseball's Grand Old Man.

Mack acquired several of the crack wartime minor-leaguers of the country and Canada, trying especially to put more punch in his outfield. His new acquisitions included Outfielders Mayo Smith of Buffalo and Jack Houck of Lancaster, batting champions of the International League and Inter-State League, respectively, and Hal Peck, batting star of the Milwaukee Brewers.

Connie's effort to buy the Minneapolis club as a Class AA farm for the A's failed to materialize, but an agreement was entered with Toronto, another Class AA outfit, to serve as a feeder and development center for the Athletics. Toronto pitchers Al Jarlett, Woodrow Crossin, and Luther Knerr were added to Mack's able pitching roster, as was Mannie Salvo of Oakland, a former National League hurler with the Giants and Braves. Catcher Jim Pruett was brought from Milwaukee—in the event that Frank Hayes can't go through another 155-game grind.

Connie and Mrs. Mack then packed their bags and took the train for California to spend the winter months. It was a disappointment for the Philadelphia sports writers, who had made Connie's birthday a festive occasion for years, and the sixteen

Mack grandchildren, who missed the beloved Patron Saint of baseball as they went through their Christmas stockings. But everyone was glad the Macks were able to duck Philadelphia's wintry blasts and bask in California's sunshine.

When will Mr. Mack retire from the active management of his club? Well, not in the immediate future.

"What would I do if I didn't have the Athletics to manage?" he asked. "I've seen a lot of men retire, lose interest, and just wither away. Besides, I am not a wealthy man and must still make a living for my family. I could retire, yes, and not be in want; but it wouldn't be any fun. Do you know, I still enjoy traveling around the country, meeting new people, seeing new things."

And then Connie got a little confidential as his blue eyes twinkled. "I'll tell you when I think I'll retire: when I find myself repeating myself—telling the same thing over and over again. I've noticed that when some people get older, they acquire the bad habit of repeating themselves; they tell you the same thing they told you yesterday, and then repeat it tomorrow. Well, when I catch myself doing that, I'll say it's about time to step down."

But he doesn't think he'll be doing that for some time to come, and so, as President Roosevelt wired him on his managerial Golden Jubilee, "Long may his scorecard wave."

INDEX